45.

ALASKA'S

SOUTHEAST

Help Us Keep This Guide Up to Date

Every effort has been made by the authors to make this guide as accurate and useful as possible. However, many things can change after a guide is published—establishments close, phone numbers change, facilities come under new management, etc.

We would love to hear from you concerning your experiences with this guide and how you feel it could be improved and kept up to date. Although we may not be able to respond to all comments and suggestions, we'll take them to heart, and we'll make certain to share them with the author. Please send your comments and suggestions to the following address:

The Globe Pequot Press
Reader Response/Editorial Department
P.O. Box 480
Guilford, CT 06437

Or you may e-mail us at:
editorial@GlobePequot.com

Thanks for your input,
and happy travels!

NINTH EDITION

ALASKA'S SOUTHEAST

TOURING THE INSIDE PASSAGE

Sarah Eppenbach

Revised and updated by

Michelle Gurney

The
Globe
Pequot
Press

GUILFORD, CONNECTICUT

45
Sitka National Historic Park . Battle of Sitka

Illustrations by Connie Hameedi
Photographs by Larry Eppenbach unless noted otherwise

ISSN: 1545-1941
ISBN: 0-7627-2797-7

Manufactured in the United States of America
Ninth Edition/First Printing

CONTENTS

The prices and rates listed in this guidebook were confirmed at press time. We recommend, however, that you call establishments before traveling to obtain the most current information.

FOREWORD

When you think of Southeast Alaska, you cannot help but conjure images of cerulean skies, snow-covered glaciers, quiet coves, hot-pink fireweed, and more wildlife than you could ever imagine. After spending time exploring Alaska's towns, villages, and wilderness areas, however, the thing that struck me most was the friendliness and generosity of its people. Unlike the author and past editors of this book, I am not a native Alaskan. In fact, I did not know a single person in Alaska before leaving on my first trip to edit this book. Before I reached Skagway, however, hikers finishing a twelve-hour running trip on the Chilkoot Trail handed me their phone number and suggested that my husband and I call them if we needed to do "laundry or anything like that" once we arrived in Juneau. Now I have traveled all over this fine earth, and never have I been invited to do laundry in a stranger's home. On the ferries Tongass Park Rangers offered all kinds of great advice on places to hike or camp. In visitor information centers I was greeted by smiles and masses of brochures and booklets on where to stay, what to eat, and places to visit. Bed-and-breakfast owners made wonderful meals and shared their knowledge about favorite leisure spots. Locals told me stories of Sasquatch sightings; I watched as kayaking guides caught salmon with their bare hands; children explained to me they were not afraid of bears; and just about everyone I met offered a sincere "good morning" as I passed them on the street.

Southeast Alaska is filled with rich Tlingit culture, fascinating remnants of the historic Gold Rush, and thriving fishing communities.

While there are lots of things to do in each community. I would be remiss if I did not highlight a few trademark Alaskan adventures: racing to Whale Park in Sitka after hearing whale sounds on Aqua Radio; kayaking along the ocean with a view of the Mendenhall Glacier (Juneau); a boat trip along the Stikine River or a trip to the Anan Bear Observatory (Wrangell); searching for bald eagles in tree tops or scanning for humpback whales while touring the Inside Passage by boat. Visiting hatcheries, fishing, leisurely walks through museums or totem parks, great cups of coffee in quaint cafes—the opportunities for enjoyment are absolutely endless, but they all begin in Alaska's Southeast. Just don't forget your rubber boots!

—Michelle Gurney

Driving south out of Haines on Mud Bay Road you may spot some wild tiger lilies near Letnikof Cove. MICHELLE GURNEY

PART ONE

GETTING ACQUAINTED WITH ALASKA'S SOUTHEAST

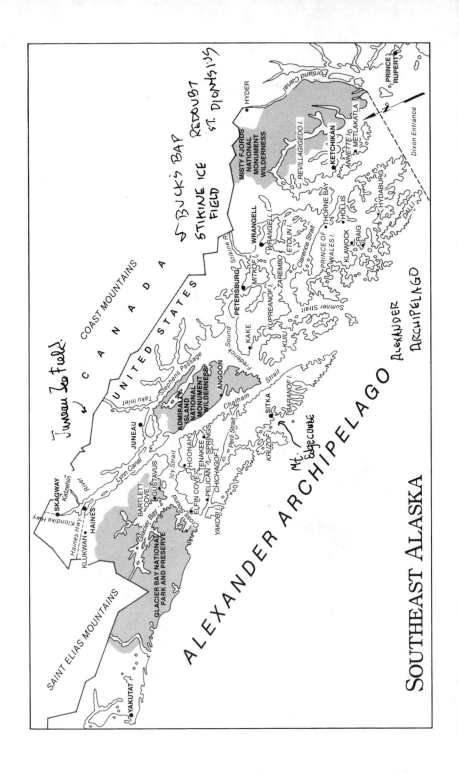

SOUTHEAST ALASKA

ALEXANDER ARCHIPELAGO

CHAPTER ONE

SOUTHEAST TRAVELER BASICS

There are ten million acres of forest in Southeast Alaska: 1,000 islands, 10,000 miles of shoreline, 50 to 70 major glaciers, as many as 5,000 brown bears, perhaps 20,000 to 25,000 bald eagles, and nearly 75,000 people. The people have left their mark here or there upon the land but on the whole have had little visible effect. When you visit this land of cascading glaciers and forested islands, you will look upon a part of the earth that has changed remarkably little in the past 1,000 years. The deep green fjords that you travel by cruise ship or ferry appeared largely the same to the Tlingit and Haida Indians who plied these shores in their cedar canoes. Now, as then, stands of giant spruce and hemlock reach toward the mountain peaks, while thickets of wild berries run rampant over the land.

We of the twenty-first century, contemplating matters from the womblike comfort of our heated living rooms, think of Southeast Alaska as prohibitively cool and wet for aboriginal dwellers, but the early Native residents knew it for what it truly is: a hospitable land. The climate was temperate—yes, temperate. The rain forest provided an environment that was pleasantly cool most of the time and seldom so cold, even in winter, that a fire and some animal skins could not provide adequate warmth within the walls of a planked enclosure.

The forest and the sea provided all the food that could be wanted, and it was easily gathered. The Tlingit and Haida Indians did not need to range far to feed their people: They went down to the mouth of the salmon stream and harvested the required amount of fish. For a change of pace, they sent a line down to the bottom and brought up a halibut. Or a snapper. Or a crab. Salmonberries, blueberries, nagoonberries, crowberries, cloudberries, thimbleberries, cranberries, currants, and more grew in profusion.

The land provided food, shelter, fuel, and transportation. There were no lions, tigers, or crocodiles to prey on helpless humans, not a single poisonous snake or insect. There was only the occasional grizzly or the icy water that could snatch a precious life in moments.

Southeast Alaska is still a hospitable land. Those of us lucky enough to live along this forested coast know that the land continues to provide food, fuel, shelter, and spiritual solace in generous portions. The cold, clear waterways—so beautiful to gaze upon—still provide the only certain link between communities. Water is our lifeline.

The waterfront atmosphere enjoyed by all Inside Passage towns is a unique aspect of Southeast Alaska. There are few places in the world where the toot of a ferry heralds an important event, but in Southeast Alaska an entire population relies upon these slow and steady boats for supplies and transportation. An automobile takes you only about 30 miles in most Southeast communities. Only one road south of Haines or Skagway connects with the outside world, at Hyder, a community of one hundred people at the head of the Portland Canal. The water is our highway. You will find the true Southeast Alaska down at the docks, where fishing boats are unloading salmon, freighters are onloading lumber, ferries and cruise ships are off-loading passengers, and tugs and barges are delivering appliances and automobiles to a grateful population.

WHEN TO GO

No matter what month of the year you make your trip, you probably will not be able to escape some of the soggy weather that keeps Southeast Alaska so deliciously green. There is no dry season in Southeast. Statistically speaking, May and June are the sunniest months of the year and October the wettest, but picking the right time to travel in Southeast is a little like betting on horses—you can study the racing forms all you like, but you still need a measure of luck. Traveling in May gives you the added advantage of beating the crowds, but temperatures can be in the fifties and below. Many areas will be recently emerged from the winter snow cover, and the scenery may not be at its prime. For most people, June is the best choice, followed by July and August.

More and more visitors are venturing into Southeast in winter for a less conventional view of the country. Besides the weather, the obvious disadvantage to winter travel is that many exhibits, shows, and excursions (including Glacier Bay) will be unavailable. Cruise ships do not travel the Inside Passage in winter, so you must fly or take the Alaska state ferry. Winter sports enthusiasts, however, find Southeast at its best in this season, when the snow transforms alpine meadows and open muskegs into vast, sparkling playgrounds for snowshoes and cross-country skis. Eaglecrest Ski Area in Juneau provides downhill skiing for all skill levels. Winter is also the time to view the world's largest gathering of bald eagles at the Chilkat Bald Eagle Preserve near Haines, to see the various Southeast communities in their everyday dress, and to take advantage of lower fares and guaranteed staterooms on Alaska state ferries.

WHAT TO BRING AND WEAR

Southeast Alaska is a casual place, where formal dress has little practicality. The most important factor for residents and visitors alike is comfort, which means dressing to stay warm and dry. Southeast Alaska can be damp and cool—with temperatures in the fifties even in summer—and wet plus cold makes an unpleasant and even dangerous combination. You will not enjoy walking around to see the sights unless you are adequately dressed.

Alaskans find that dressing in layers offers the optimum protection against the elements. Whatever time of year you visit, your most important article of clothing will be something to keep you warm. For example, wear a wool or fiberfill coat over a layer of moderate weight, such as a cotton turtleneck and sweater. Or, choose a warm underlayer—a heavy wool sweater, polyester fleece pullover, down or fiberfill vest—and top with a lighter jacket or windbreaker. Your outermost layer should be water-repellent. If your jacket or coat does not offer sufficient protection, bring a fold-up poncho or raincoat

A good raincoat is a must when traveling to Alaska's Southeast. MICHELLE GURNEY

for rainy days. If you will be traveling in the shoulder seasons, equip yourself with a set of ultra-lightweight long underwear (such as silk) in case you need an extra layer.

Footgear should be comfortable for walking in wet conditions. Good choices include rubber- or crepe-soled walking shoes, athletic shoes, lightweight day-hikers, and rubber-soled moccasins. Rubber rain boots are always in fashion in Southeast Alaska. Bring a rain hat and also a warm hat and gloves for shipboard and for sightseeing around glaciers, even in summer.

Other items to consider bringing include a folding umbrella, insect repellent, and sunscreen. Good binoculars are a must. Cruising along the quiet waterways of the Inside Passage, you will want to look closely at eagles, whales, glaciers, fishing boats—so many things. And if you are at all interested in catching these images on film, now would be a good time to purchase that 75–300 zoom lens you have been thinking about.

USING THE ALASKA
STATE FERRIES

Although the territory and the state of Alaska operated the tiny ferry *Chilkat* (fifteen vehicles, seventy-five passengers) earlier between Juneau and Haines, the Alaska Marine Highway System began regionwide service in 1963, when the motor vessels *Malaspina, Taku,* and *Matanuska* came on line—the first of the popular state ferries. Each of the blue-hulled ships was outfitted to carry 108 cars and 500 passengers on the regular service between Prince Rupert (British Columbia) and Haines/Skagway. At present the Southeast fleet has expanded to five main-line ferries and two smaller ferries (the *Aurora* and *LeConte*). The 382-foot ferry, *Kennicott,* began service in 1998. All of the state's ferries are named after glaciers in Alaska.

The main-line service operates year-round, connecting the major communities of Southeast Alaska with one another and with the Lower 48 and Canada. The *Columbia* and the *Matanuska* (during high season) travel between Bellingham, Washington (85 miles north of Seattle), and Skagway, Alaska. The *Kennicott* and *Taku* travel between Prince Rupert, British Columbia (linking with the provincial ferry system), and Skagway. All the major Inside Passage towns, including Ketchikan, Wrangell, Petersburg, Sitka, Juneau, Haines, and Skagway, are served on both the Bellingham and Prince Rupert routes. The *Kennicott* also makes a monthly run from Juneau to

THE SOUTHEAST FLEET

Name of Vessel	Cruising Speed	Length	Passengers	Vehicles	Staterooms
Columbia	17.3 knots	418 feet	625	134	104
Malaspina	16.5 knots	408 feet	500	88	73
Matanuska	16.5 knots	408 feet	500	88	107
Kennicott	16.75 knots	382 feet	750	120	100
Taku	16.5 knots	352 feet	450	69	44
Aurora	14.5 knots	235 feet	250	34	—
LeConte	14.5 knots	235 feet	250	34	—

south-central Alaska, docking at Valdez and Seward before returning to Southeast. The *Malaspina* now operates as a day boat, making daily runs to the northern Panhandle communities of Skagway, Juneau, and Haines.

The smaller vessels fill in the gaps with short-distance hauls to the smaller communities of Metlakatla, Hollis, Kake, Angoon, Hoonah, Tenakee Springs, Pelican, and Stewart/Hyder (summer only) off the main route. All the vessels carry automobiles (including campers and trailers) as well as passengers.

The main-line vessels operate just like regular passenger ships except that transportation, not luxury, is their aim. They feature functional staterooms, deck chairs, movies, video games, observation lounges, cocktail bars, and dining rooms. There is elevator and wheelchair access to cabins.

If you do not want to pay for a stateroom, you can doze in a reclining chair or spread your sleeping bag on the floor. (You cannot sleep in your vehicle as the car deck is off-limits between ports.) All ships are equipped with a heated, glassed-in solarium on the top deck, an ideal spot for sleeping outside without getting wet. Coin lockers and public showers are available, too, and you can rent a towel, pillow, or blanket on the larger vessels. Neither of the two smaller ferries has staterooms. Overnight passengers stretch out in the lounge chairs in the solarium, or on the floor.

The meals aboard the ferries are self-service (the *Columbia* offers both restaurant service and cafeteria meals). In general, the self-service fare tends to be plain but adequate, ranging from sandwiches, salads, fresh fruit, and yogurt to hot entrees such as pasta and seafood, as well as the standard burger and fries. Travelers from the Lower 48, especially families with children, will probably find the meals expensive. It will help to carry aboard your own supply of fresh fruit, snacks, and sandwich makings. (Passengers are welcome to bring food aboard any of the Alaska state ferries, but cooking is not permitted.)

In summer U.S. Forest Service interpreters are onboard the mainline ferries to point out sights along the route, answer questions, and enhance your enjoyment of Alaska's scenic wilderness. Musicians, storytellers, or other artists from the Pacific Northwest might also be aboard to inform and entertain passengers.

Fares are charged from the port of embarkation to the port of debarkation. There is only a slight increase in the cost of your trip if you stop over along the way. Passenger and vehicle fares are reduced during the off-season, from October 1 through April 30. Depending on the season, discounted rates may also be available to senior citizens and to passengers with disabilities.

You can design your whole trip around the state ferry system if you are willing to plan in advance. You can leave for Alaska from either Bellingham or Prince Rupert and stop at ports along the way to Skagway, and back. Another option is to drive the Alaska Highway to Skagway or Haines and travel south to Prince Rupert. Get off and spend a few days in each town; then resume your trek on another ferry, provided you have made reservations if you have a vehicle or want a stateroom. With judicious planning, however, you can schedule your travels so that you make virtually every leg of the trip in the daytime and do not need a stateroom at all. In this case, foot passengers will need reservations for passage only if traveling during a heavy traffic period such as the weekend of the Southeast State Fair in Haines in August or the Little Norway Festival in Petersburg in May.

You can use the small vessels to make side trips from the major communities and investigate what most tourists miss. You can take the *Aurora* from Ketchikan to Prince of Wales Island, for example, and explore for days. There are several hotels and lodges where you can stay on the island. Take a day trip to Metlakatla; you can go over and back from Ketchikan in one day. Go to Tenakee Springs and spend a few restful hours in the hot sulfur baths, or go to Angoon on Admiralty Island and watch the tide boil through the narrow entrance of Kootznahoo Inlet. (See "Angoon," page 306, for additional information.)

You can take your car or camper on the ferry, but should you? If you are interested only in visiting the towns, or in taking trips from the towns, I would recommend against it. However, if you want to see more of community life, camping is a good and inexpensive alternative.

Once arrived in each town, you will probably want to do most of your exploring on foot. If you decide to do some sightseeing outside the city center, you can always rent a car or hire a taxi. It is decidedly more expensive to take a car, and you will spend precious time waiting in ferry lines—especially if you plan to get off and on at several communities.

Reservations for peak-season travel present something of a catch-22. Summer sailings from Bellingham are so popular that you need to reserve early, but the summer sailing schedule does not come out until mid-November, with bookings typically opening on December 1. The Alaska Marine Highway reservations office accepts written requests for reservations at any time, but since the schedule will not be available yet, you will have to give the approximate dates you want to travel. Telephone requests are accepted as of the first working day in December. On that date written and telephone requests are processed simultaneously, written ones in the order received. Because telephone lines are usually jammed, your best chance is to send in your written request well before the first of December.

Ideally you should begin planning your trip a year in advance by writing for current schedule and tariff information. Even though the schedule will be out-of-date for your trip, you can get an idea of the itinerary you want to work out. Then, as far in advance as possible, put in your written request for reservations. Keep in mind that ships

Ferries link towns along the Inside Passage. Smaller vessels like the Aurora *serve communities off the main line.*

APPROXIMATE MILEAGE AND SAILING TIME BETWEEN PORTS ON THE ALASKA MARINE HIGHWAY SYSTEM

Ports	Sailing Time	Statute Miles
Bellingham to Ketchikan	37 hours	595
Prince Rupert to Ketchikan	6 hours	91
Ketchikan to Wrangell	6 hours	89
Wrangell to Petersburg	3 hours	41
Petersburg to Juneau	8 hours, 30 minutes	123
Juneau to Haines	4 hours, 30 minutes	68
Haines to Skagway	1 hour	13
Petersburg to Sitka	10 hours	156
Sitka to Juneau	8 hours, 45 minutes	132

departing from Prince Rupert are usually less booked than those leaving from Bellingham, and southward-bound ferries are usually less booked than those heading north. Try to be flexible in your planning and provide the reservations office with several alternative dates. For current schedules and reservations, write **Alaska Marine Highway,** P.O. Box 25535, Juneau, AK 99802-5535; telephone (907) 465-3941 or toll-free (800) 642-0066 from both the United States and Canada. The ferry system also has an official Web site at www.state.ak.us/ferry. As a last straw, try telephoning one or more of the Alaska Marine Highway terminals (see "Information Sources," beginning on page 355, for telephone numbers). Any of the ferry terminals can handle reservations and information requests; however, they usually are staffed only during ferry arrivals and departures. Ellen Searby, a former Marine Highway employee, details the workings of the Alaska ferry system in her book, *Alaska's Inside Passage Traveler.*

Ferry passengers often fly kites on the observation deck. It's a good way to pass the time on long voyages. MICHELLE GURNEY

You may be able to save on ferry travel by purchasing a multiday **AlaskaPass.** Similar to European rail passes, the AlaskaPass entitles you to unlimited passage on Alaska and British Columbia ferries as well as rail and motorcoach services in Alaska and Canada. The program offers several options, including family and senior citizen rates. Write **AlaskaPass,** P.O. Box 351, Vashon, WA 98070-0351; telephone (800) 248-7598 or (206) 463-6550; Web site at www.alaskapass.com.

Private ferries that operate between Juneau and Gustavus, the gateway to Glacier Bay National Park, and between Skagway and Haines are another option for ferry travelers who find that the state ferry schedule doesn't fit their itinerary.

TRAVELING BY CRUISE SHIP

The number of ships cruising the Inside Passage during the mid-May through September cruise season increases every year. Most of the ships embark from Vancouver and follow one of two basic itineraries: a seven-day round-trip cruise through the Inside Passage, or a ten-day or longer cruise that takes in the Inside Passage and then crosses the Gulf of Alaska to south-central Alaska ports. A few sailings leave from Seattle or other West Coast ports, and a number of the smaller ships operate entirely within Southeast Alaska.

Although itineraries differ, the typical Inside Passage journey includes stops at Ketchikan, Juneau, Skagway, and Sitka in addition to cruising Glacier Bay. You often have the option of cruising in one direction and connecting with a land tour and/or flying in the other. Ships stay in port from several hours to all day; you can disembark and sightsee on your own or purchase shore excursions from the ship (more expensive in most cases).

The ships cruising Alaska come in virtually every size and style, from the most sumptuous vessel with all-outside staterooms and private balconies to a serviceable "university at sea." The trend in recent years has been to the two extremes. At one end of the spectrum, increasingly larger ships (carrying 1,200 to 2,400 passengers) resemble floating resorts. They emphasize the luxury-cruise experience of fine dining, shipboard activities, and Las Vegas–style

CRUISE SHIPS TRAVELING ALASKA'S INSIDE PASSAGE

Companies that travel to and from Southeast Alaska
(usually departing Vancouver)

Cruise Line	Ship	Passengers	Feet
Alaska Sightseeing Cruise West	*Sheltered Seas*	70	90
(800–580–0072)	*Spirit of Alaska*	78	143
www.cruisewest.com	*Spirit of Columbia*	78	143
	Spirit of Discovery	84	166
	Spirit of Endeavor	102	217
	Spirit of '98	96	192
	Spirit of Oceanus	114	295
Carnival Cruise Lines	*New Spirit*	2,124	963
(800–438–6744)			
www.carnival.com			
Celebrity Cruises	*Infinity*	1,950	965
(800–CELEBRITY)	*Mercury*		
www.celebrity.com		1,870	866
Crystal Cruises	*Crystal Harmony*	940	791
(800–804–1500)			
www.crystalcruises.com			
Holland America Line Westours	*Ryndam*	1,266	720
(877–724–5425)	*Statendam*	1,266	720
www.hollandamerica.com	*Veendam*	1,266	720
	Volendam	1,440	780
	Zaandam	1,440	780
Norwegian Cruise Line	*Norwegian Sky*	2,002	853
(800–327–7030)	*Norwegian Wind*	1,748	754
www.ncl.com			
Princess Cruises	*Coral Princess*	1,950	856
(800–774–6237)	*Dawn Princess*	1,950	856
www.princess.com	*Ocean Princess*	1,950	857
	Sea Princess	1,950	856
	Star Princess	2,600	951
	Sun Princess	1,950	856
Royal Caribbean Cruise Line	*Legend of the Seas*	2,076	867
(800–398–9819)	*Vision of the Seas*	2,435	915
www.royalcaribbean.com			
World Explorer Cruises	*Universe Explorer*	732	618
(800–854–3835)			
www.wecruise.com			

Cruise companies that operate primarily in Southeast Alaska

Cruise Line	Ship	Passengers	Feet
American Safari Cruises	*Safari Escape*	12	112
(888-862-8881)	*Safari Quest*	22	120
www.amsafari.com	*Safari Spirit*	12	105
Glacier Bay Cruiseline	*Wilderness Adventurer*	72	157
(800-451-5952)	*Wilderness Discoverer*	94	104
www.glacierbaytours.com	*Wilderness Explorer*	32	112
Clipper Cruise Line	*Yorktown Clipper*	138	257
(800-325-0010)			
www.clippercruise.com			
Lindblad Expeditions	*Sea Bird*	70	152
(800-397-3348)	*Sea Lion*	70	152
www.lindblad.com			
Society Expeditions	*New World Discoverer*	160	354
(800-548-8669)			
www.societyexpeditions.com			

NOTE: The cruise picture in Alaska changes every season. Check with your travel agent for current information regarding specific cruise lines and schedules.

nightclubs. At the other end of the spectrum, the small ships (138 passengers or fewer) trade glamour for flexibility and focus on the locale. They visit smaller, more out-of-the-way ports and travel some of the more picturesque waterways of the Inside Passage. Holland America Westours and Princess Cruises are the giants of the luxury-cruise industry, whereas Alaska Sightseeing/Cruise West dominates the small-ship scene.

In addition to ships cruising the Inside Passage from Vancouver, Seattle, or other southern ports, a number of small vessels make overnight or day cruises within Alaska to such scenic locales as Glacier Bay and Tracy Arm Fjord. You'll find many of these cruise opportunities mentioned later in chapter 8, "Main-line Ports of the Inside Passage."

BEFORE YOU GO

As a useful first step in planning your trip, write for the *Official State Guide and Vacation Planner* from the Alaska Division of Tourism/ Tourism Marketing Council. This free color publication introduces all the regions of Alaska and includes more than 1,100 listings for hotels, campgrounds, sightseeing opportunities, charter companies, and other services, as well as local chambers of commerce and visitor centers, state and national parks, and other government offices. Write **Alaska Division of Tourism,** P.O. Box 110801, Juneau, AK 99811-0801; telephone (907) 465-2010. Another excellent planning resource is the Southeast Alaska Tourism Council Web site. The address is www.alaskainfo.org. See "Information Sources" at the back of the book for other useful trip-planning information.

IF YOU WANT TO HUNT OR FISH

If you plan to hunt or fish, you should consult directly with the Alaska Department of Fish and Game for regulations concerning the particular quarry you have in mind. Write Public Communications Section, **Alaska Department of Fish and Game,** P.O. Box 25526, Juneau, AK 99802-5526; telephone (907) 465-4112. Several types of fishing, hunting, and trapping licenses are available. In general, a fishing license is required for anyone sixteen years or older fishing in fresh or salt water. For nonresidents of Alaska, five types of license are available: a one-year license ($100), fourteen-day license ($50), seven-day license ($30), three-day license ($20), and one-day license ($10). Licenses are available at most sporting-goods stores in Alaska. You must also purchase a King Salmon stamp for $10 to $100 (depending on the number of days) if you intend to fish for kings (chinook).

Hunting licenses and appropriate tags are required for nonresidents of any age. Fees are $20 for a one-year small game license (grouse, hare, ptarmigan, waterfowl, cranes, and snipe), $85 for a one-year hunting license, or $185 for a one-year combination hunting and sportfishing license. Tag fees, seasons, and bag limits vary with the species, so check with the Fish and Game Department in advance. Those wishing to hunt brown bear, mountain goat, or Dall sheep must be accompanied by either a registered guide or an Alaskan blood relative who is over age nineteen and either a parent, grandparent, sister, brother, child, or grandchild. This rule is strictly interpreted and enforced. Visitors from other countries should check with the Fish and Game Department for special regulations pertaining to them. A list of registered guides is available for $5.00 from the **Alaska Department of Commerce and Economic Development, Division of Occupational Licensing,** P.O. Box 110806, Juneau, AK 99811-0806.

The Alaska Department of Fish and Game publishes free sport-fishing guides for various locales, as well as a fishing atlas of Southeast Alaska, *Salmon Holes and Halibut Hills,* printed on weather-resistant paper, which sells for $12.

IF YOU WANT TO CAMP

There are federal, state, or city campgrounds in all the major Inside Passage communities. A list of campgrounds is included in the *State Guide and Vacation Planner,* or you can write the appropriate chamber of commerce or visitor bureau. In addition, you can camp almost anywhere in the Tongass National Forest (which encompasses much of Southeast Alaska). Exceptions include sensitive areas such as archaeological sites. No permit is necessary to camp or to build a fire, but you should be cautious about fires, even in the rain forest. Many serious fires have been caused by campers who mistakenly thought the rain would put out their campfires for them. Use the same precautions you would camping anyplace else. Also be extremely wary of bears anywhere in the Tongass. Do not camp on known bear paths, and do not leave food in or near your tent. Write the U.S. Forest Service or Alaska Department of Fish and Game for advice about camping and hiking in bear country.

There is a Forest Service office in almost every community along the Inside Passage. Staff members are glad to recommend places to camp, hike, or otherwise enjoy the national forest. Before striking out into the wilderness, it is a good idea to call or visit the local Forest Ser-

Hiking Basics

Most trail guides recommend rubber boots for many of the Panhandle's paths for good reason. The rainy climate can make for some muddy, swampy trails. It's also a good idea to pack rain gear whenever you venture into the woods because chances are there'll be some rain in your future. Having said all that, there's still beauty to find along Southeast's forest, alpine, and beach paths.

If you are a novice hiker, it makes sense to contact the local visitor bureau for the names of guiding services that offer hikes in the area. In Juneau, Gastineau Guiding (223 Gold Street, Juneau, AK 99801; 907–586–2666) may be the most active. Try to contact them a week in advance for the best selection of trip availability. The city also sponsors hikes on local trails Saturday and Wednesday mornings. (In the winter these hikes turn into cross-country ski trips.) Check with the Juneau Parks and Recreation Department for the hike schedule (907–586–5226). Hikers are supposed to bring their own food and gear on these journeys.

It also is helpful to check with the U.S. Forest Service about trails in the area. Another helpful guide is Margaret Piggott's *Discover Southeast Alaska with Pack and Paddle*.

NOTE: Before going out on a hike in Southeast Alaska, hikers should be sure they are equipped with rain gear, extra food and water, a compass, a map of the route, a first-aid kit, and a fire starter. It's also important to let other people know where you are hiking and when you plan to return, in case troubles develop.

vice office to ask their advice and let them know your plans.

For a wilderness adventure at a bargain price, consider renting a U.S. Forest Service recreational cabin. There are more than 145 from which to choose in the Tongass. Most are situated in remote locales: along saltwater inlets or freshwater lakes, accessible only by floatplane or boat. One, a converted railroad caboose, can be reached by rail from Skagway. A couple are wheelchair accessible.

All cabins have a wood-burning or diesel stove, wooden bunks, and a table. Firewood is provided but not stove oil. Many lakeside cabins are supposed to be equipped with a skiff and oars, but you should not depend upon either. For other equipment and food, you are on your own. In fact, you are on your own, period, once the floatplane leaves, so plan accordingly. The cost is $35 per night for your entire party, but you can spend $200 to $300 for your round-trip transportation from the nearest town. Cabins can be reserved up to 180 days in advance for a maximum stay of seven nights (in summer). The Forest Service has contracted with a vendor to handle cabin reservations on the Internet at www.reserveusa.com or by calling toll-free (877) 444-6777. For a map of the cabin locations and other information, write **U.S. Forest Service,** Centennial Hall, 101 Egan Drive, Juneau, AK 99801; telephone (907) 586-8751.

The state Division of Parks also has four cabins for rent in Southeast Alaska, including two reachable by short hikes along the roadside in Juneau. Another cabin is on an island near Ketchikan, and another is on Admiralty Island near Juneau. The rules and costs for the state parks' cabins are similar to those of the Forest Service. For information on state cabin rentals, write **Department of Natural**

Renting a recreational cabin is a great way to have a wilderness adventure. COURTESY USDA FOREST SERVICE

Favorite Hiking Trails

Looking for a memorable hike in Southeast Alaska? Here are a couple of favorite trails throughout Southeast:

Perseverance Trail in Juneau. The trail is built on the remains of an old mining road that ventures into the Gold Creek valley and Perseverance Basin behind downtown Juneau, where gold used to be mined. The trail crosses Gold Creek several times and joins up with the Granite Creek and Mount Juneau Trails.

Rainbow Falls near Wrangell. This steep trail runs nearly a mile up to the falls, through tall trees and forest. The falls are picturesque, and when the skies are clear, this spot offers good views of some of Wrangell's surrounding islands. At the falls you can hook up with another trail that takes a hiker to Shoemaker Hill, which overlooks the water. There is a U.S. Forest Service shelter here. The trailhead for both routes is about 4 miles from town on the Zimovia Highway.

The Chilkoot Trail out of Skagway. This 33-mile trail is laden with history of the Klondike Gold Rush. I first hiked the Chilkoot in 1997 in a race that reenacted the 1897–98 Klondike Gold Rush. We carried fifty-pound packs over the Chilkoot and then paddled across Lakes Bennett, Tagish, Nares, Marsh, and Labarge as we followed the footsteps of the Klondikers. Once past the lakes, we paddled the Yukon River to Dawson, Yukon Territory. In all, it took us eight days, about twice as long as the winners took. Even so, the day we spent racing over the Chilkoot was my favorite, and it's a place I'll continue to go back and hike.

Oliver's Inlet Tram Trail on Admiralty Island. This mile-long trail is interesting because you can use the tram car to carry your kayaks from Oliver's Inlet to Seymour Canal. The excursion on the tram is something. At the end of the tram trail, the state Division of Parks has a public-use cabin that it rents out. Oliver's Inlet is about 5 miles from Douglas Island, across Stephens Passage.

> **The Totem Walk in Sitka.** This trail is about a mile long. The draw here, besides the great coastal views, is the sight of eighteen totem poles in Sitka National Historical Park, spaced along the forested path. The park is the site of the Tlingit and Russian battle of 1804.

Resources, Public Information Center, 3601 C Street, Suite 200, Anchorage, AK 99503-5929 or call (907) 269-8400. The **state parks system's** Internet site at www.dnr.state.ak.us/parks also offers cabin information.

VIEWING WILDLIFE

The Inside Passage abounds with wildlife: humpback and orca whales, bears, eagles, otters, deer, and more. The glossy brochures marketing Alaska destinations imply that you will see these creatures, up close and personal, practically at every turn. The truth is that you may see some spectacular wildlife displays, but you will probably not see as much wildlife as you would like, or as close as you would like, unless you travel into the more remote areas of Southeast. If you cruise the Inside Passage by tour ship or ferry, you will certainly see bald eagles—more, in fact, than you can imagine— and plenty of other birds. You will very likely see humpback whales, orca, and porpoise, although they may be in the distance. If you are very lucky, you may see a bear or black-tailed deer feeding onshore.

If wildlife viewing is a priority, you need to consider travel options that take you away from urban centers and heavily traveled waterways to places where wildlife congregates. This doesn't mean you have to go it alone in the wilderness. Wilderness lodges, simply as a function of their isolation, generally offer excellent wildlife-viewing opportunities, as do smaller cruise ships and excursion vessels that travel the lonelier inlets and fjords. These include day trips to such locales as Tracy Arm near Juneau, overnight excursions into Glacier Bay or around Admiralty Island, and longer Inside Passage cruises. Finally, guided wilderness or nature trips offered by reputable companies such as Alaska Discovery take you safely into the wild country to observe the Southeast Alaska habitat and the creatures that live there.

There are three major designated wildlife-viewing sites in Southeast Alaska, where animals can be observed in their natural habitat under conditions that optimize safety for both animals and humans. They are the Stan Price Bear Sanctuary at Pack Creek on Admiralty Island, the Anan Creek Bear Observatory near Wrangell, and the Chilkat Bald Eagle Preserve near Haines. Travelers seeking information about watchable wildlife can purchase the book *Alaska Wildlife Viewing Guide* from the state Department of Fish and Game for $10.50 (which includes postage). The address is P.O. Box 25526, Juneau, AK 99802; telephone (907) 465-4190.

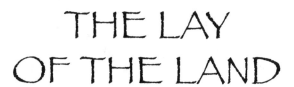

CHAPTER TWO

THE LAY
OF THE LAND

I f you look at a map of Alaska, you will see that the Southeast region consists of a narrow strip of coast wedged between the Pacific Ocean and the Canadian border and a multitude of sizable islands that lie offshore. The rest of Alaska is positioned far to the north in a distinctly separate chunk. The awkward shape of the state has been likened to that of a frying pan, which is why Southeast Alaska is frequently called the Panhandle.

Most of Southeast Alaska, whether island or mainland coast, is covered with either permanent snow and ice (10 percent) or with dense rain forest of spruce and hemlock (45 percent). The only exceptions are the alpine zones above tree level that are snow-free in summer, the marshy estuaries, and the river valleys that cut through the mountains to the sea.

THE PANHANDLE

The Panhandle extends from Dixon Entrance, which separates the Queen Charlotte Islands that lie in Canadian territory from their Alaska counterparts, to Icy Cape, on the western edge of Malaspina Glacier—a distance of some 600 miles. The mainland strip and the islands offshore average 120 miles across and are bounded by the Coast Mountains and the border between the United States and Canada, which follows the line of the mountain peaks. These Coast Mountains are actually part of the Pacific Mountain System that continues along the coast to the north to take in the Saint Elias

Mountains near Yakutat, the Chugach Mountains that border Prince William Sound, the Kenai Mountains that extend southward from Anchorage, the Kodiak Mountains on Kodiak Island, and the Aleutian Range. In total this mountain system wraps 1,000 miles around the Pacific Coast. In Southeast the most rugged of the Coast Mountains are those of the Fairweather Range, which forms the western edge of Glacier Bay, separating the national park and preserve from the Pacific Ocean. Mount Fairweather rises to 15,300 feet, one of the highest mountains in Southeast Alaska.

The coastal mountains extend into the Pacific Ocean to form a complex arrangement of mountainous islands called the Alexander Archipelago. Close to 1,000 in number, these islands constitute a major portion of the land mass of Southeast Alaska and contain four of the major communities in the area (Ketchikan, Wrangell, Petersburg, and Sitka) and most of the smaller ones as well. Several of the islands are more than 1,000 square miles in area. The largest is Prince of Wales Island, across Clarence Strait from Ketchikan, with 2,770 square miles.

Separating the islands from the mainland and one another is a veinlike system of waterways that has come to be known as the Inside Passage. Many of the waterways are fjords—narrow, deep, sheer-sided troughs that were scraped out by advancing glaciers thousands of years ago and subsequently flooded by the sea. Some, such as Chatham Strait and Lynn Canal, follow faults that formed millions of years ago. The Inside Passage has served as a transportation and communication network since humans first settled in Southeast Alaska. Even now, there is no road system to connect the communities along the Panhandle, and the waterways have taken the place of highways.

The rugged face of Southeast Alaska was carved during the Great Ice Age one million years ago. During this era, the Pleistocene, thick plates of ice covered all of the Panhandle except the very tops of the highest mountains and extended miles into the Pacific Ocean. Glaciers flowed down the natural drainage courses in the Coast Mountains, scouring the trenches into deep, narrow channels as they moved. When the Ice Age ended some 10,000 to 15,000 years ago, Southeast was frozen in place. As the climate warmed, the ice receded and ocean water flooded into the glacial trenches to form the fjords we see at present. There followed other periods of cooler climate when the glaciers surged forward once again. The most recent was the Little Ice Age, which culminated in the seventeenth and eighteenth centuries. Now all but a few of the glaciers continue to retreat.

GLACIER FACTS

A glacier is an accumulation of snow and ice that continually flows from a mountain ice field toward sea level. Glaciers are formed when successive snowfalls pile up, creating pressure on the bottom layers. Gradually, the pressure causes the snow on the bottom to undergo a structural change into an extremely dense form of ice called glacier ice, a process that may take several years. Once the ice begins to accumulate, gravity causes the mass to move downhill. Glaciers usually take the path of least resistance, following stream beds or other natural channels down the mountain. As they move, they scrape the surface of the earth, picking up rocks and other sediment on the way. The ice and the debris carve a deep U-shaped valley as they proceed down the mountain. If they advance far enough, they will eventually reach the sea and become tidewater glaciers that break off, or calve, directly into salt water. Alaska is one of only three places in the world where tidewater glaciers exist (Scandinavia and Chile are the others). Other glaciers, called hanging glaciers, spill out of icy basins high up on valley walls and tumble toward the valley floor.

Glaciers are in a constant state of flux because of increases or decreases in precipitation and temperature. Minor changes can cause significant buildup or reduction in the accumulation of snow on the glacier. When the buildup of glacier ice is greater than the amount lost to melting or calving at the terminus, the glacier will gain ground and is said to advance. If the reverse is true and the ice melts faster than new ice accumulates, the glacier will lose ground and is said to retreat. Some glaciers are simply in a state of equilibrium, the new accumulation roughly equaling the degree of loss. Glaciers can stay in a state of equilibrium for years. Regardless of whether a particular glacier is advancing, retreating, or in a state of equilibrium, the ice continues to flow down the mountain at a measurable rate. Only the total length of the glacier is affected.

The surface of a glacier is interrupted by fissures that develop as the mass moves downhill. It also accumulates a dark layer of dirt and rocks and other debris that falls from the valley walls. This sediment, called a lateral moraine, usually occurs in two distinct dark stripes, one on each side of the glacier. When two valley glaciers meet and merge into one, the inner lateral moraines merge into a single medial moraine that can be seen in the middle of the new superglacier. The moraines of some glaciers are so prominent that they look like asphalt highways from the air.

Glaciers are not blue, although they certainly look blue, especially where a new wedge of ice has just calved from the face. The blue appearance is attributable to a trick of light: The molecules of ice absorb all the colors of the spectrum except blue, which is reflected outward. The blue color is more noticeable on overcast days.

The Mendenhall Glacier is a must-see attraction just 13 miles from Juneau. At 12 miles long, it retreats at a rate of 30 to 50 feet a year. MICHELLE GURNEY

Glaciers exist only in areas that provide the heavy snowfall needed to accumulate into glacier ice. Most of the glaciers in Southeast Alaska are born out of two massive ice fields in the Coast Mountains: the Stikine and the Juneau ice fields. The Stikine Ice Field, which starts in the mountains north of Wrangell, has spawned at least a dozen sizable glaciers, many of which can be seen from the water. The best known is the Le Conte Glacier, which empties into salt water at the head of Le Conte Bay, between Wrangell and Petersburg. The Le Conte is the southernmost tidewater glacier in North America. Although the glacier was in a state of equilibrium from the 1960s until 1994, it receded about half a mile between the winter of that year and the spring of 1996. It appears now to be stable again. In any case, it continues to flow downward into the sea and discharges icebergs into the bay.

The Juneau Ice Field consists of approximately 1,500 square miles of ice and snow sprawling in back of Juneau, over the border into Canada, and north nearly to Skagway. The ice field has produced more than thirty glaciers, including the famous Mendenhall. The Mendenhall Glacier measures approximately 12 miles long, 1.5 miles wide, and 30 to 40 feet high above water level at the face where it terminates in a deep lake. Below the surface of the water it descends an additional 150 feet. The glacier is retreating at the rate of 30 to 50 feet a year.

Reached by highway north of Juneau, the Mendenhall is one of Alaska's most accessible glaciers. A splendid view can be had even from the parking lot. The Forest Service operates a visitor center, which was recently expanded, and maintains trails to the flanks of the glacier. A self-guided nature walk illustrates features of the glacier-carved terrain.

Other glaciers visible from either the highway north of Juneau or from the water include Lemon Creek Glacier, Herbert Glacier, and Eagle Glacier. None of these glaciers descends to tidewater. Presently some 260 square miles in size, Taku Glacier is the largest from the Juneau Ice Field. Forest Service experts say that the Taku now appears to be stabilized and "digging itself in" at the terminus, growing as much as 13 feet thicker a year.

The sixteen tidewater glaciers of Glacier Bay National Park and Preserve course out of the massive Saint Elias Mountains. As recently as 200 years ago, when Captain George Vancouver charted the Southeast Alaska coast for England, glaciers completely filled the area now known as Glacier Bay. The various glaciers that flow into the bay have retreated to the point that the bay presently measures 60 miles long. Presently the Johns Hopkins and Grand Pacific Glaciers on the west arm of the bay are slowly advancing; the others in the area are stabilized or retreating.

Traveling up Glacier Bay is like taking a trip back in time: The farther you proceed toward the active glaciers at the head of the bay, the more primitive the plant forms become. A retreating glacier leaves behind a deposit of rock and other sediment that was scraped along its advancing path. This deposit, called glacial till, is composed chiefly of ground-up rock with little or no organic content—only limited organisms such as lichens and mosses are able to establish themselves. With time, however, such low-growing pioneer plants as dwarf fireweed and dryas gain a foothold and begin improving the soil for other species. Next come low shrubs and broadleaf trees such as willow and alder, which improve the soil still further. Finally evergreens take root and develop into the common spruce and hemlock forest of Southeast Alaska. At present, established forest exists only at the entrance to Glacier Bay, where the land has been ice-free the longest.

Despite the barren environment left in the wake of receding glaciers, a surprising number of organisms exist on or near the ice. Scientists report more than seventy species of wildflowers growing in the vicinity of the Juneau Ice Field. A variety of insects thrive there, too, among them the snow flea, a species seemingly impervious to heat, cold, and moisture. Small black glacier worms, called ice worms, live off the algae that grows on glacier ice or on other organic matter that falls onto the ice. First noted in Alaska on the Muir Glacier in 1887, the ice worm is the only species of earthworm known to inhabit snow and ice.

THE WEATHER FORECAST

Contrary to popular belief, Southeast Alaska enjoys a mild climate: cool in summer and moderate in winter (the average winter temperature is 33 degrees Fahrenheit). The sea provides a warming influence in winter when the water is warmer than the air, and a cooling influence in summer when the air is warmer than the water. In every season, the ocean pumps quantities of moisture into the air. The moisture is gathered by storm clouds borne across the Pacific on the jet stream and released as rain and snow when they contact the steeply rising slopes of the Coast Mountains. In winter the dense cloud cover over coastal Alaska also acts as a layer of insulation to retain the heat generated by the land and water. In summer the effect is reversed, and the clouds insulate the cool landmass from the sun's rays.

The temperature varies little from one Southeast community to another. The average year-round temperature is 40 degrees Fahrenheit, with the coldest weather usually in January and the warmest in July. Besides being moderate, the temperature is also quite constant in Southeast, normally varying fewer than ten degrees in the course of the day. In winter temperatures usually range from the high teens to the low forties. In summer the mid-fifties to the mid-sixties is the norm, although the thermometer can soar to the eighties on a sunny day.

Extreme temperatures can occur in winter, too. For example, in Juneau the winds usually blow out of the southeast. But occasionally they blow across the ice fields of the Coast Mountains and rush down the glacier valleys in gusts of more than 100 miles per hour. This bitter wind, known as the Taku, occurs in clear, cold conditions, and it sends the windchill factor plummeting.

Although temperatures vary little from place to place, precipitation varies quite a lot. Most of Southeast Alaska is a rain forest, averaging more than 100 inches of rain and snow a year (as a rule of thumb, 10 inches of snow is the equivalent of 1 inch of rain). But the southern third of the Panhandle is rainier than the rest. Ketchikan usually takes credit for being the "liquid sunshine" capital of the state with an average yearly precipitation of 152 inches, but the record is actually held by Little Port Walter, near the southeast tip of Baranof Island, at 221 inches of precipitation a year. Things become drier as you move north: 106 inches in Petersburg, 70 in Juneau, and only 26 in Skagway. In winter most of this precipitation falls as snow. In the northern part of the Panhandle, much of the snow stays on the ground and accumulates, even at sea level. In the mountains Southeast is able to produce more than 200 inches of snow a year, which is what fuels the pretty glaciers.

Southeastern residents, then, experience a predominance of cool, moist days with overcast skies. June is usually the driest month and October the wettest. Winters, not at all unpleasant, produce moderate temperatures and lots of snow for skiing and sledding. Snow typically begins falling in late October. Heavy snowfalls can accumulate as late as April.

What drives southeasterners "Outside" for periodic respites is the gray cloud that seems to hang overhead for weeks at a time. When the cloud moves on, however, and the sun reappears, the beauty of the lush, green forests and the snowcapped mountains blots out all memories of overcast skies and winters that endure through spring.

THE WATERS

Alaska is a land of enormous tides, and Southeast is no exception. The height of the tide increases as it moves over the continental shelf and squeezes up the narrow passages of the Alexander Archipelago. The tide reaches as high as 21.2 feet in Haines, at the north of Lynn Canal, and falls to as low as –5.0. In Juneau the tides can reach highs of 20.7 feet and lows of –5.0 feet. At Sitka the tidal range is more moderate, from 12.9 feet to –2.9. There are two high tides and two low tides within every twenty-four-hour period.

The large tides cause powerful currents as the water ebbs and flows through the tight waterways. In Wrangell Narrows south of Petersburg and Sergius Narrows en route to Sitka—two of the most scenic stretches of water along the Inside Passage—the current has been clocked at more than 8 miles an hour. If you are traveling by canoe or kayak, the tidal currents can prove dangerous. Always check the tide table before starting through a narrow channel and talk with local residents about the conditions. Make the passage when the tide is slack—either high or low—and not on the change, and don't camp too near the waterline. Tide tables are available at most sporting-goods shops in Southeast.

The temperature of the water kills. Though warmed by the Japanese current that keeps Southeast ports ice-free in winter, the coastal water is too cold to support human life for more than a few minutes. The surface temperature of the water varies from place to place, but the range is typically as follows: winter, 42.5 to 45 degrees; spring, 45 to 47 degrees; summer, 55 to 57 degrees; fall, 45 to 47 degrees.

When a human is immersed in such waters, body heat is lost into the water, causing hypothermia, or subnormal body temperature. If the body temperature drops far enough, the victim becomes unconscious and death will follow. Survival time in the water varies according to the size, shape, physical condition, and mental attitude of the victim, but the table in this section shows the approximate survival time of a human immersed in the ocean.

In sum, the cool climate of Southeast Alaska can turn a normal situation into a dangerous situation in a hurry. Be cautious whenever you are facing the elements, whether boating, hiking, skiing, fishing, or simply walking around on the docks.

SURVIVAL TIME

WATER TEMPERATURE (FAHRENHEIT)	EXHAUSTION OR UNCONSCIOUSNESS	EXPECTED TIME OF SURVIVAL
32.5 degrees	15 minutes	15 to 45 minutes
32.5 to 40 degrees	15 to 30 minutes	30 to 90 minutes
40 to 50 degrees	30 to 60 minutes	1 to 3 hours
50 to 60 degrees	1 to 2 hours	1 to 6 hours
60 to 70 degrees	2 to 7 hours	2 to 40 hours
70 to 80 degrees	3 to 12 hours	3 hours plus (indefinite)

EVERLASTING DAYS
AND NIGHTS

Southeast Alaska is far enough north to enjoy some of the Arctic "midnight sun" effect. In the course of the year, the number of daylight hours ranges from seven to eighteen and a half hours. At summer's peak, however, most of the remaining five and a half hours are in twilight, so the effective daylight is more like twenty-two hours. If you step outside at midnight on a clear night in midsummer, you can read a newspaper in the available light. On June 21, the longest day of the year, you can expect more than seventeen hours of daylight in Ketchikan and more than eighteen hours in Juneau and Skagway.

In winter the opposite conditions prevail. On the shortest day of the year, December 21, Ketchikan residents will see the sun for about seven hours. Juneau gets about six and a half hours of sun that day and Skagway about six hours. It is dark going to work in the morning and dark again going home.

Although minimal compared with the Arctic, the seasonal fluctuations in daylight make themselves felt in people's attitudes and levels of activity. People seem to become increasingly energized as the days lengthen. By summer's peak, with near-perpetual daylight, it is not unusual to put in a full day at the office and then spend several more hours fishing or working on the house or yard. The streets ring with the voices of children playing late into the evening. With the onset of winter's darkness, the pace slows and people seem to need more sleep.

CHAPTER THREE

~~~~~~~~~~

SOUTHEAST PAST TO PRESENT

Fifteen thousand years ago, the watery trail now known as the Inside Passage was locked in an icy embrace. Glaciers flowed down the 10,000-foot peaks and scoured the valleys below. As the land warmed, the ocean waters gradually thawed. Rivers sprang from melting glaciers and coursed across the land, carrying a succession of unknown peoples who lingered along the coast as many as 9,000 years ago. Eventually—perhaps some 1,500 years ago, perhaps longer—groups of Tlingit Indians followed the waterways out of Interior Alaska and Canada and into the lush coastal forests of Southeast Alaska.

The Tlingit lived comfortably off the land. They formed small villages along the coast, where they could harvest the resources that the sea and land placed within their reach. They fished for salmon and halibut, collected seaweed from the beach, and picked the blueberries, salmonberries, and nagoonberries growing wild along the Southeast shore. They learned to use the forest cedar and spruce for shelter, tools, and complex works of art.

The Tlingit traveled the length of their 600-mile domain by wooden canoe. Occasionally they contacted the Haida Indians, who lived to the south of them, or the Athapaskans, who ranged across Interior Alaska to the north. Secure in their rain-forest environment, the Tlingit peoples prospered and increased. By the middle of the eighteenth century, the Southeast Alaska coastline was one of the most heavily populated regions north of Mexico.

No white person had yet set foot upon the shore. On the day that the first sailing ship appeared off the Southeast coast, according to one Tlingit tradition, the villagers had sent several boys to the beach to see if the wild celery shoots had reached the height that meant the seaweed was ready to harvest. The boys came running back with the news that a huge white Thunderbird—in Tlingit mythology, a powerful spirit that created thunder by beating his enormous wings and lightning by blinking his eyes—was approaching from the sea. Most of the villagers fled. Those who stayed behind watched as the Thunderbird folded his wings and white men came ashore for the first time in Southeast Alaska.

In that instant, life along the Inside Passage changed irrevocably. The future of Southeast Alaska would be governed by the harvesting of resources as first furs, then gold, fish, timber, and even the ice itself brought wave after wave of fortune hunters into the coastal wilderness.

FIRST CONTACT

The men who rowed ashore from the white "thunderbird" might have come from the *Saint Paul,* one of two Russian ships that set out on an exploratory expedition under the command of Vitus Bering in 1741. The North Pacific coast was an unknown entity in the 1700s. European expeditions had unraveled the mysteries of much of the rest of North America (the English had been settled in Hudson's Bay since 1670, and the Spanish were on the California coast), but the northern region had remained obscure. In 1725 the Russian czar Peter the Great had sent Bering on a preliminary voyage to find out what lay to the east of Russia: Were the continents of Asia and North America one and the same, or were they separate? Sailing from the mouth of the Kamchatka River in Siberia, Bering passed through what would come to be called Bering Strait but turned back without sighting the Alaskan coast. On his second voyage, in 1741, Bering left with two ships: the *Saint Peter,* under his own command, and the *Saint Paul,* captained by Alexei Chirikof. Fifteen days out they became separated and never sighted each other again.

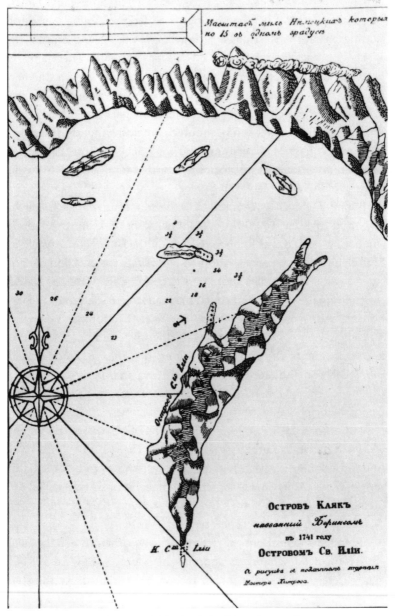

A 1741 Russian map shows Kayak Island and cloud-capped mountains. CENTENNIAL COLLECTIONS, ALASKA HISTORICAL LIBRARY

Chirikof, in the *Saint Paul*, was the first to glimpse the North American continent. He sighted high wooded mountains near Cape Addington off the west coast of Prince of Wales Island on July 15, 1741. Two days later he anchored in a bay (possibly where Sitka is presently located) and sent an armed party ashore. When the men failed to return, a second landing party went to investigate. They did not return either. On the day after that, two parties of Tlingit paddled out to the ship in canoes, shouted something that the Russians, of course, could not understand, and went back to shore. Having no other landing boats at his disposal, Chirikof turned back to Russia without learning the fate of his men.

Bering, meanwhile, proceeded in the same east-northeast direction and sighted 18,000-foot Mount Saint Elias near Yakutat. Anchoring near Kayak Island, to the southeast of Prince William Sound, he sent two parties ashore to investigate the area and replenish the water supply. The shore parties found a few deserted Native dwellings made of logs and rough planks, some underground storehouses, and signs of a recent cooking fire. They took away several household items, such as bundles of dried fish and a wooden box, and left some of their own possessions in exchange, among them reportedly some tobacco, a pipe, cloth, and an iron kettle.

One of the members of the shore expedition was the naturalist Georg Wilhelm Steller. In the short time that Bering allowed him to remain ashore, Steller collected specimens of plants and birds that were not native to Europe or Asia, among them a most important find: a dark blue jay with a high head crest known to be an inhabitant of North America. Steller realized that this bird—now called the Steller's jay—was proof that the new land was part of the North American continent and separate from Asia.

Bering, anxious about the deteriorating weather, turned the *Saint Peter* toward Kamchatka as soon as the water casks were full but encountered a massive storm in the Aleutians that drove the ship hundreds of miles off course. After battling the Aleutian weather throughout late summer and fall, he made a landing on one of the Commander Islands (west of the Aleutian chain) in November. The crew scraped pits in the bank of a ravine for shelter, collected driftwood for a roof, and settled in to try to survive the winter, keeping themselves warm with pelts from blue foxes and other animals that were plentiful around the island. The *Saint Peter* was blown ashore, and they salvaged what they could from the wreck. Bering died in December, like so many of his crew, a victim of exhaustion, exposure, and scurvy, the scourge of early seafarers.

When spring came the survivors built a 40-foot craft from the wreckage of the *Saint Peter* and reached home port in little more than two weeks. Among their baggage were 900 sea otter pelts that had been collected during the stay in the Commander Islands. Richly colored, glossy, and luxurious, the pelts fetched astonishingly high prices from Chinese merchants, and before long the first wave of Russian fur traders set off to find the mysterious fur-rich lands to the east and their small marine inhabitant, the sea otter.

THE EUROPEAN EXPLORERS

In the years following the return of the Bering expedition, word trickled through the courts of Europe that the Russians had discovered a great land in the North Pacific that was rich in furs and possibly other treasures as well. A progression of exploratory voyages was soon under way to find this land and to find the Northwest Passage between the Pacific and Atlantic Oceans that rumors persistently claimed to exist. Between 1774 and 1800, sailing ships from Spain, Britain, France, Russia, and America glided among the misty waterways of Southeast Alaska. Some of them reached tentatively northward along the Gulf of Alaska to Prince William Sound and Cook Inlet, then passed through the Aleutian Chain to the Bering Sea and proceeded into the Arctic. Eventually, all came to the same conclusion: If the Northwest Passage lay in that direction, it would not be usable anyway. (It took until 1837 to prove that there was a passageway from the Arctic Ocean to the Atlantic, but it was so clogged with ice for much of the year that it was of little practical use.)

The early explorers bartered with the local inhabitants they encountered along their route, paving the way for the trading vessels that would soon follow. Besides the coveted furs, the sea captains brought out of Alaska the first examples of Southeast Alaska Native art and culture, as well as detailed sketches of Native villages. These

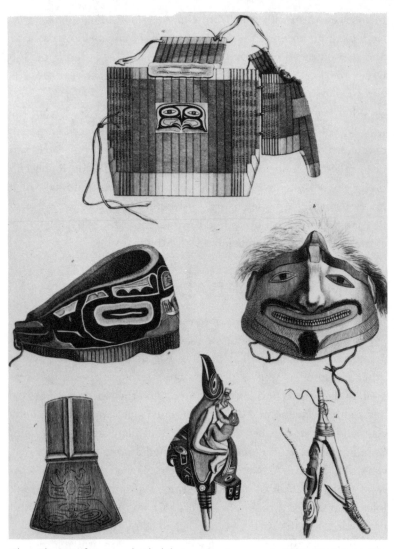

These Tlingit artifacts were sketched during a Russian voyage in 1805. CENTENNIAL COL-
LECTIONS, ALASKA HISTORICAL LIBRARY

items—woven blankets and baskets, carved wooden feast dishes,
fishing equipment, and household tools—which are now displayed
in museums of European capitals, give us a priceless portrait of the
Tlingit and Haida peoples at the time of their initial contact with
European culture. Among the legacies of the explorers were the place

names they gave to many of the landforms in Southeast Alaska. Juan Pérez was the first of the international boating community to follow the Russians into Alaska, sailing from Spain in the *Santiago* in 1774. With holdings in Mexico and California, the Spanish were in an excellent position to continue their explorations northward along the Pacific coast. Pérez proceeded far enough to sight Prince of Wales Island, which he named Santa Maria Magdalena. The following year he returned with two ships. He turned back because of a storm before reaching Alaska, but Lieutenant Juan Francisco de la Bodega y Quadra, in the second vessel, sighted Mount Edgecumbe at Sitka before scurvy forced him to retreat. On the way home he entered and named Bucareli Bay on the outside coast of Prince of Wales Island.

English sea captain James Cook reached Southeast in 1778 on the third of his remarkable explorations to the Pacific (the first two had taken him to New Zealand, Australia, and the Antarctic). In the ships *Resolution* and *Discovery,* he sighted and named Mount Edgecumbe off Sitka and Mount Fairweather off the Gulf of Alaska and then continued along the coast to the north until he was stopped by the Arctic ice. He then headed south to winter in the Hawaiian Islands, preparatory to continuing the search for the Northwest Passage the following summer, but was killed there in a dispute with the indigenous people.

The French explorations were carried out by Jean François Galaup de la Pérouse in the ships *Astrolabe* and *Boussole.* La Pérouse arrived in Southeast in June 1786. He sighted Mount Saint Elias and anchored for some days at Lituya Bay (south of Yakutat), surveying the inlet and trading with the local Tlingit. The trip ended in disaster when two of the survey boats were swept into the breakers at the entrance to the bay and all hands lost. La Pérouse left Alaska after the catastrophe and journeyed to the Kamchatka Peninsula, where he arranged for his journals to be sent on to Paris, which was a good idea because when he turned south again, the *Astrolabe* and *Boussole* vanished in the southern oceans.

The British returned to Alaska in 1793. Captain George Vancouver sailed from England with instructions to verify Cook's findings and make one more search for the Northwest Passage. Cook's voyages had pretty much convinced the British government that no practical waterway existed north of latitude 60° (to the north or west of the Gulf of Alaska), but rumors persisted that the elusive passage lay to the south of latitude 60° (that is, in Southeast Alaska). Vancouver was also charged with charting the coast from the Columbia River to Cook Inlet. Having served with Cook on the last voyage, he was no stranger to the territory.

Vancouver's ships, the *Discovery* and *Chatham,* arrived in Southeast Alaska in July 1793. Throughout that summer he and his four-man survey teams worked along the inlets and passageways of the Alexander Archipelago. They ran south in the fall to winter in the Hawaiian Islands, returned the following summer, and mapped their way south from Cook Inlet. When they left for England in August 1794 (arriving the following year), Vancouver took with him a set of charts so accurate that they were used for years after Alaska became a U.S. possession. Vancouver also provided many of the names we presently use for geographical features (among them Chatham Strait, which he named for English statesman William Pitt Chatham, the Earl of Chatham, and Lynn Canal, which he named for his birthplace, King's Lynn, in Norfolk) and proved conclusively that there was no usable passage through North America between the Pacific and the Atlantic below or above latitude 60°. Besides successfully completing his mission, Vancouver accumulated a remarkable safety record. During the four and one-half years that the expedition was gone from England, the *Discovery* lost only six men out of a crew of one hundred: five through accidents and one from disease. The *Chatham* did not lose a single man.

THE RUSSIAN OCCUPATION

When the survivors of the *Saint Peter* staggered back to Saint Petersburg with their souvenir pelts of lustrous sea otter that fetched fabulous prices from Chinese traders, they touched off a fur stampede to the North Pacific. The onslaught consisted mainly of *promyshlenniki*—gangs of toughs who moved through the mountains of Russia, conquering villages and forcing villagers to pay a tribute in furs to the czar. The *promyshlenniki* had reached the coast of Kamchatka by the time of Bering's expedition, and when they saw the rich furs com-

The unassuming sea otter caused a fur stampede to the North Pacific. CENTENNIAL COL-LECTIONS, ALASKA HISTORICAL LIBRARY

ing in from the unknown waters to the east, they recognized an unparalleled opportunity for profit.

The *promyshlenniki* built boats out of anything they could find and set out for the Commander Islands, where Bering's party had been shipwrecked. The *promyshlenniki* were mountain men, not seamen, and many were swamped at sea in their unseaworthy crafts, but those who managed to complete the trip found their dreams come true—acres of sea otter available for the taking. The Russian opportunists gradually worked their way along the Commander Islands and onto the Aleutian chain, harvesting the sea otter as they went. They met little resistance from the indigenous Aleuts, who were gentle and unwarlike in nature. The Russians made it their practice to take the Aleut women and children hostage and force the Aleut men to hunt sea otter. In their lithe skin kayaks, which the Russians called *bidarka,* the Aleuts were much more efficient hunters than the Russians were, anyway.

Kodiak Colony

The Russian expeditions traveled farther and farther from Kamchatka as the hunting grounds were depleted, and the excursions became more costly. The fur traders gradually banded together in small companies to make the trips economical. In 1783 a merchant named Grigor Shelikof decided to establish a permanent hunting base on the Aleutian Islands that would make the fur-gathering business more efficient still. That summer Shelikof, his wife, Natalie, and a small party of settlers founded the first Russian colony in Alaska on the southeast part of Kodiak Island. The Russians soon had a working settlement with houses, offices, and outbuildings. They organized the indigenous population into work parties to hunt sea otter, gather food, and perform other menial tasks. The idea worked tolerably well, and the storehouses filled up with furs. Shelikof's company was the forerunner of the Russian-American Company, which would ultimately be granted a royal charter with exclusive rights to all trade and properties in Alaska.

By 1790 Shelikof had concluded he needed someone to manage the Alaska colony for him. Alexander Baranof was a natural organizer, gutsy and efficient, and experienced in trading with Siberian natives. When at last he arrived at Kodiak, after a shipwreck in the Aleutians, he set about trying to improve conditions in the settlement. Sea otter were growing scarce, and supplies, which had to be shipped out from Russia, were constantly running out. There was also the increasingly serious problem of trying to prevent traders from other countries, now familiar with the Alaska coast, from encroaching upon the Russian position. Baranof began to scout for a better location for the colony.

Saint Archangel Michael

The Russians established a small agricultural settlement at Yakutat in 1795, but Baranof's choice for a new headquarters was a natural harbor on the outside coast of Baranof Island. In April 1799 a convoy of Russians and Aleuts crossed the Gulf of Alaska to the new site in Southeast Alaska. Baranof negotiated with the chief of the local Tlingit Indians for land on which to build a fort. The site was on the harbor about 6 miles north of the present town of Sitka. The Russians and a detachment of Aleuts stayed to start the building, while the rest of the Aleut hunters went back to Kodiak with instructions to hunt along the way. Two days after their departure, they had rounded the northern shore of the island and were camped on the beach when they ate a meal of purple-black mussels that grew there in great profusion. Many of the Aleuts became violently ill, and more than one hundred died—the first known case of paralytic shellfish poisoning in Southeast Alaska. From this event the body of water became known as *Pogibshii*, the Russian word for deadly, and has come down to us as Peril Strait.

The Russians quickly completed a two-story barracks and various outbuildings, all enclosed within a wooden stockade. Baranof named the new settlement Saint Archangel Michael. The Russian outpost was simply a foothold in the midst of what had become an international trading center on traditional Tlingit ground. French, Spanish, British, and Yankee vessels had visited Sitka Sound for years. They traded cloth, beads, blankets, metal, and anything else they could get the Tlingit to take as payment for the profitable furs they had come to find. During the 1790s, twenty to thirty trading ships a year anchored at various harbors along the northern coast. Eventually some of the sea captains found two other items that the local Indians would readily accept in exchange for furs: alcohol and arms.

The Sitka Indians tolerated the Russian settlement initially but became increasingly angry about the way the Russians treated them, especially their women, and they got into disputes with the Aleuts as well. The situation became volatile. When Baranof left on a trip back to Kodiak three years after founding the Sitka settlement, he gave strict instructions to avoid giving offense to the Tlingit and to be continually on the alert.

On Sunday, June 20, 1802, when most of the Russians and Aleuts were away from the fort hunting, fishing, or picking berries in the woods, the Tlingit attacked. Wearing their fierce-looking wooden helmets and armed with guns and spears, the warriors emerged from the forest, where they had been hiding, and quickly overran the stockade. The Russians resisted the attack, but almost all were killed or captured. A few of those in the woods escaped to the water and were rescued by English and American boats anchored in the sound. The Tlingit burned the buildings, and the post was completely destroyed.

Retaking Sitka

Baranof immediately made preparations to retake the Sitka outpost. In the summer of 1804, a second convoy left Kodiak for Sitka Sound. This time the party consisted of some 400 *bidarkas* carrying 800 Aleuts, plus two small sailing ships with 120 Russians. The expedition stopped at Yakutat to pick up two additional vessels that Baranof had commissioned for the attack. When they arrived at Baranof Island, they found the frigate *Neva* had arrived from Kodiak to assist. The Tlingit retreated to a stronghold when the Russians began their cannon assault. The Russians landed 150 men on the beach but were repulsed with ten killed and twenty-six wounded, including Baranof, who took a shot in the arm. After several days of alternating negotiations and bombardment, the Tlingit quietly abandoned

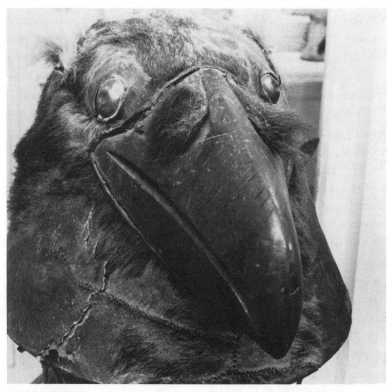

Chief Katlean's Raven helmet, worn in the 1804 battle with the Russians, is displayed in the Sheldon Jackson Museum in Sitka.

their fort during the night and slipped away to Chichagof Island to the north. Baranof ordered the Tlingit stronghold burned. He built a new stockade with houses, storehouses, and other buildings within, calling the settlement New Archangel.

For the Tlingit, the hero of the occasion was the young chief Katlean, who led the battle against the Russians, fighting fiercely hand to hand and, according to tradition, swinging at his enemies with a mighty hammer. Remarkably, Katlean's raven-shaped helmet can be seen now in the Sheldon Jackson Museum in Sitka. (At Sitka National Historic Park, the actual battle site, you can view a film about the contest and the Russian settlement at Sitka.)

New Archangel

The year after retaking Sitka, the Russians had completed eight new buildings and cleared ground for gardens and livestock. Baranof had concluded a treaty with part of the Tlingit tribe, and although others remained hostile, relations had improved to the point that the Indians were invited to the settlement occasionally for feasting and presents. The main worry continued to be food. The climate was cool and damp, the Russian settlers were not farmers by trade or inclination, the soil was unproductive, and the crops were not a success. Baranof developed a penchant for buying ships with cargoes intact from Americans who happened into port.

Baranof invited the Tlingit to return to Sitka in 1821. In the intervening years, they had caused periodic trouble for the colonists by interfering with the Aleut hunting parties, and Baranof thought the wisest course would be to let them return to their ancestral home. Besides, he needed their skills to provide game and fish for the Russian larders. The Indians settled around the Russian fort. They outnumbered the Russians, and the colonists were in constant fear of another uprising, but an uneasy truce prevailed.

In 1834 the Russians established a second outpost in Southeast Alaska. Redoubt Saint Dionysius was built to prevent the British Hudson's Bay Company, a fierce competitor for the Native fur trade, from using the Stikine River to gain access to the fur-rich Interior. The post was placed close to the mouth of the Stikine, at present-day Wrangell.

The 1840s were the height of development for the colonists at New Archangel. The physical plant had grown to include a governor's residence atop Castle Hill, a clubhouse for lower officials, barracks and other housing, a library, an observatory, churches, a hospital, an arsenal, a wharf, and three schools, including an academy that trained students in surveying, navigation, engraving, and accounting as well as a finishing school for young ladies and a theological seminary. There were shipyards that built steam vessels, a forge that fabricated plow blades and spades for Spanish farmers in California, and a foundry, sawmill, flour mill, and fish saltery. New Archangel was not only the center of commerce for the twenty-four Russian settlements that then existed in Alaska, the town was the largest port on the entire North Pacific coast. In the days when San Francisco was still a muddy hole in the Pacific, Sitka was a haven of culture for trading vessels from all over the world.

In the 1850s a new industry was born: ice. Enterprising capitalists discovered that lake ice from Southeast Alaska could be packed in sawdust deep in a ship's hold and arrive in San Francisco intact. Over the next decade, tons of ice were sawed from freshwater lakes at both Sitka and Kodiak and shipped south. Fish and lumber were sent south, too, for sale in California, Mexico, and Hawaii. Other ships came north to be repaired in Sitka's well-equipped shipyards. On occasion there were fifteen vessels in the harbor at once, loading and unloading wares.

The Russians Opt Out

At length, Russia's expenses of maintaining the Alaska colonies began to outweigh the benefits. The fur trade diminished to almost nothing as the supply of pelts grew scarce. Provisioning remained a constant headache, as did the difficulties of maintaining a political presence so far from the mother country. Treaties had fixed the boundary between Russian-America and Canada in 1824 and 1825, but both British and American traders were pushing past the Russian boundaries into the Alaska Interior. Renewal of the Russian-American Company charter was in question, too. The Russian government had proposed to renew the charter for a twenty-year term beginning in 1862, but company officials were not pleased with new conditions that would exempt Aleuts and all other Alaska Natives from forced labor and allow them to participate in other industries.

The Russian government had never really intended to occupy Alaska. The settlements had come about through the activities of first the fur traders and then the Russian-American Company, which had represented the government's interests there while it gathered in the rich harvest of Alaska resources. If the company was no longer interested in governing the new settlements, neither was the government. The czar decided to give up the Alaska colonies. The question was, to whom? Both Britain and America were likely prospects. The czar opted to have the United States for a neighbor instead of England, Russia's enemy in the Crimean War.

The treaty of purchase was concluded by U.S. Secretary of State William Seward on March 30, 1867, and ratified that May. The purchase price was $7.2 million. The boundaries between the new possession and Canada would be the same as were agreed upon in the 1824–25 treaties between Russia and Great Britain, with the lower extreme fixed at 54°40' north latitude and then following the natural boundaries of the Portland Canal and the Coast Mountains before turning due north at Mount Saint Elias.

At Sitka the Russian flag was exchanged for the American on October 18, 1867. The Russians were promised citizenship rights in the new American territory, but most went home to Russia. The Aleuts went back to their native islands, and the Tlingit Indians were left to wonder what new indignities this new development would bring.

RACING FOR GOLD

Thousands of miles to the south of New Archangel—now called Sitka—gold had been struck near Sacramento, California, and the gold rush was under way. Prospectors fanned across California, exploring the creek beds and mountain canyons for gold. The search took them northward through Oregon and Washington and on into Canada and its bordering neighbor, Alaska.

In 1858 a discovery was made on Canada's Fraser River, and thousands of prospectors surged into this area. The first strike to affect Alaska came three years later. A Hudson's Bay Company trader named

Buck Choquette found gold on the upper Stikine River in Canada at a spot that came to be known as Buck's Bar. Prospectors flocked to Southeast Alaska to get to the new Stikine strike. Their destination was Wrangell, at the mouth of the Stikine in Russian territory. William Moore, an enterprising riverboat captain, was running a steamer upriver to the strike site with cargoes of optimistic prospectors.

The Cassiar

In 1873 word of a huge, new strike in Canada brought another wave of opportunists up the Stikine on their way to the Cassiar goldfields in the Interior. This time Wrangell ballooned from a quiet outpost to a booming tent city of 15,000. Captain Moore was on the scene again to move prospectors and their gear upriver, where they could pack the 200-odd miles to the diggings. Other steamers, both British and American, carried passengers and goods as well. At the end of the season, the prospectors came downriver to Wrangell to patronize the stores, saloons, dance halls, and other boomtown delights. At the time, Wrangell was the busiest place in Alaska.

Prospectors picked around in both Canada and Alaska, searching for that next big strike. The first find in Alaska came in 1870 at Windham Bay on the mainland, 65 miles south of Juneau. Forty

Exhaustion was the only certainty about the Klondike rush for gold. P. E. LARSS COLLECTION, ALASKA HISTORICAL LIBRARY

thousand dollars in gold is said to have been taken from the placers in that region. Gold mining was carried out near Sitka shortly thereafter, and, in 1880, ore samples from Silver Bow Basin on Gastineau Channel led to the founding of Juneau, Douglas, and Treadwell and, ultimately, the largest gold-mining operation in the world.

But the biggest gold boom was yet to come. The gold trail led onward to a region close to Canada's western border called the Klondike. At its center was the boomtown of Dawson on the Yukon River. The route to the goldfields lay through Southeast Alaska, and the migration of men and equipment was one of the greatest in history.

Klondike Madness

The Klondike story began in August 1896 when George Washington Carmack and his two Indian companions, Skookum Jim and Tagish Charlie, found gold on a tributary of the Klondike River in the Yukon Territory of Canada. That winter, rumor spread that rich gold deposits had been found in the Yukon, and a few prospectors working nearby managed to get into the area by spring. On July 17, 1897, headlines in the *Seattle Post-Intelligencer* screamed that the steamer *Portland* was on its way with a "ton of gold" from the Klondike.

All through that summer and fall, prospectors stampeded to the Klondike and the fields of gold. There were at least seven ways to get into the Klondike, and not one of them was easy. The safest route was also the longest: the all-water route that led from Seattle to the port of Saint Michael on the far western coast of Alaska where the Yukon River exited into the Bering Sea. There prospectors boarded Yukon River steamers for the 2,000-mile journey upriver to the goldfields. All the other possibilities involved a combination of water and land travel. There was the White Pass Trail, which left from Skagway at the head of Lynn Canal, and the shorter but steeper Chilkoot Pass from nearby Dyea. Both terminated in a system of treacherous waterways that led to the Yukon River and Dawson. Or there was the Dalton Trail from Haines, which also led to the Yukon headwaters; the old Stikine River route; the Edmonton route through Canada; and finally the gruesome climb over Valdez Glacier and into the Interior river systems from Prince William Sound.

Those who reached Dawson had a lot of panning to do. P. E. LARSS COLLECTION, ALASKA HISTORICAL LIBRARY

The most popular routes were the White Pass and Chilkoot Trails. In the summer of 1897, Dyea, at the foot of the Chilkoot Trail, consisted of a trading post and a couple of saloons. At Skagway a log cabin had been put up by a homesteader by the name of Captain William Moore. (Now there was a man with vision.) Dyea and Skagway turned into boomtowns overnight as some 25,000 people prepared to pack up the gold trails with the required year's worth of provisions. Over the Coast Mountains in Canada, the trails came together at Lake Bennett. Twenty thousand would-be prospectors camped around the lake that spring of '98, constructing boats to

Prospectors trudge to the summit of Chilkoot Pass in 1898. P. E. LARSS COLLECTION, ALASKA HISTORICAL LIBRARY

carry them downstream to the Yukon. As soon as the ice gave way on the lakes, 7,000 boats headed downriver on the next leg of the journey. By midsummer 18,000 people had arrived at Dawson. By summer's end many had started for home—broke. Others went on down the Yukon to the next big strike in 1899. The place was Nome, where, rumor had it, there was gold on the beach, just waiting to be picked up.

WHEN SALMON WAS KING

Simultaneously with the gold strikes, a new industry was launched in Alaska: salmon. The first salmon canneries were built in 1878 at the Tlingit village of Klawock, on Prince of Wales Island, and at Sitka. The canneries spread like wildfire up and down the Southeast coast. Ketchikan grew from an Indian summer fishing camp to a salmon saltery in 1883 and a cannery in 1887. The next year the nearby Loring Cannery was finished. Prince of Wales Island developed canneries at Craig, Kasaan, and other sites. Three canneries were started near Haines in the 1880s. Wrangell got one in 1887 and another in

In the late 1800s Southeast's supply of salmon seemed limitless. H. G. BARLEY COLLECTION, ALASKA HISTORICAL LIBRARY

1889. In 1900 the town of Petersburg was born, with a salmon cannery and an equally lucrative halibut industry that kept the fishing crews occupied over the winter.

Southeast waters were choked with salmon, and Ketchikan was at the center—the "Salmon Capital of the World." More than a dozen canneries operated there in the 1930s. During the peak years the Ketchikan district alone packed more than two million cases a year. The piper had to be paid, however, and by the 1940s the years of over-fishing had taken their toll. At present the empty, sagging remnants of the great cannery buildings can be seen in many quiet Southeast coves—picturesque but forlorn reminders of plentiful days gone by.

One result of the decline in the salmon runs has been the development of aquaculture. Fish hatcheries were introduced in Alaska around 1900, but most projects were busts. Research and experimentation have since led to successful techniques for rearing salmon. The Alaska Department of Fish and Game built several hatcheries during the 1970s. Today there are two state hatcheries, twenty-nine nonprofit corporation hatcheries, and two federal or Bureau of Indian Affairs hatcheries. Hatcheries in Southeast Alaska rear and release all five species of salmon (plus steelhead, lake, and rainbow trout, arctic char, and grayling) and contribute significantly to the commercial and sport harvest, although there were signs of a decline in commercial fishing in 2002.

There are several opportunities for touring salmon hatcheries in Southeast. Two of the most accessible facilities are the Deer Mountain Hatchery in Ketchikan and the Gastineau Salmon Hatchery in Juneau.

The majority of the operating mariculture, or ocean ranching, farms produce Pacific oysters, grown from spat imported from the Lower 48. There is limited farming of blue mussels as well. Most mariculture takes place in the southern part of the Panhandle, particularly in the areas of Wrangell Narrows, Clarence and Sumner Straits, and Prince of Wales Island.

CASHING IN THE FOREST

The wood-products industry has played a role in the Southeast economy since Russian times. The Russian-American Company harvested the local timber for shipbuilding and for fuel. (Evidence of their clear-cutting practice can still be seen around Sitka.) They also operated sawmills and exported lumber to South America and China.

After the United States' purchase of Alaska, additional sawmills were constructed to provide lumber for packing boxes needed by the salmon canneries. Development of the industry was hindered, however, by the absence of a civil government in Alaska to regulate ownership of the land being logged. The situation was clarified somewhat in 1884 when Congress passed the Organic Act, providing machinery for the regulation and administration of government in Alaska according to the laws of Oregon. In 1907 the federal government created the sixteen-million-acre Tongass National Forest—

Rafted logs await milling at the Tsimshian village of Metlakatla on Annette Island.

the largest national forest in the United States (since expanded to seventeen million acres)—incorporating most of the timber in the Alexander Archipelago. With management of the forest in the hands of the U.S. Forest Service, which could hold timber sales, private timber companies were able to get into business.

World War I brought demand for strong and lightweight Sitka spruce for building fighter planes. Mills at Craig and Ketchikan cut spruce for the war effort and supplied lumber for local fishing and mining operations. The demand for spruce reappeared during World War II for the same reason. The Alaska Spruce Log Program called for 100 million board feet of timber to be cut annually from Prince of Wales Island. The logs were tied into enormous oceangoing rafts called "Davis Rafts," 280 feet long by 60 feet wide and 30 feet deep, which were towed to Puget Sound mills. In the 1950s the forest industry began to surpass the declining salmon industry. The annual timber harvest in Southeast doubled and doubled again as pulp mills were constructed at Ketchikan and Sitka.

The pulp mill in Sitka closed in 1993, and an ancillary sawmill in Wrangell closed soon after. From 1993 through early 1997, most of the timber cut from the Tongass went to Alaska's sole remaining pulp mill in Ketchikan. But it, too, closed in March 1997, having failed to reach agreement with the U.S. Forest Service to extend its fifty-year contract. Gateway Forest Products built a veneer mill on the site in 1999, but low lumber prices forced its closure in 2002. High-quality logs go to sawmills for processing into cants or dimensional lumber, usually for export. There are three primary sawmills, located in Metlakatla, Ketchikan, and Klawock, which may or may not continue to operate depending on negotiations between the Forest Service and mill owners. Dozens of mom-and-pop operations start up and close down according to the timber supply. In 1998 the wood products industry accounted for slightly more than 3 percent of the jobs in Southeast Alaska. Recent times have brought the Alaska forest products industry to its lowest point in fifty years. Three factors have caused this decline: the slowdown in Japan, Alaska's primary export market; a decrease in the allowable harvest from the Tongass National Forest; and a decrease in harvesting on privately held Native Corporation lands.

In recent years logging in the Tongass has engendered a storm of protest from environmental and commercial fishing organizations, with far-reaching results. Like all national forestlands, the Tongass is open to many different activities, from tourism and recreation to logging and mining—a policy known as Multiple Use Management. In other words, the U.S. Forest Service is charged with managing the land in such a way that all these activities can be carried out simultaneously without damage to timber, water, wildlife habitat, or recreational values. Critics have charged the Forest Service with catering to the needs of the timber industry, especially the two pulp mills, at the expense of other values. At the heart of the controversy were prime watersheds—lush river valleys that contain the largest and most valuable stands of old-growth timber; prime wildlife and scenic habitat prized by hunters, tourists, and local recreationists; and important fish-spawning grounds that the commercial fishing community depend upon for their livelihood.

The public controversy reached a climax in the late 1980s with a series of bills submitted to Congress to amend the policies governing timber sales and logging in the Tongass. Previous legislation, the Alaska National Interest Lands Conservation Act of 1980, had specified that a certain amount of timber per decade would be made available for harvest in the Tongass, regardless of market demand. Congress revoked that stipulation in the Tongass Timber Reform Act of 1990 and directed that the timber supply would be based on market considerations. They also addressed environmental and fishing concerns by declaring slightly more than one million additional acres in the Tongass, including a number of key watersheds, as wilderness areas or otherwise off-limits to logging. The act tightened requirements for no-logging buffer strips along salmon streams and repealed an automatic $40 million annual appropriation that had been used for road building and other activities supporting the timber program. By 1997 both pulp mills and at least one sawmill that had operated in the Tongass had closed down.

Not all the logging in Southeast Alaska takes place on national forest land. The Alaska Native Land Claims Settlement Act of 1971 added a new dimension to the timber industry by granting Southeast Native corporations some 600,000 acres of land selected from the Tongass National Forest. Several Native corporations selected prime timberland and entered the logging and timber export business. Unlike timber cut from the national forest, which must undergo "primary processing" prior to export (usually into squared-off logs called cants), Native-owned logs can be exported in the round; most of the high-quality Native timber goes as raw logs to Japan.

SHORT-LIVED VENTURES

Through the decades, numerous other ventures have stirred the economy in various locales, but they have been short-lived. Whaling was one of the industries that touched Southeast Alaska briefly. In 1880 Northwest Trading Company of Portland, Oregon, built a shore-based whaling station on Killisnoo Island opposite the Tlingit village of Angoon. The company harvested whales from local waters and reduced the carcasses to oil, bone meal, and fertilizer. A second company started a whaling station on the southeast tip of Admiralty in 1907, and a third set up shop at Port Armstrong on the southern end of Baranof Island. All had shut down by 1923.

The Killisnoo plant, however, turned to another resource that proved profitable for several more years: herring. In 1882 the whaling station was converted to a herring reduction plant to process the plentiful small, oily fish into fish meal. Quite a market developed for the meal, first as fertilizer and then as a food additive for livestock and poultry. A second product, herring oil, was valued as a superior industrial oil for manufacturing such varied products as leather, cosmetics, and ink. Eventually seventeen herring reduction plants operated in Southeast Alaska and processed millions of pounds of herring a year. The industry gradually declined as the herring were fished out, and the last plant closed in 1966. Herring also figured in food industries. Herring salteries had operated on a small scale at least since 1894. The 1920s saw a great demand for salted and pickled herring, but this industry declined as competition appeared from East Coast and foreign producers. Commercial production ended in 1953. Today's limited herring industry consists of two products: bait, which is processed whole and frozen, and roe, exported to Japan as a delicacy.

Copper provided a fleeting boom in the Ketchikan area. Copper claims had been located on Prince of Wales Island as early as 1867, and mining was under way on both sides of the island by 1900. The boomtowns of Coppermount and Hadley grew up around the copper industry. High costs and depleted ores closed the smelters by 1908, and the copper-mining industry faded away, taking Coppermount and Hadley with it.

Marble provided a flurry of activity in the same region in 1912, when the Vermont Marble Company began quarrying at Tokeen on Marble Island, off the west coast of Prince of Wales. The white Tokeen marble was used in many buildings in the Pacific Northwest, including the Alaska Capitol at Juneau. The industry folded when the Depression cut into the building market.

Fox farming swept Southeast in the 1920s. With furs fetching high prices, some bright entrepreneur realized that the little, tree-studded islands in Southeast Alaska would make ideal fox pens. Food would be easy to come by in the form of scraps from the many nearby salmon canneries, and the water perimeter would prevent the foxes from escaping. The U.S. Forest Service leased the islands for as little as $25 per year. One or two pairs of blue fox—which provided pretty, sooty brown pelts with bluish hairs beneath—could stock the entire farm in just a few years. Many fox farms operated in the Tongass in the 1920s, but by the mid-1930s the price of furs had dropped again and the foxes were left to run wild.

SOUTHEAST TODAY

Mining, timber, and fish—the traditional resource-extractive industries operating in Southeast Alaska—continue to form a cornerstone of the economy. But now they operate in a much more heavily regulated environment than in the past. Increasingly they compete with one another and with other industries, such as tourism and mariculture, for the most valuable resources of the forest and sea. Wilderness—valued historically for the extractable elements it contained—has itself become a resource, with a vocal, national constituency.

Together, the wood-products industry and the commercial fishing/seafood-processing industry account for roughly one tenth of the 37,500 jobs in Southeast Alaska. At present mining produces fewer than 1 percent of Southeast Alaska's jobs, most of them coming from the Greens Creek Mine on Admiralty Island, which reopened in 1996. Initially opened in 1989, Greens Creek generated more than eight million ounces of silver a year, making it the largest lode-silver mine in the United States, but suspended operation in the spring of 1993 pending higher metal prices. Several former gold-mining properties are being actively explored and evaluated for possible redevelopment; a development company has begun the work of reopening the Kensington Mine in Berners Bay near Juneau.

The tourism industry was born in Southeast Alaska soon after the great naturalist John Muir visited the country for the first time in 1879. Muir landed in Wrangell and canoed into Glacier Bay with his Presbyterian missionary friend Hall Young. Muir's accounts of the ice-locked wilderness were so inspiring that steamship companies began to offer summer tours up the Inside Passage. The first was the steamer *Idaho,* which came north in 1883. Onboard was a twenty-

The City of Topeka *rides at anchor while tourists step ashore at Glacier Bay in 1895.*
ALASKA HISTORICAL LIBRARY

seven-year-old journalist named Eliza Ruhamah Scidmore, whose descriptions of the voyage appeared in national newspapers and magazines and later in a guidebook to Alaska. The tourism industry was launched.

The early steamships were oases of comfort, with carpeted lounges, crystal chandeliers, starched linen, and elegant food. The ships, along their route to deliver supplies, called at mining towns and cannery sites, which passengers found interesting and entertaining. By 1889, 5,000 tourists a year were making the trip up the Inside Passage. The practice continues, but the number of visitors who pass along the same route has swelled to nearly half a million a year, substantially impacting local economies. Juneau, for instance, regards tourism as the number-two job maker of the community—after government.

The number-one employer in Southeast Alaska today is government. Roughly one-third of the Southeast workforce earn their annual wages from federal, state, or local government. In Juneau, the capital of Alaska since 1906, nearly one out of every two working people is an employee of either state, federal, or local government.

SOUTHEAST HISTORY IN BRIEF

1741   Alexei Chirikof, sailing for Russia with the Bering expedition, makes the first recorded sighting of Alaska on July 15, 1741. Two landing parties go ashore, possibly near Sitka, but fail to return. Vitus Bering anchors at Kayak Island. Shore parties inspect deserted Native dwellings and collect several household items.

1774   Spanish explorer Juan Pérez sights Prince of Wales Island.

1775   Spanish explorer Bodega y Quadra sights Mount Edgecumbe.

1778   Captain James Cook visits Southeast Alaska on his third voyage of exploration in the Pacific for England.

1783   Russian merchant Grigor Shelikof establishes a Russian settlement on Kodiak Island.

1786   La Pérouse sights Mount Saint Elias and surveys Lituya Bay for France.

1793–   Captain George Vancouver charts the Alexander Archipelago
1794   for England.

1795   Russians establish a small agricultural settlement at Yakutat.

1799   Russians settle at Old Sitka.

1802   Sitka Tlingit attack and destroy the Russian post.

1804   Russians retake Sitka and build a new fort at the present site.

1824–   Treaties fix boundaries between Russian-America (Alaska)
1825   and Canada.

1834   Russians establish Redoubt Saint Dionysius at Wrangell.

1839   British lease mainland coast from Russia; Redoubt Saint Dionysius passes into British hands as Fort Stikine.

1861   Buck Choquette discovers gold on the upper Stikine River in Canada; prospectors flock to Wrangell.

1867   United States purchases Alaska from Russia.

1873   Wrangell balloons to 15,000 people with a new gold strike in the Canadian Cassiar.

1877	First mission school in Alaska opens at Wrangell.

1877   First mission school in Alaska opens at Wrangell.

1878   First salmon canneries in Alaska built at Klawock and Sitka.

1879   S. Hall Young founds a Presbyterian mission at Haines.

1880   Joe Juneau and Richard Harris find gold on the Gastineau Channel and stake the townsite of Juneau. First Southeast whaling station begins operation on Killisnoo Island.

1882   U.S. Navy vessels shell and burn village of Angoon.

1883   Steamer *Idaho* brings tourists up the Inside Passage.

1884   Congress passes Organic Act, providing minimum framework for administering government in Alaska.

1887   Father William Duncan and Tsimshian followers found Metlakatla on Annette Island.

1896   George Washington Carmack, Skookum Jim, and Tagish Charlie strike gold in Yukon Territory, precipitating a rush to the Klondike.

1897   Skagway takes shape as a tent city of 10,000 people. Peter Buschmann homesteads along Wrangell Narrows to found Petersburg.

1898   Porcupine becomes the center of a rich gold-mining district.

1900   White Pass and Yukon Route is completed from Skagway to Whitehorse. Copper mining booms on Prince of Wales Island.

1903   U.S. Army constructs Fort William H. Seward at Port Chilkoot, Haines.

1906   Capital of Alaska transferred from Sitka to Juneau.

1907   New sixteen-million-acre Tongass National Forest is largest in the United States.

1912   Alaska is granted territorial status. Marble quarries begin production on Marble Island.

1913   First territorial legislature's first law gives women the right to vote.

1917   Cave-in floods all Treadwell mines except one.

1925   Glacier Bay is proclaimed a national monument.

1941 Sitka hosts 30,000 military personnel with an army base and naval air station.

1943 Haines Highway links Haines with the Alaska Highway.

1944 Closure of the Alaska-Juneau Mill ends hard-rock mining in Juneau.

1948 Steve Homer initiates ferry service between Haines, Skagway, and Juneau.

1954 Alaska's first pulp mill constructed in Ketchican.

1959 Alaska achieves statehood.

1960 Alaska Pulp Corporation builds mill at Sitka.

1963 First vessels of the Alaska Marine Highway fleet come on line.

1971 Alaska Native Land Claims Settlement Act awards Southeast Native corporations 550,000 to 600,000 acres of land.

1978 Klondike Highway connects Skagway with the Carcross and the Alaska Highway. Presidential proclamation designates Misty Fiords and Admiralty Island national monuments to be managed by the Forest Service.

1980 Alaska Lands bill reaffirms national monument status for Misty Fjords and Admiralty Island and designates these areas and twelve others as wilderness. Wilderness lands within the Tongass National Forest now equal 5.5 million acres.

1982 Alaskans rescind vote to move state capital from Juneau to Willow. White Pass and Yukon Route railway suspends operations.

1989 White Pass and Yukon Route reopens as summer excursion train to Fraser. Greens Creek Mine, the largest lode-silver mine in the United States, begins production on Admiralty Island.

1990 Congress passes Tongass Timber Reform Act, which designates an additional 296,080 acres of wilderness in the Tongass National Forest and makes major changes to Tongass timber program.

1993   Greens Creek Mine suspends operation; Alaska Pulp Corporation Mill closes at Sitka.

1994   Alaska Pulp's sawmill at Wrangell closes.

1996   Greens Creek mine reopens on Admiralty Island near Juneau.

1997   Ketchikan Pulp Company closes its pulp mill, though its sawmill remains open.

1998   Newest Alaska ferry, the *Kennicott*, begins serving the communities of Southeast and south-central Alaska. Klondike Gold Rush National Historical Park reaches its centennial. To mark the occasion, the park was designated an International Historical Park.

1999   Ketchikan sets aside $2 million to study the feasibility of building a wood-veneer plant in the community.

2000   Klondike Gold Dredge Tours opens in Skagway.

2001   Sea Life Discover Tours, with the Southeast's only submersible boat, becomes the newest adventure in Sitka.

2002   Juneau's Visitor Information Center moves to Centennial Hall.

2004   Wrangell completes construction on its new $6 million James Nolan Center. This new civic center will also house the visitor center, chamber of commerce, U.S. Forest Service, and museum.

CHAPTER FOUR

SOUTHEAST'S NATIVE HERITAGE

M any thousands of years ago when the North Pacific Ocean was still in the grip of the Great Ice Age, groups of humans ventured out of Asia and Siberia, across the bridge of land that is now the Bering Sea, and into Alaska and northern Canada. As the glaciers withdrew and the great rivers were freed of ice, these peoples and their descendants were able to range throughout the Canadian and Alaskan Interior and southward to California and Mexico.

Among these early wanderers were the ancestors of all of Alaska's Native peoples: the Eskimos of the Arctic coast, the Aleuts of the Aleutian Chain, the Athapaskan Indians of the Interior region, and the Tlingit, Haida, and Tsimshian Indians of Southeast Alaska. Over the next several thousand years, these different groups settled into their own geographic regions and developed distinct and complex cultures. Historians have estimated that at the time of the first recorded European voyage to Alaska in 1741, the total Native population numbered 60,000 to 80,000 people, of which perhaps 10,000 were located in Southeast. At present the total Native population is approximately 67,380 and declining.

FIRST INHABITANTS

The coastal Indians of Southeast gradually migrated out of Interior Canada, following the river valleys through the Coast Mountains until they reached the saltwater shore. The Tlingit (*klink*-et) settled into villages along a 600-mile stretch of coast between Yakutat Bay and the Portland Canal (now the southern boundary of Alaska) and inhabited several of the islands of the Alexander Archipelago. The Haida (*hy*-dah) established themselves to the south of the Tlingit on the coast of British Columbia and on the Queen Charlotte Islands. Later, in the late seventeenth or early eighteenth century, the Haida extended their range farther north and took over the southern end of Prince of Wales Island in Alaska from the Tlingit.

By contrast, the Tsimshian (*sim*-shee-anne) did not settle in Southeast until twenty years after the Alaska Purchase and even then were isolated from the mainstream of Southeast Native society. Their people lived initially along the Nass and Skeena Rivers in British Columbia. Some relocated near the Hudson's Bay Company trading post at Port Simpson in the 1830s. In 1857 William Duncan, a twenty-one-year-old missionary, arrived in Canada to educate the Tsimshian in the ways of the Church of England. He founded a church there but decided that liquor and other unhealthy activities around the post were leading his flock astray. Duncan and his followers left the community and returned to original Tsimshian lands to establish a new model village called Metlakatla.

In 1881 Duncan fell into disagreement with his church leaders and was dismissed from the missionary society. The U.S. government gave him permission to relocate his community on Annette Island in Southeast Alaska. Duncan moved to Annette with 825 Tsimshian in 1887 and built a new town that they named New Metlakatla. Like the old village, the new Metlakatla community was designed to be self-sufficient and self-contained. Duncan encouraged his followers to break from the past and pursue a new lifestyle in wooden frame houses and geometric streets. The community continues as a part of the self-governing Annette Island Indian Reserve.

SEAGOING CULTURE

The Tlingit and Haida Indians were able to live well on their coastal land and islands. The climate was moderate, and the constant precipitation favored the lush rain forests that provided most of their necessities. They built permanent villages along riverbanks or on protected coves or inlets facing the sea and, in summer, moved to temporary fishing camps that were convenient to the salmon supply.

They developed into expert seamen. In their cedar canoes they traveled throughout their watery realm, harvesting the sea's resources, visiting allied communities, and trading or warring with other Native groups. The Haida were the unquestioned masters of canoe building. Red cedar, the preferred wood for dugout canoes, was more plentiful in the southern region where they lived, and they were known up and down the Northwest coast for their large, well-built, beautifully decorated craft. A Haida seagoing canoe could easily measure 70 feet in length and carry fifty to sixty men. (The early European explorers frequently found their vessels overshadowed by the Indian canoes.) The Tlingit and Haida regularly canoed down the coast of British Columbia to Puget Sound, some 700 miles away.

Housing

The traditional Native houses were each shared by several families. They were constructed of rough cedar planking set horizontally and notched at the corners. The structures contained a low doorway, but no windows, and a bare earth floor. An opening at the top let out smoke from the central fire pit that served for both cooking and heating. A raised wood platform around the perimeter of the house provided space for seating during the day and sleeping at night. Some houses contained two of these platforms, one above the other. The platforms were also used to store wooden boxes, sleeping mats, blankets, clothing, weapons, hunting and fishing gear, and other belongings. Dried fish, meat, and other foodstuffs hung from the ceiling.

With no ventilation except the smoke hole, these traditional dwellings were aromatic. The early traders who observed some of these structures before the houses were adulterated with European goods and ideas reported themselves much bothered by the darkness and acrid smoke that permeated the interior. The visitors felt invariably either too hot or too cold, depending upon their distance from the fire.

Replicated Native community houses can be seen at Haines (Port Chilkoot), Wrangell (Chief Shakes Island), and Ketchikan (Saxman and Totem Bight). Another, at Kasaan on Prince of Wales Island, will be outside your itinerary unless you are traveling in your own boat. A replicated house interior is part of the permanent display at the Alaska State Museum in Juneau.

Food Gathering

Food was plentiful and varied along the Northwest coast. The primary staple was fish: salmon, halibut, herring, trout, and a small, oily member of the smelt family called eulachon (*hoo*-li-gan). The forests were generous with bears and deer, and mountain goats were available for the price of a climb. There were birds of all types and bird eggs. In addition to fish, the sea provided several types of seaweed, seals, the occasional whale, and all manner of shellfish. The land produced wild rhubarb, wild peas, wild rice, and nearly every imaginable form of berry. If necessary, even the hemlock forest could be eaten. With the bark peeled away, the soft cambium layer beneath could be scraped off, cooked, and consumed.

The Tlingit and Haida Indians were superb fishermen. The European explorers quickly discovered, to their astonishment, that the Natives could outfish them handily, even with their "primitive" gear of wood and bone. In fact, the Indian fishing equipment, while fabricated from natural materials, was highly efficient. Nets were fashioned out of twined cedar bark or spun nettle fibers, and lines were made from spruce roots, cedar bark, or kelp stems. Fishing methods depended upon the quarry. Salmon were speared, netted, or trapped. Herring and eulachon were netted or brailed out of the water with long-handled rakes. \ hoo-li-gan

The breadth of the Indian ingenuity can be seen in their method of catching halibut. The traditional halibut set consisted of a wooden hook with a stone or bone barb (later metal, fashioned from nails), a stone weight to hold it down because halibut are bottom dwellers, and a line leading to the surface with an inflated seal bladder or wooden float at the end to mark the location of the set. Two men in a canoe could watch over several halibut sets at once. The hooks were baited with squid or octopus, lowered into position, and left to do their work. When a halibut took the bait, the surface float would bob and jerk, signaling the fishermen to paddle over and haul the fish aboard. The wooden hooks discriminated between halibut, a flat fish, and other bottom feeders and even controlled the size of halibut that could be caught.

Tlingit and Haida halibut hooks were objects of beauty as well as efficiency. The unbarbed arm of the V-shaped hook was carved in the figure of an animal or human. Perhaps the carvings represented spirits that were called upon to assist the fishing effort, or perhaps they simply attracted the halibut's eye. The wooden floats that marked the lines also were carved into shapes, usually of animals or birds. Most of the museums in Southeast Alaska have displays of carved halibut hooks and other Native fishing gear.

The Tlingit and Haida smoked or dried most of their fish for preservation. The eulachon, however, was valued most for its oil. The flesh of this small fish is so oily that a dried eulachon can be lighted like a candle, hence the nickname "candlefish." Southeast Alaska Natives used eulachon oil as a dipping sauce and mixed it with berries and other foods to preserve them over the winter. To

Carved wooden halibut hooks in the Wrangell Museum show the beauty that accompanied an efficient design.

obtain the oil, the fish was allowed to decompose for several days and was then boiled in water. Most of the oil collected on the surface of the water, where it could easily be skimmed off. The remainder was obtained by pressing the cooked fish in a basket. In the old days, eulachon oil was frequently stored in the long, hollow kelp stems that are plentiful in Southeast waters.

The Tlingit and Haida were not the only Alaska Natives to enjoy the oil: So much eulachon oil was traded to the Athapaskans that the trade routes to the Interior became known as the "grease trails." Dietitians now know that eulachon oil is rich in iodine and vitamins and was important to the Native diet. It is still a precious commodity among Southeast Natives.

Until the Europeans came, Southeast Natives had no iron except the few bits that drifted ashore from distant shipwrecks, and no pottery. Their cooking vessels consisted of wooden boxes and tightly woven baskets. They placed water and the food to be cooked in a basket or box and dropped in stones that had been heated in the fire. They also practiced pit cooking, wrapping or layering their fish with seaweed or leaves.

SOCIAL STRUCTURE

The Southeast coastal Natives observed a rigid social structure that emphasized kinship lines. The concept of lineage permeated every aspect of their lives and was manifested in their works of art. It is thanks to this strong adhesion to kinship that we can admire today the great totem poles, the beaded blankets, the carved serving dishes, and all the other items, both ceremonial and quotidian, that have been marked with the animal crests denoting family line.

Eagle and Raven

As you travel throughout Southeast Alaska and observe the artifacts of Tlingit and Haida culture, you will quickly notice that Eagle and Raven are the dominant motifs. Every individual in Tlingit or Haida society was (and still is) born into one of two great social divisions, known as Eagles and Ravens (northern Tlingit use Wolf interchangeably with Eagle). These two groups are called *moieties* or *phratries*—

anthropological terms meaning tribal subdivisions. Tlingit and Haida societies are matrilineal, so each child automatically assumes the moiety of the mother but must marry into the opposite moiety. Thus every set of parents consists of one Eagle and one Raven, with all of the children belonging to the mother's group.

Kinship Clans

Both Eagle and Raven moieties are subdivided into several kinship clans that identify themselves by totems: animal names and crests that were adopted long ago because they had special significance for the groups they represent. For example, Frog and Beaver are common clans of the Raven moiety, whereas Grizzly Bear, Killer Whale, and Wolf are Eagle clans. Clans represent specific lineages, like branches of a family tree, that theoretically could be traced back to the time of their migration to and throughout Southeast Alaska. Thus each individual is born into one moiety and one clan, for example, Eagle and Killer Whale, both according to the mother's group.

Traditionally, clans controlled such property rights as were acknowledged by the coastal Indians. They owned the right to use specific salmon streams, berry patches, hunting grounds, and house sites, as well as the right to employ the clan crest and other designs, songs, dances, and names. The head of each clan was an important and powerful chief whose responsibility was to look after the clan and its property and act as spokesman.

House Groups

Clans were further subdivided into as many house groups as were necessary to accommodate all the clan members and their families in a particular village. The community house was the minimum political and social unit in all Southeast Native societies, and all houses were ranked according to prestige and importance. The head of the most important house in a village was automatically the village chief. Within each house lived various families and individuals of like clan and moiety. Each house had a name, usually relating to one of the clan's totemic crests or to a physical feature of the structure. Dog Salmon House, House of Many Levels, and House with Sand All Around would be examples. Because of intermarriages between clans, the same clan might own houses in several different villages, and each village was made up of at least two and usually several different clans, all of which vied to be most important.

Kwans

Historically, the Tlingit, the largest of the Native groups, were arranged into several different geographical groups called kwans. The precise number of kwans in Southeast Alaska that existed at the time of the first contact with Europeans is uncertain but seems to have been at least thirteen. The kwans took their names from prominent rivers or bays in their region. Each contained a number of permanent villages.

Tlingit kwans were fairly cohesive units. The Chilkat Tlingit, for example—the Chilkat kwan—from the Klukwan area were reputed to be fierce and warlike, the most powerful of all the kwans. Their principal village of Klukwan, on the Chilkat River north of Haines, is still an important Tlingit village. The Chilkat controlled the mountain passes that lead to the Interior, traded with the Interior Athapaskans, and were known up and down the coast for their skill at weaving the famed Chilkat blankets from the hair of mountain goats. Other well-known kwans included the Stikines, near Wrangell, who controlled the river trade that passed up the Stikine River to Interior Canada, and the Sitka Tlingit.

Class

Underlying the fabric of moiety, clan, house group, and kwan was the fundamental question of social class. Southeast Native society ranked all individuals into roughly three classes: nobility, including clan chiefs and their heirs and families; commoners, who comprised the majority of the population; and slaves, who were born into servitude, purchased from neighboring groups, or captured in raids on other villages. Social status was of the utmost importance to Southeast Natives. Rank could always be improved through the acquisition of wealth and prestige, the pursuit of which was a continuous and passionate undertaking.

The Potlatch

The various Tlingit and Haida groups did not live in isolation but traveled around Southeast and beyond on trading missions or social visits. Sometimes they went to war against other groups to capture slaves or property or to avenge a past slight. Occasionally they journeyed to another village to attend a potlatch, which was a party thrown by a clan chief on some meritorious occasion (perhaps to erect a totem pole, celebrate a marriage, dedicate a new house, or perform memorial rites) for the purpose of bringing honor to himself, his house, and his clan.

In the old days a potlatch could go on for weeks, with feasting, singing, dancing, and storytelling. Gift giving was an important aspect of the potlatch, and the esteem of the potlatch chief was measured by the amount of wealth he distributed to his guests. Clans saved for years to accumulate the wealth necessary to throw a potlatch, and often the rise in status was about the only thing they had left when it was over. It was more than enough, however, because an astute potlatch host could expect to get everything back, with interest, by the time the necessary reciprocal potlatches had been held.

Potlatches are still given on occasion in Southeast Alaska, and they are an apt reflection of a culture balancing the traditional with the contemporary. Feast dishes of roast turkey and sheet cakes might be presented alongside smoked salmon, pickled kelp, and berries served with eulachon oil. Gifts could be blankets, cases of soda, or cash.

Summer was the trading season. The coastal Tlingit followed the Stikine, Taku, and Chilkat river systems into the mountains to trade with the Interior Athapaskans. They exchanged eulachon oil for such items as durable moose and caribou hides, then went south to barter these things plus thick Chilkat blankets for the superior cedar canoes of the Haida. When the Hudson's Bay Company established a trading post in British Columbia in 1831, the Tlingit and Haida ventured even farther for the chance to trade furs for manufactured goods such as iron tools and cooking utensils, cloth blankets, beads and buttons, rifles, tobacco, sugar, molasses, and flour.

THE RAVEN CYCLE AND
OTHER MYTHS

The Southeast Coast Indians enjoyed a rich tradition of stories and myths, passed down orally from one generation to the next, that helped to explain the natural phenomena that surrounded their forested home. Prior to contact with the Russian colonists, their religion centered on trying to stay on the right side of the various spirits that inhabited the earth in the form of animals, fish, trees, water, winds, and other natural elements. They did have a shaman among them whose job was to interpret spirit signs and, in his role as healer, to intercede with the supernatural beings on behalf of the sick.

The most important myths involve Raven, who winged his way into the mythology of many Indian cultures, both inside Alaska and out. In Tlingit mythology there are actually two Ravens. Yehl, the Great Raven, also called Nass Raven, is the creator figure. From his home above the Nass River (at the southern border of Southeast Alaska), which the Tlingit believe to be their original homeland, he controlled the sun, the moon, and the stars. Scamp Raven, his grandson, is known as the trickster, and most of the Raven stories pertain to him and his usually comical adventures. It was Scamp Raven who manufactured the earth out of mud and rocks and then stole the sun, moon, and stars away from Nass Raven so that the world would have light. He also acquired fire, got the tides under control, painted birds their various colors, and accomplished many other feats. Scamp Raven is a much-beloved character. He has a rather coarse sense of humor and something of a mean streak; he loves to play tricks on people. He is basically lazy and a glutton, in an endearing, human sort of way.

Many totem poles in Southeast depict characters and episodes from the Raven myths. So that you can better appreciate these poles on your travels through Southeast, here are very abbreviated versions of some of the best-known tales.

"How Raven Stole the Stars, the Moon, and the Sun"

All of the light in the world was kept by a man (Nass Raven) who lived at the head of the Nass River. He kept the light hidden in various boxes and bundles inside his house and guarded them closely. Scamp Raven wanted some light for the world, and he thought and thought how to go about getting the light away from the man on Nass River. The man had a beautiful daughter, but she always had her slaves with her, so Raven was not able to approach. Finally he thought of turning himself into a hemlock needle and slipping into her glass of water. She swallowed the needle and then grew large with child, which is how Scamp Raven happened to be born into the household.

The girl's father loved the baby dearly and gave him everything he asked for. One day the baby cried and cried and simply would not be comforted until his grandfather reluctantly let him play with the bag of stars. Raven rolled the bundle around and around on the floor and when he was positioned beneath the smoke hole in the roof, quickly untied it. All the stars flew out the smoke hole and escaped into the heavens.

Raven's grandfather was extremely cross about losing his precious stars, but when again the baby cried and cried, he relented a second time and gave him the moon to play with. The same thing happened, and the moon took its place in the sky. When Raven finally got hold of the box of daylight, he flew with it up the smoke hole and enjoyed his new world full of light.

"How Raven Stole Water"

In the beginning there were no lakes, no streams, and no rivers; no water anywhere except at Petrel's house, where there was a natural spring. Raven wanted water for the world, and he thought and thought of a way to get some of that water from Petrel.

Raven went to visit Petrel, who was courteous but very suspicious. He would not let Raven anywhere near the spring. In desperation, Raven invited himself to spend the night at Petrel's house, but still he was not able to approach the spring. The next morning he got up very early and found a pile of dog excrement that he smeared over the poor sleeping Petrel and his blankets. Then he woke Petrel up and, with a great show of commiseration, pointed out that the unfortunate bird had dirtied himself in the night. Petrel, humiliated, went off to bathe. Raven took the opportunity to drink as much water as he could and then escaped out the smoke hole. As he flew, Raven spat out the water in his beak and the Nass, the Stikine, the Chilkat, the Taku, and the Alsek—all the great rivers of Southeast Alaska—took shape beneath him. Little drops fell here and there as well, forming the smaller salmon streams.

"Raven and Tidewoman"

Tidewoman, or Tidewatcher, lived high on a cliff, where she controlled the tide. Raven decided that she kept the tide too high and people could not gather enough food on the beach. He vowed to do something about that. He went down to the water and gathered some sea urchins, then approached Tidewoman and asked her to lower the tide. When she refused, he pricked her bottom with a sea urchin spine. "Ouch!" she cried, and she let the tide down just a little bit. Raven stuck her with another sea urchin spine. "Oh! Ouch!" she cried. "Please don't stick me anymore!" The tide receded a little farther. Raven stuck more spines in her bottom until Tidewoman promised to make the tides rise and fall every day so that the people could collect the food they needed.

"Raven and the Daughters of the Fog"

Raven created the salmon streams when he stole the water from Petrel, but unfortunately, the salmon refused to go up them, and the people could not catch the fish to eat. One day when Raven was wondering what to do about this, he noticed a fine-looking woman sitting beside one of the streams. He decided to place her at the head of the stream so that all the salmon would rush upstream to look at her. This worked just fine, and now all of the salmon travel up the streams every fall to see the beautiful women, the Daughters of the Fog, who live there.

Other Tales

Both Tlingit and Haida mythologies include tales of the giant Thunderbird responsible for lightning and thunder. The Thunderbird had enormous wings and a large, curved beak. He lived on a mountaintop and when he was hungry flew down to the sea and returned with a whale in his talons. The thunder was caused by his great wings beating the air, and lightning flashed from his eyes when he blinked. One Raven story explains why something does not exist, in this case "Why There Is No Large River Near Sitka." According to this tale, Raven alighted one day near Sitka in a place that he thought would make a fine river. The tide was out, and there were clams all over the beach. As Raven walked about to get the lay of the land, the clams kept squirting, making so much noise that Raven could not hear himself think. "Stop squirting, you clams!" he yelled, becoming increasingly irate, but the clams paid no attention. Next Raven picked some blueberries and stuffed them down the necks of the clams, but that did no good either. Finally he flew away in a huff, vowing not to make a river there after all.

This last Raven story, "How Raven Lost His Beak," concerns Scamp Raven, who was hungry one day and looking for an easy meal. He noticed some men fishing for halibut and decided to make his dinner from the bait on their hooks. For a long while he succeeded at this and was feeling very pleased with his cleverness when his beak caught on one of the hooks and came completely off. The fishermen took home the curious object they had brought up on their halibut hook. That night Raven turned himself into human form, wrapped himself with a blanket to cover the hole in his face, and went to their house. He asked to examine the object they had found, pretending he might be able to identify it. When they showed him the beak, Raven clapped it back on his face and flew away.

ART AND ARTIFACTS

Food was so easily gathered in the coastal forest that the Tlingit and Haida had time for other pursuits. One of them was art, which they managed to integrate into virtually every aspect of their daily lives. There is a fine line between producing a utilitarian object such as a basket or a wooden bowl that is beautiful for its workmanship and design and making a functional object beautiful by enhancing it with decorative design. The Southeast Indians did both, and some of the most delightful art objects in modern museums were created for everyday use. The Tlingit and Haida also used their sophisticated design sense to create objects that were strictly ceremonial, such as totem poles, or strictly decorative, such as carved metal bracelets. These art forms have undergone a revival in recent years and continue to be practiced.

Men were the artists and artisans in traditional Tlingit and Haida culture, with one exception: Basketry was women's work. Women also wove the fabulous Chilkat blankets, but men created the pattern boards that the women followed to make the design.

Basketry

Southeast Alaska Natives produced two types of baskets: cedar-bark baskets, woven from the stringy inner bark of the cedar tree, and spruce-root baskets. The latter were the most difficult, requiring years of practice and immense skill, not just in the weaving but in preparing the materials. First the roots had to be collected; the smaller roots were preferred. These were roasted in the fire so that their outer covering could be removed by pulling the roots through a forked stick. Then each root was split into still smaller strands with the aid of a long thumbnail. The smooth and shiny outer portion

Years of practice were required to weave a spruce-root or cedar-bark basket. ALASKA STATE MUSEUM, ALFRED A. BLAKER

was set aside for the part of the design that would show, and the inner layer was used for the rest of the weaving.

Spruce-root baskets could be woven watertight. Before contact with other civilizations brought pottery and iron vessels, the Natives used baskets for carrying water and for cooking. Special needs called for special shapes. Very small baskets were carried around the neck when berrying, leaving both hands free to pick the fruit. When full, the small basket was upended into a larger basket borne on the back, which was in turn emptied into an even larger model for transporting the berries back to camp. The Indian women of the northern Panhandle were known for weaving large, flat, floppy baskets that they placed beneath the bushes to catch the berries as they fell. Their baskets were so finely woven and flexible that they could be folded and stored for the winter. To decorate their baskets, the women bleached or dyed tall grasses and overlaid the woven spruce roots with stripes, zigzags, or other geometric designs. For a black pattern, they buried the grass in black mud or steeped it in a solution of hemlock bark. Yellow dye could be made from moss, blue from a solution of urine and copper ore, red from urine that had stood in an alder dish.

Spruce root was also used for weaving hats. Ordinary hats were roughly lampshade-shaped, made of coarser roots, and left undecorated. Wealthy and important people wore larger hats that were more finely woven and decorated with a painted crest design. The weaver's talent was put to the test with the potlatch hats worn by clan chiefs on ceremonial occasions. The potlatch hat was one of the most important symbols of Southeast Indian society. They also were decorated with painted crests, but their distinguishing feature was a series of flat cylinders stacked one on top of the other to form a topknot over the crown. These potlatch rings signified the number of potlatches that the wearer had given during his lifetime and thus symbolized his status in Tlingit or Haida society.

The museum collections of Southeast Alaska, especially the Alaska State Museum in Juneau, Sheldon Jackson Museum in Sitka, and the Tongass Historical Society Museum in Ketchikan, contain fine examples of cedar-bark and spruce-root basketry.

The rings on top of ceremonial potlatch hats indicated the status of the wearer. ALASKA STATE MUSEUM, ALFRED A. BLAKER

Bentwood Boxes

Southeast Alaska and other Northwest Coastal Indians crafted a style of wooden container known as the bentwood box. The boxes, used for storage, packing, carrying, and cooking, were formed out of a single cedar plank that was folded or bent in three places and joined at the fourth corner. The artist added a bottom and some-times a removable lid and decorated the finished box with carved or painted crest designs.

To construct a bentwood box, the artist first chiseled or adzed the plank to the correct thickness and then routed out the inside sur-face opposite the points where the bends would be made. The board was steamed until it could be bent to shape and the ends joined with wooden pegs or spruce-root stitching (also used to mend wooden canoes). Iron nails were used in later years. This method of con-struction produced a sturdy but beautiful box with the soft lines of rounded corners. Look for the seamed corner and nearly invisible spruce-root stitches when you see bentwood boxes in museums.

Chilkat Blankets

Art historians look upon Chilkat blankets as the crowning glory of Tlingit artistic design. The shawl-shaped ceremonial and dance robes featured a complicated geometrical pattern that demanded extraordinary skill to achieve. Only a handful of contemporary weavers have mastered this nearly lost art.

Chilkat blankets were woven from mountain-goat hair. The weaver spun the wool by hand by rolling the strands of hair between the palm of her hand and her thigh. For added strength, the yarn of the warp (the fixed, vertical part of the weave) was wound around a strand of cedar bark. (You can see the reddish-brown bark in the long fringe that hangs from the bottom of the blanket.) The yarn was worked with the fingers—not shuttles—on a simple, upright frame, following a pattern board created by one of the male artists of the village.

The colors of the intricate design were black, yellow, and blue-green, set against the cream background of the natural goat hair. To obtain the colors, the wool was dyed in various concoctions similar to those used to dye grass for decorating baskets. Black usually came from hemlock bark, yellow from a type of moss, and blue-green from urine and copper.

The art of weaving the Chilkat blanket was not limited to the Chilkat Tlingit, but they were considered the masters of the craft. The goat wool was more readily available to them in their northern villages than to some of the other Tlingit groups. The original art form is thought to have originated with the Tsimshian peoples, who used a similar technique to create a different type of robe. It is not known when the present style of blanket was first developed, but Captain Cook acquired geometrically styled goat-hair robes that may represent the early stages of the art form when he visited the Northwest coast in 1778.

Chilkat blankets have always been coveted by Southeast Natives as objects of beauty and status. They signified wealth and were very valuable trade items. Present-day collectors covet the prized blankets. You will find several on display in museums and cultural centers.

Button blankets came into use after traders introduced plain woolen blankets to Southeast Alaska late in the eighteenth century.

The shawl-shaped Chilkat blankets are the highest expression of Tlingit art.
JORGEN SVENDSEN

The Indians adapted the blankets for ceremonial use by decorating them with red trade cloth and bits of abalone shell. When commercially manufactured buttons, glass beads, and sequins became available, they were added to the crest designs.

Totem Poles

Totem poles are at once the most familiar and most misunderstood form of Southeast Native art. Part of the false impression can be attributed to the grotesque and gaudily painted poles in curio-shop windows, seeming as they do to symbolize some mysterious religion or primitive Native rite. In fact, traditional Haida and Tlingit poles were never worshipped as religious objects, and they were not gaudy. For the most part, they were bare cedar with painted accents of the typical Southeast Alaska palette: black, red, and blue-green. As the poles aged, they were allowed to return gracefully to their natural state, never being touched up or restored, so that in time they sprouted bits of grass and woolly moss blankets. In later years, when the art form was in danger of being lost, efforts were made to retrieve and rehabilitate the best of these poles.

Many visitors, upon seeing a particular totem pole, will ask what it "says." What is the story carved in the pole? For many poles there is no story at all; for others the answer can be given only by the carver or the person who commissioned the pole.

Totem poles were carved and erected for several different purposes or occasions. None of them involved worship in any sense; they were not religious objects. Some were memorial poles erected to honor important individuals upon their deaths. Many memorial poles were comparatively simple: a plain shaft topped by a crest figure representing the individual's clan. The crest figure might be Eagle, Raven, or one of the other totems such as Bear, Beaver, or Frog. Some early poles were mortuary poles, which were similar to memorial poles except for a niche carved in the back of the pole to contain the ashes of the deceased.

Totem poles also were carved to commemorate a particular event, such as the building of a new house, the giving of a potlatch, or an occasion of even more widespread significance. One of the most famous poles in Southeast was commissioned by a Tongass Island chief around 1883 to commemorate his clan's first sighting of a white man many years before. The carver evidently used a likeness of Abraham Lincoln as a model for the figure of the white man at the top of the pole, which is why the pole has come to be called the Lincoln totem pole. The pole is more properly known as the Proud Raven pole from the Raven crest carved at the base. The original carving, weathered but still Lincolnesque, stands in the State Museum in Juneau. (There is a replica at Saxman Totem Park in Ketchikan.) A last type, the ridicule pole, was erected to shame publicly a family or individual who had failed to pay a debt or otherwise broken a trust. When the debt was paid, the pole was taken down.

The Lincoln totem pole, carved around 1883, bears likeness to the U.S. president.
R. N. DE ARMOND

Whatever the type of pole, the dramatic carvings on the column served to remind the Native viewers of events, people, and legends from their collective history. With no written language, this was a significant contribution to the continuation of the culture. Totem poles are "story poles" only in the sense that the figures carved on them acted as symbols or memory aids to remind the storyteller of the principal characters and events he was relating.

Totem poles were carved by artists commissioned by the clan chief. The chief decided what figures he wanted on the pole, and the artist executed the design. Red cedar was the preferred wood, although yellow cedar (Alaska cedar) was acceptable in the north, where red cedar was not available. The Haida, especially, who had very large trees at their disposal, frequently hollowed out the back of the log to reduce weight and guard against splitting. The artist was left with a half-round shell approximately 10 inches thick on which to carve his designs. (Be sure to look at the backs of totem poles, too.) The artist shaped the figures on the pole by chipping off small, uniform bites of wood with an adze. The Southeast Natives look upon fine-textured, even adzing as an indication of the carver's skill.

The next step was paint, applied sparingly. In earlier days the paint was a version of egg tempera using pulverized salmon eggs for a binding medium. Soot, graphite, or charcoal ground and mixed with the salmon eggs produced black paint. Red was made from red ochre, and the blue-green came from copper sulfide. Originally wood-carving tools were polished stone, bone, or shell, but trade with the Europeans brought sharp iron blades that cut through the cedar like butter. The metal blades enabled carvers to create larger and more complex designs, culminating in totem poles up to 65 feet tall. Most of the poles now seen in Southeast Alaska were carved in the latter half of the nineteenth century, when trade with Europeans and Americans had brought considerable wealth to local Native groups and touched off a renaissance of Native carving.

Once erected, totem poles were generally not taken down (except for ridicule poles), even if the villagers moved to a new site. The poles were simply abandoned. Most of the totem parks around Southeast today stem from the 1930s when the Civilian Conservation Corps, working in conjunction with the U.S. Forest Service, undertook collecting old poles from abandoned sites and restoring them to public view. Over the course of the project, more than one hundred totem poles were restored, duplicated, or carved from memory and placed in parks around Southeast.

Southeast's largest and most accessible totem pole collections are at Sitka National Historical Park and at Saxman Totem Park and Totem Bight State Historic Park in Ketchikan. At Sitka the poles are spaced along a beautiful trail within the historic park. There is an exhibit center where you can watch carvers and other craftspeople work and can see a film about the history of Sitka and the Tlingit culture. The Totem Bight site in Ketchikan has a spectacular beach setting, but Saxman is closer to downtown. Ketchikan also houses the state's largest collection of original, unrestored totem poles at the Totem Heritage Center. Totem parks also can be found at the villages of Hydaburg, Kasaan, and Klawock on Prince of Wales Island.

There are also many individual poles to be seen as you walk around Southeast towns, and several new poles have been erected in recent years. Alaska's tallest totem pole—132 feet, 6 inches—stands in the village of Kake on Kupreanof Island. The pole was carved in the 1970s at the Alaska Indian Arts Center in Haines.

Other Carving

The Tlingit and Haida carvers—always men in those days, but no longer—were kept busy. Besides bentwood boxes and totem poles, many other utilitarian and ceremonial objects were decoratively carved with clan crests or other significant totemic designs. The posts supporting the house roof beams frequently were patterned in designs that celebrated the history of the clan. There were elaborate wooden serving dishes for special feasts, "grease dishes" to hold eulachon or seal oil, enormous sheep-horn spoons with handles carved of black goat horn, dance rattles shaped like birds, and ceremonial wooden hats with crest animals carved on top. Intricate dance masks, some with moving parts that the wearer controlled by strings, represented birds, animals, or spirits. All these objects, and more, are displayed in museums throughout Southeast Alaska.

In the early 1800s the Haida developed a new art form: argillite carving. Argillite is a black shalestone that was discovered around

1820 on the Queen Charlotte Islands of British Columbia. The Haida artists found that the new substance could be carved and polished to a high luster that the traders frequenting the Northwest coast found attractive. The Natives began carving boxes and ceremonial dishes from argillite, sometimes adding decorations of ivory, abalone shell, or operculum to the traditional crest designs. Later they found that miniature totem poles of argillite proved profitable in the tourist trade. Haida argillite carving is considered one of the highest art forms of the Northwest coast.

BASIC COMPONENTS OF TOTEMIC DESIGN

Almost every object in Southeast Native life, whether ceremonial or strictly utilitarian, lent itself to adornment. Sometimes the design was carved into the wood of the object, and sometimes it was painted on top. The designs were generally totemic, meaning that they represented the clan totems, or crests. The crests served to signify ownership of the object, and they engendered a sense of pride, in much the same way that a coat of arms created pride and allegiance in medieval Europe. Perhaps more than anything else, they turned plain household implements into objects of beauty and delight. Looking at an exquisitely carved halibut hook or a perfectly proportioned dish, in the shape of a seal, for example, it is easy to believe that these early artists worked primarily out of love for the materials, their tools, and the designs they were creating. Surely they felt great joy in filling their workaday world with beautiful objects.

Tlingit and Haida designs may all look the same to you at first; you may not be able to distinguish one totem from the next. In time, though, you will become practiced at picking out the identifying characteristics of each totem, which will add enormously to your pleasure in viewing Native art.

If you want to learn more about totemic design, I strongly recommend Hilary Stewart's *Looking at Indian Art of the Northwest Coast* (University of Washington Press). The author uses wonderfully

Standing near the entrance of Sitka National Historical Park, this 27-foot pole depicts 200 years of Pacific Northwest Coast Indian cultural history. MICHELLE GURNEY

Visited this 06.12.04

explicit illustrations to break down the elements of totemic design into understandable bits.

The Totems

Whether painted on canoes or spruce-root hats or carved into the soft cedar of totem poles or storage chests, Native designs consist of the same basic totemic motifs. Only the format differs according to the shape of the object. The basic crest figures are most easily recognized in three-dimensional form as they appear on totem poles. Whether the carving is Tlingit, Haida, or Tsimshian, there are certain distinguishing features that you can look for in each crest animal. Usually the identifying characteristic is a particular body part, but a characteristic pose or an object frequently associated with that animal may be part of the design convention as well.

Raven: Raven can probably be considered the most important design figure because he appears so frequently, either as one of the two major totems or in his mythological guise. Either way, Raven is usually portrayed as birdlike with wings. His distinguishing feature is a long, straight beak.

Eagle: Eagle's beak is shorter than Raven's and curved downward. Frequently he is shown with large claws. Occasionally you will see a

This sea lion feasting bowl, from the Sheldon Jackson Museum, is a fine example of the carver's art.

ᏞᏁ ᏚᏆᎢᏦᎪ

double-headed eagle, such as the one on the totem pole in front of the Pioneers' Home in Sitka. This does not represent the Eagle crest, but the Russians in Alaska.

Bear: Bear is an important family crest. He is usually sitting upright on his haunches, in the attitude of a begging dog. He has upright ears, prominent teeth, large nostrils, and no tail. Sometimes a bear represents not a clan crest but a story, such as "Kats and His Bear Wife." This popular Tlingit legend tells of Kats, whose life was saved by a female grizzly bear that appeared to him in human form. Kats and the bear woman lived together as husband and wife, but he was killed by their cub children.

Beaver: Beaver is similar to Bear in overall shape and begging-dog attitude, but he has very large front teeth for gnawing. He also has a distinctive paddle-shaped tail that frequently is turned up in front of him and decorated with cross-hatching. Beaver sometimes holds a stick between his front paws.

Wolf: Wolf often assumes the begging-dog pose, with these differences from Bear or Beaver: a pointed snout, pointed ears, and a long tail. Sometimes his tongue lolls out of his mouth.

Frog: Frog generally looks exactly like a frog, with a large, toothless mouth, short legs, and a squat body, sometimes with spots.

Killer Whale: Killer Whale is the easiest totem to identify. Look for a blunt head sometimes with prominent teeth, a forked tail, and a circular blowhole. The telling dorsal fin protrudes from his back. Usually Killer Whale is placed vertically on the totem pole, head down, but sometimes he rides crosswise on top.

Halibut: Halibut does not appear as frequently as some of the other totems but is eminently recognizable with close-set eyes that are off-center, mouth to one side, and flatfish body.

Humans: Humans are occasionally portrayed on totem poles as figures from legends or notable events. They can be distinguished from animals by their ears, which are located on the sides of the head instead of the top. White men are typically given beards, clothes, and curly hair. Native women wear lip ornaments called labrets, which were popular in early days. Haida poles are frequently topped by one or two human figures wearing tall potlatch hats. They are the "watchmen" on the lookout for enemies.

Raven

Double-headed Eagle

Grizzly Bear

Beaver

Wolf

Frog

Killer Whale

Halibut

White Man

Applied Designs

The same techniques for carving animal designs onto a log could be applied to other surfaces and shapes, such as wooden serving vessels. A bowl could be shaped like a halibut, for example, with a broad tail at one end, a head with two offset eyes and crooked mouth at the other end, and the body hollowed out to form the cavity. Or a grease dish made to hold seal oil could be formed in the shape of a seal, with head protruding from one end and flippers on the sides.

When the totemic patterns were applied to flat surfaces, such as painted house screens, the designs had to be adjusted to fit. Once the principle was established of letting each totem be represented by stylized body parts, however, the problem was solved. The body parts were simply rearranged as necessary to fill up the given space in a pleasing manner. Sometimes the animal was simply "split" down the backbone and spread open to create a symmetrical design in one plane. The head appeared at the center of the design, with one side

Killer Whale is portrayed with a double profile on a painted housefront in Angoon.

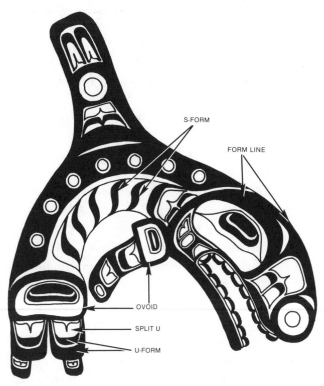

S-FORM

FORM LINE

OVOID

SPLIT U

U-FORM

Jumping Killer Whale patterned after the design on a Tlinget hide shirt in the Berne Historical Museum.

of the body shown to the left and the other side to the right. Many silver bracelets are carved this way.

Sometimes the totem was just shown in a single profile or as a double profile. Sometimes all the necessary features were there, but out of order. This rearrangement of body parts can approach pure abstraction, as in the case of Chilkat blanket designs, which only experts can interpret.

INTO THE CORPORATE ERA

After the first contact with the Russians when Chirikof's party went ashore, presumably near Sitka, in 1741, the Indians of Southeast Alaska saw ships from many nations. They traded furs for articles they did not have, such as cloth, iron tools, kettles, and pots. These manufactured goods, and the practice of trading with the outsiders, changed the pattern of their lives. They began to fit canvas sails onto their seagoing canoes; they adopted white men's garments in place of their own sewn skins and cedar-bark shirts. But even when the Russian-American Company settled into Sitka, forcing the local Tlingit to abandon their homeland and camp in the shadow of the Russian community, the lifestyle of the majority of the Tlingit and Haida Indians living on the coast was not severely disrupted.

Clear, cataclysmic devastation came in the form of smallpox, the scourge of aboriginal peoples. The English sea captain Nathaniel Portlock believed he saw many pockmarked faces when he visited near Sitka in 1787. He concluded the Spanish had brought the disease with them a dozen years before during the Pérez explorations. In 1836 smallpox broke out among the Tlingit in the southern range of the territory, perhaps spread northward from the British territories in Canada. This time the disease ran rampant through the Southeast coast and island chain. An estimated 50 to 60 percent of the Indian population—thousands of people—died. The smallpox spread from settlement to settlement along the coast to the north, eventually reaching the peoples of Bristol Bay, the Kuskokwim River, the Yukon River, and Norton Sound.

The United States' purchase of Alaska from Russia had little immediate effect upon the Tlingit and Haida. The trading posts were more of an interruption to their lifestyle, as was the coming of missionaries. The discovery of gold and the birth of the commercial fishing industry in the late 1800s brought a substantial increase in the white population of Southeast Alaska and the development of new permanent communities. The Indians moved from their traditional villages to camp near the bustling mining towns or canneries, where they could barter for goods or earn wages.

In the first years of U.S. possession, there were few laws to protect the white population and even fewer for Natives. In 1902 the Tlingit petitioned to attend white schools in Juneau and Ketchikan but were refused entrance. In 1912 they organized the Alaska Native Brotherhood with the aim of winning citizenship. This right was finally recognized in 1924. The same year, Tlingit attorney William Paul Sr. won a seat in the territorial legislature.

Native peoples from all over Alaska gradually gained political sophistication and power. In 1971 their long efforts were rewarded by passage of the Alaska Native Claims Settlement Act, which awarded a cash and land settlement to reimburse the various Native groups for aboriginal lands that had been usurped by the U.S. government. Village, urban, and regional corporations were formed to manage the new resources. In Southeast Alaska the final land selections for Native corporations will total 550,000 to 600,000 acres. Much of the acreage has been selected from prime timberland, and many Native corporations have entered the logging industry on a large-scale basis.

CHAPTER FIVE

COMMON PLANTS
OF THE
INSIDE PASSAGE

The topography of the Inside Passage region consists of deep saltwater passages adjacent to mature coastal forests and high mountains, all occurring within a few thousand feet. This wide range of habitats existing in close proximity is one of the principal characteristics of Southeast Alaska.

HABITATS

From shipboard the flora of the Inside Passage appears to consist solely of evergreen forest, but there are actually five distinct communities of vegetation. Marshlands or tidal flats made up of grasses, sedges, and other herbs lie close to the saltwater shore and along estuaries and riverbanks. Small willows and alders also grow at this low elevation and, in some locales, tall black cottonwoods.

The evergreen forest extends from sea level to timberline at 2,000 or 3,000 feet. The coastal forest of Southeast Alaska is the natural extension of the forest that stretches all along the Pacific coast from northern California to Cook Inlet in south-central Alaska. The southern forests are composed primarily of Douglas fir, but the dominant species in Alaska are western hemlock and Sitka spruce. There is also a scattering of red cedar, Alaska cedar, and mountain hemlock.

Except where they have been disturbed by humans, Southeast forests are generally more than 150 years old. Some of the mature trees are more than 200 feet tall. Shrubs, ferns, and young trees grow beneath the tall cover, and the forest floor is littered with a thick layer of fallen logs and moss. These mature old-growth forests are called climax forests. They are in a natural cycle of growth and decay, which means that every stretch of woods contains many large, healthy trees; some small, young trees; and the remains of dead and dying trees that eventually will decompose to nourish the next generation.

 In the forest openings are wet muskegs with pools of freestanding water. This community is characterized by natural bonsai—stunted, deformed trees that may be 200 years old—as well as mosses, sedges, and low shrubs such as Labrador tea, bog and mountain cranberry, blueberry, and crowberry. The primary trees are lodgepole pine (also called shore pine) and mountain hemlock.

Above the spruce and hemlock forest lies a subalpine transition zone of scrubby trees such as mountain hemlock and a mat of low-spreading vegetation. Past the tree line, above 2,500 feet, begins the true alpine tundra community of tiny, low-spreading plants, such as heather, crowberry, nagoonberry, and alpine azalea, which grow among the rocky outcrops.

Vegetation grows rapidly with the increasing daylight of spring. Within the space of a few weeks, muddy hillsides are transformed into impenetrable salmonberry thickets that tower overhead. In autumn the process is reversed. The leaves linger on the berry bushes, turning yellow and mottled brown, until a late fall wind blows up, baring trees and bushes to winter.

The five most important conifers and some of the other common plants of the Inside Passage follow.

TREES

Western Hemlock

Western hemlock is the most prevalent tree in Southeast, forming more than 70 percent of the coastal spruce/hemlock forest. These tall evergreens can grow to 190 feet with a 5-foot-diameter trunk. The needles are dark green and shiny on top, dull on the underside.

Unlike spruce needles, they are short, soft, flexible, and rounded at the tip. They grow along two sides of the twig only, so the western hemlock twig is flat. The branches have a feathery appearance compared with the stiffer spruce; the tips are slender and curve down, especially when the ⅝- to 1-inch cones have formed on the ends.

Western hemlock

Better-quality hemlock logs are used for general construction lumber. Poor-quality hemlock is used for pulp. Although hemlock makes one of the best paper pulps, the mills in Southeast produce dissolving pulp, which is further processed into rayon, cellophane, and plastics.

Sitka Spruce

The Sitka spruce is Alaska's official state tree and makes up 20 percent of the Southeast coastal forest. The tree can attain 225 feet in height and 8 feet in diameter, although 160 feet high and 3 to 5 feet in diameter is more typical. The needles are dark green on top, but silvery blue below. They are short, stiff, and sharp and grow all around the twig, like a bottlebrush. If you squeeze your hand around a spruce tip, you will say "Ouch!"

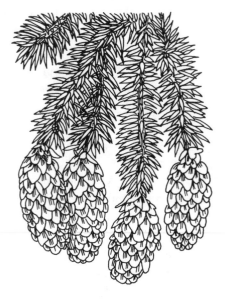

Sitka spruce

Not so with the hemlock. The 2- to 4-inch cones—considerably larger than the hemlock's—hang from the branch tips.

The fast-growing Sitka spruce is one of the most valuable trees in Alaska. Like hemlock, better-quality spruce is cut into lumber. Spruce is an important wood for aircraft and glider construction, boats, ladders, and other items that require strength combined with light weight, and its excellent acoustical properties make it suitable for guitar faces and piano sounding boards. Lesser-quality wood goes into dissolving pulp.

Mountain Hemlock

Mountain hemlock is the alpine counterpart to western hemlock. Although found at sea level, the mountain hemlock's habitat extends to 3,500 feet—higher than the western hemlock and Sitka spruce care to grow. The tree is smaller than the western hemlock, normally 50 to 100 feet high, but capable of stretching to 125 feet. In muskeg bogs and subalpine communities where soils are infertile, the tree takes on a severely stressed shape with very short branches, bonsai bends, and weathered gray bark. At times mountain hemlock hugs the ground, spreading horizontally as a low-lying shrub. The needles of mountain hemlock are similar to those of western hemlock: shiny green, short, and soft. The difference is that they grow around the entire circumference of the twig. The cones resemble those of western hemlock but are longer. They are dark purple before they mature, deepening eventually to brown.

Western Red Cedar

Western red cedar grows in the southern part of the Panhandle, approximately from Petersburg south, mixed in with the rest of the spruce/hemlock forest. The foliage of this aromatic tree is much different than that of either spruce or hemlock, the needles forming flat, fanlike sprays with ½-inch elliptical cones appearing near the ends of the twigs. The wood from the red cedar resists rot and insects and is widely used for fence posts, shakes, shingles, and boats. The Tlingit and Haida Indians used this wood for their canoes, houses, and totem poles, and they wove mats and baskets out of the stringy bark. The red cedar commonly grows to 100 feet and sometimes to 130.

Alaska Cedar

Alaska cedar, known also as Alaska cypress or yellow cedar, exists throughout the coastal forest but is not nearly as common as spruce or hemlock. Smaller than the western red cedar, the Alaska variety grows to a maximum height of 100 feet. The leaf structure consists of the same flat, fanlike spray, but the tiny cones (less than

Alaska cedar

½-inch in diameter) are nearly round and more gray-colored than brown. The durable wood is soft and easy to work—the Coastal Indians habitually used Alaska cedar for their carved canoe paddles. Presently Japan imports quantities of Alaska cedar, and U.S. manufacturers use the lumber for windows, doors, and boats.

Lodgepole Pine

Lodgepole pine, or shore pine, is the only pine native to Alaska. In Southeast Alaska it usually appears as a twisted, scrubby specimen growing in the muskeg swamps of forest openings. In this mode the pine attains only a few feet of height, often spreading horizontally rather than vertically. In better growing conditions, though, lodgepole pine can shoot straight up to 40 feet. An inland variety found around Haines and Skagway grows to 75 feet. The tree is dark green, with typical pine needles growing in pairs with a sheath at the base. The cones are up to 2 inches long. Many local residents prefer this resinous pine at Christmastime, but they are too few to be harvested commercially.

Alder

Alder is the most common deciduous tree in Southeast Alaska. It appears from the size of a shrub to a small tree in places where the ground has been disturbed: along roads and ditches, on avalanche scars, by rivers and streams, on logging sites, and where glaciers

Red alder

have retreated. The smooth, gray-barked wood has long been used for smoking fish and game and is easily gathered for firewood. Alder is also preferred for some types of Native carving.

Three species of alder are present in Southeast. All have smooth, gray bark; shiny, dark green leaves with serrated edges; and small, dark, nutmeg-shaped nuts. The largest and most abundant species is red alder, which grows to 40 feet. Sitka alder is slightly smaller, growing to 30 feet. This species grows along with red alder at lower elevations but exists by itself at elevations above 1,000 feet. The third variety, thinleaf alder, is found only in the northern part of the Panhandle, from Juneau to Skagway, where it grows mixed in with willows along streams.

Alder is known as a pioneer species, meaning that it follows disturbances to the ground such as avalanches or road building, quickly takes root, and improves soil conditions. When the evergreens appear and overtake them in size, the shade-intolerant alders disappear.

Willow

Willows grow along with alders beside stream beds, beaches, and roads. Like alders, they quickly take over sites that have been logged, burned, or otherwise cleared. Their light, gray-green leaves are smooth and oblong. In spring they develop fuzzy caterpillar-shaped catkins that spread tufts of white fluff everywhere. There are many varieties of willow in Southeast. The Scouler willow is most common, followed by the Sitka willow and Barclay willow. In size, the willows range from shrubs to small trees.

Black Cottonwood

The stately black cottonwood, the largest deciduous tree in the area, reigns over the river valleys on the mainland of Southeast Alaska, including the Stikine, the Taku, and the Chilkat. The black cotton-wood grows alongside the alder and willow trees but towers above both at 80 to 100 feet. In 1965 a champion specimen was found near Haines (about 5 miles west of Klukwan on the Klehini River). The tree measured 101 feet in height with a circumference of 32 feet, 6 inches.

At first glance the cottonwood might be taken for an alder, since the two usually grow side by side. The cottonwood is much larger, though, and the leaves are smooth around the edges, in contrast with the toothed leaves of the alder. The handsome cottonwood provides welcome color in fall, when the leaves turn golden. In late autumn and winter, bald eagles gather by the thousands in the cot-tonwoods along the Chilkat River near Haines to feed on spawned-out salmon.

Mountain Ash

The colorful European mountain ash, introduced as an ornamental in many Southeast towns, grows to 40 feet. Its clusters of tiny white flowers are among the first blooms to appear in spring; in fall its scarlet berries attract flocks of Bohemian waxwings and other migrating birds. The delicate foliage contains numerous small, yellow-green leaves on a slim stem. The leaves turn bronze in fall. The bark is light gray and smooth. A rare native species of mountain ash grows as a tall

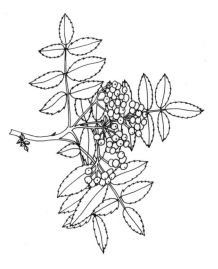

Mountain ash

shrub to about 15 feet in forest openings. It is smaller and less showy than the introduced tree.

A handful of other trees exist in Southeast Alaska but are less commonly seen or exist only in isolated spots. They include the dwarf Douglas maple (the only maple in Alaska), Pacific silver and subalpine firs, Pacific yew, quaking aspen, western paper birch, and Pacific serviceberry.

BERRIES AND OTHER
FOREST PLANTS

Berrying is an important recreational and subsistence activity in Southeast Alaska. It's also an excuse to be with friends and enjoy the wild forest trails. Around late June the berry fanatics begin cruising the roads and trails to sniff out the best patches for the summer's gathering. A two-pound coffee can makes an excellent berrying pail. You punch holes in the sides, thread them with a long scarf, and knot the ends. The scarf goes over your neck and the pail hangs in front of you, freeing both hands for picking. The bounty in Southeast Alaska includes blueberries, salmonberries, thimbleberries, and nagoonberries. Southeasterners bake them in pies, shortcake, and crisps and freeze a supply for muffins and sourdough pancakes throughout the winter. The remainder goes into jam and jelly—Christmas presents for favored friends and relatives in the Lower 48.

Berry picking is more than recreation for some older Alaska Natives, whose culture was at one time heavily influenced by the cycle of food gathering. For them, collecting a quantity of berries in summer and preserving them for winter use is virtually a ritualistic necessity. I once was acquainted with an elderly Tlingit woman who had the use of only one eye and such severe arthritis that she could barely hobble with the use of a cane. At berrying time she asked to be carried to the berry patch where she would spend hour upon hour gathering her winter's fruit.

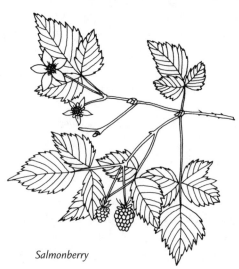

Salmonberry

Salmonberry

The pink, star-shaped blossoms of the salmonberry peek through the bright green leaves in early May, a welcome sign of spring. These berries grow profusely along trails, on open hillsides, and in forest clearings. When the prickly canes reach their full summer height—easily 10 feet—they form a nearly impenetrable barrier. The fruit, which appears around July, appeals to both humans and bears. The large, pendulous berries, shaped like boysenberries or blackberries, vary in color from salmon-orange to dark red. The mild flavor is slightly tangy.

Pacific Red Elder

When the salmonberries are already blossoming, the red elder, or elderberry, springs to life with clumps of lacy, white blossoms. This berry reaches the size of a small tree in Southeast, with brittle, woody branches and long, narrow leaves. In late summer grapelike clusters of shiny red berries form in place of the flowers—much to the delight of the crows. But the bitter fruit affects some people adversely. (The European elderberry that forms the basis for the excellent elderberry wines is not present in Southeast.)

Red elders add color and grace to many Southeast gardens. They are common in open areas of the forest and on the fringes of communities: a scarlet splash against the dark green spruce and hemlock.

Blueberry

Several varieties of blueberry and huckleberry thrive in Southeast. All the varieties form compact shrubs that can reach 6 feet in height. The stems are woody; there are no thorns or prickles. The oval leaves are small and light green, and the spring blossoms, yellow-pink to bronze-pink, depending upon the variety, hang down in the shape of a bell. The berries vary in color from blue to nearly black.

The fruit of the early blueberry is covered with a light-colored powder, or bloom, whereas that of the Alaska blueberry, often called a huckleberry, is shiny blue-black. Both varieties grow together. The red huckleberry, much appreciated for its bright color and good jam-making qualities, is rarer. Most people simply mix the various varieties together since they grow side by side in the woods. Two dwarf varieties grow on the muskeg at higher elevations: the dwarf blueberry and the bog blueberry. Both are low, spreading shrubs that never attain more than a couple of feet in height.

Sometimes the blueberries have a tendency toward worminess. Nothing to be squeamish about—just dump your berries in a pail of water when you get back from the woods and soak them for a few hours. The worms (which are minuscule) become starved for oxygen and crawl out.

Other Berries

Blueberries and salmonberries may be the most plentiful berries in the Panhandle, but they are by no means the only ones. Wild cranberries are a tangy bounty in fall. There are two creeping varieties that grow in bogs and alpine areas, and a highbush variety that appears in the forest and grows to 12 feet. The sparse, three-lobed leaves turn color with the seasons. The large ($\frac{3}{8}$ to $\frac{1}{2}$ inch), elliptical, translucent fruit is a beautiful yellow-orange in summer and turns brighter with time. Locals prize the highbush cranberries for jelly or syrup. Unfortunately they are not plentiful except along streams on the mainland. The western thimbleberry has large, maple-shaped leaves. The flat, white blossom forms an edible pinky-red berry shaped like a thimble. The shrub grows to 5 feet.

Southeast has several edible currants and gooseberries and several ground berries. The latter include the crowberry (sometimes called mossberry), a low, heatherlike plant with shiny, round, black berries that grows in bogs and upper tundra regions, including the rocky cliffs of the Juneau Ice Field at 5,600 feet. The rare nagoonberry appears in low-lying meadows and bogs. This is a delicate little plant, growing 2 to 10 inches off the ground, with three-lobed leaves and a red fruit shaped like a rounded, shiny raspberry—coveted for jam, jelly, or wine (Southeasterners have been known to share anything except the location of their secret nagoonberry patch). Small wild strawberries can be found in beach areas.

Avoid the poisonous baneberry, which has large, coarsely toothed, lobed leaves and round red or white fruit, several to a stem. The bush grows in woods and thickets to 4 feet high. As few as six berries have been known to cause dizziness, increased pulse, and stomach pain.

Devil's Club

Devil's club might be called the ogre of the woods: a primitive-looking plant with enormous leaves and treacherous spines. This common inhabitant of the spruce/hemlock forest undergrowth grows to 10 feet. The elephantine leaves, which measure up to a foot in diameter, are prickly on the underside. Even worse, the tall, snaking stalks are equipped with sharp, poisonous spines that

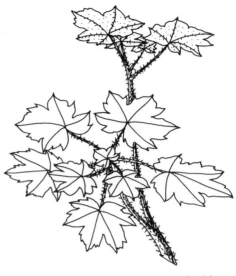

Devil's club

can make a painful sore if they become embedded in your skin. Devil's club needs this protection because its leaves are rich in protein and could otherwise be heavily used by forest animals. Although it can block your path through the forest very unpleasantly, the plant is quite handsome at a distance. In spring pale greenish-white flowers develop on tall stalks and turn into bright red berries (not edible) in fall. Devil's club is one of the few hazardous plants in the Southeast woods. There is no poison ivy or poison oak in Southeast forests.

Cow Parsnip

The cow parsnip also has gigantic leaves. This plant appears along roadsides and in meadows, forest clearings, and many a domestic garden where it is not wanted. The hollow green stem is striated like celery or rhubarb, hence the plant's two other names: wild celery and Indian rhubarb. Cow parsnip bears tight clusters of tiny white flowers in spring—so large and compact that they resemble a flat head of cauliflower.

Cow parsnip smells strongly "weedy," and the scent lingers on skin and clothing for hours. Many people are allergic to this plant; for particularly susceptible people, even superficial contact can cause painful blisters on the skin. For those not allergic, the stems are edible and formed part of the Native diet in earlier times. But beware of confusing cow parsnip with deadly poison water hemlock, which has a similar-appearing flower.

Skunk Cabbage

Bright yellow skunk cabbage is the unsung champion of the boggy forests of Southeast Alaska, the first plant to appear through the waning snow in spring. The flower appears first, shaped like a yellow

calla lily, with a green stalk in the center. The leaves come up later. They are bright green, and they grow, and grow, and grow throughout spring and summer until they are nearly 5 feet tall.

Skunk cabbage thrives in wet conditions. You will see the familiar shape in drainage ditches, swamps, and bogs. The plant sometimes gives off a strong odor, hence the name. Although the Tlingit used skunk cabbage for pit baking, the leaves contain large amounts of oxalic acid and should not be eaten.

Skunk cabbage

WILDFLOWERS

Despite a rainy disposition, Southeast Alaska grows a full complement of wildflowers. A list of the commonly appearing varieties appears on pages 110–12. Below are a few of the better-known specimens that you may encounter during your rambles through the coastal forest.

The lovely blue-violet lupine grows to 4 feet tall along the coastal shore, along highways and roads, and in alpine areas. One of the most extravagant displays appears opposite the highway just north of the Juneau airport, in the vicinity of Brotherhood Bridge. The showy fireweed, with magenta blossoms, grows to 9 feet along roadsides, riverbanks, and in meadows. Along forest trails the bunchberry, a dwarf form of dogwood, forms a single greenish-white flower with four petals in spring and a red fruit in fall. This common ground cover in the spruce and hemlock forest stands no taller than 8 inches.

Both the yellow stream violet and the blue Alaska violet grow in Southeast. They prefer damp loca-tions. Southeast has many

Chocolate lily

varieties of buttercup, a red-orange columbine, a purple-blue wild flag, or iris, a wild rose, the delicate blue forget-me-not—Alaska's state flower—and a wild beach pea with red-violet flowers. Among the other species, one has special interest: a rare (outside of coastal Alaska) chocolate lily that grows in open grassy flatlands. This purple-brown lily grows to 24 inches. The bulb is covered with rice-like pellets that are edible when cooked. The local Native peoples included the pellets in their diet, accounting for the lily's other name: Indian rice.

If you visit Southeast in early fall, you might enjoy searching for clumps of Alaska cotton grass. Local residents like to use this tufted grass in dried floral arrangements.

COMMON WILDFLOWERS OF
SOUTHEAST ALASKA

- [ ] Cotton grass/Alaska cotton, *Eriophorum* species *
- [ ] Skunk cabbage, *Lysichitum americanum* *
- [ ] False hellebore, *Veratrum eschscholtzii*
- [ ] Indian rice/chocolate lily, *Fritillaria camschatcensis* *
- [ ] Alp lily, *Lloydia serotina*
- [ ] False lily-of-the-valley, *Maianthemum dilitatum*
- [ ] Wild iris/wild flag, *Iris setosa* *
- [ ] White bog orchid, *Habenaria dilitata*
- [ ] Ladies' tresses, *Spiranthes romanzoffiana*
- [ ] Heart-leaf twayblade, *Listera* species
- [ ] Fairy slipper/Calypso, *Calypso bulbosa*
- [ ] Coral root, *Corallorrhiza mertensiana*
- [ ] Moss campion/cushion pink, *Silene acaulis*
- [ ] Dwarf water lily, *Nymphaea tetragona*
- [ ] Yellow pond lily, *Nuphar polysepalum*
- [ ] Mountain marigold, *Caltha leptosepala*
- [ ] Marsh marigold, *Caltha palustris*
- [ ] Western columbine, *Aquilegia formosa* *
- [ ] Monkshood, *Aconitum delphinifolium*
- [ ] Yellow anemone, *Anemone richardsonii*
- [ ] Narcissus-flowered anemone, *Anemone narcissiflora*
- [ ] Cut leaf anemone, *Anemone multifida*
- [ ] Cooley buttercup, *Ranunculus cooleyae*
- [ ] Eschscholtz buttercup, *Ranunculus eschscholtzii*
- [ ] Creeping buttercup, *Ranunculus repens* *
- [ ] Western buttercup, *Ranunculus occidentalis* *
- [ ] Sundew, *Drosera* species
- [ ] Roseroot/king's crown, *Sedum rosea*
- [ ] Grass of Parnassus, *Parnassia palustris*

- [ ] Fringe cup, *Tellima grandiflora*
- [ ] Alaska boykinia/bear flower, *Boykinia richardsonii*
- [ ] Laceflower, *Tiarella trifoliata*
- [ ] Purple mountain saxifrage, *Saxifraga oppositifolia*
- [ ] Luetkea/Alaska spirea, *Luetkea pectinata*
- [ ] Goatsbeard, *Aruncus sylvester* *
- [ ] Marsh fivefinger/cinquefoil, *Potentilla palustris*
- [ ] Silverweed, *Potentilla egedii* var. *grandis*
- [ ] Yellow dryas, *Dryas drummondii*
- [ ] Eight-petaled dryas/mountain avens, *Dryas octopetala*
- [ ] Nootka lupine, *Lupinus nootkatensis* *
- [ ] Prickly wild rose/Nootka rose, *Rosa nutkana* *
- [ ] Beach pea, *Lathyrus maritimus*
- [ ] Cranesbill/northern geranium, *Geranium erianthum*
- [ ] Touch-me-not, *Impatiens noli-tangere*
- [ ] Stream violet/yellow violet, *Viola glabella* *
- [ ] Alaska violet, *Viola langsdorffii* *
- [ ] Fireweed, *Epilobium angustifolium* *
- [ ] Dwarf fireweed, *Epilobium latifolium* *
- [ ] Western/poison water hemlock, *Cicuta douglasii*
- [ ] Cow parsnip, *Heracleum lanatum* *
- [ ] Ground dogwood/bunchberry, *Cornus canadensis* *
- [ ] Pink pyrola/wintergreen, *Pyrola asarifolia*
- [ ] Single delight/shy maiden/wax flower, *Moneses uniflora*
- [ ] Labrador tea, *Ledum groenlandicum*
- [ ] Alpine azalea, *Loiseleuria procumbens*
- [ ] Aleutian heather/mountain heather, *Phyllodoce glanduliflora*
- [ ] Alaska moss heather, *Cassiope* species
- [ ] Bog rosemary, *Andromeda polifolia*
- [ ] Pixie eyes/wedge-leaved primrose, *Primula cuneifolia*
- [ ] Rock jasmine, *Androsace septentrionalis*

- [ ] Star flower, *Trientalis europaea*
- [ ] Shooting star, *Dodecatheon* species
- [ ] Broad-petaled gentian, *Gentiana platypetala*
- [ ] Jacob's ladder, *Polemonium pulcherrimum*
- [ ] Forget-me-not, *Myosotis sylvatica* *
- [ ] Monkey flower/wild snapdragon, *Mimulus guttatus*
- [ ] Coastal paintbrush/yellow paintbrush, *Castilleja unalaschcensis*
- [ ] Mountain paintbrush, *Castilleja parviflora*
- [ ] Lousewort, *Pedicularis* species
- [ ] Poque/broomrape, *Boschniakia rossica*
- [ ] Butterwort/bog violet, *Pinguicula vulgaris* var. *macroceras*
- [ ] Twinflower, *Linnaea borealis*
- [ ] Valerian/mountain heliotrope, *Valeriana* species
- [ ] Mountain harebell/bluebell, *Campanula lasiocarpa*
- [ ] Bluebells of Scotland, *Campanula rotundifolia*
- [ ] Dandelion, *Taraxacum* species *
- [ ] Goldenrod, *Solidago multiradiata*
- [ ] Fleabane, *Erigeron* species
- [ ] Arctic daisy, *Chrysanthemum arcticum*
- [ ] Arnica, *Arnica* species
- [ ] Seabeach senecio/seabeach groundsel, *Senecio pseudo-arnica*
- [ ] Yarrow, *Achillea borealis*

* Very common

CHAPTER SIX

WILDLIFE OF THE INSIDE PASSAGE

The coastal forests and waterways of Southeast Alaska nurture a huge variety of creatures. A few of them, such as the bald eagle, grizzly bear, and humpback whale, are so seldom seen in most of the continental United States that their numbers in Alaska seem an embarrassment of riches and, for lovers of wildlife, probably worth a trip in themselves.

The continued richness of wildlife resources—biologists estimate there are as many as 5,000 brown bears and 20,000 to 25,000 bald eagles here—can be attributed to the relatively vast expanse of habitat that still exists in an undisturbed state in Southeast Alaska. Where natural habitat gives way, be it from logging, mining, road building, tourist activities, or simply the gradual encroachment of towns and marinas, wildlife decreases. Animals lose nesting areas and cease to bear young; they become poisoned by unnatural substances in their environment and die; they lose sources of nourishment or resting spots and fail to reproduce. In the case of brown and black bears, they become a threat to the safety of humans and are destroyed.

So far, wildlife populations for major species in Southeast Alaska remain strong. Even the sea otter, long missing from these coasts, appears to be returning. Living in close proximity to these wild creatures—seeing them in their natural habitat, observing their seasonal comings and goings—remains one of the greatest pleasures of living along the Inside Passage.

These are a few wildlife forms that are common to Southeast Alaska.

LAND ANIMALS

Black Bear

The black bear, the smallest and most common species of bear in America, exists in the forests of much of Alaska. In Southeast the black bear is at home on all of the mainland and most of the islands. Exceptions are the northernmost islands, including Admiralty, Baranof, Chichagof, and Kruzof. One of the highest concentrations occurs on Prince of Wales Island, across Clarence Strait from Ketchikan, where you might well glimpse one of these animals ambling across one of the logging roads that bisect the island.

An adult black bear measures approximately 26 inches at the shoulder and can weigh more than 200 pounds in summer, when feed is plentiful. Although called *black* bears, the animals range in color from deep black to brown and even cinnamon, a fact that frequently causes them to be confused with their larger brown grizzly cousins. A very rare glacier variety with smoky blue fur appears sometimes in parts of the Panhandle, especially around Yakutat.

Black bears spend most of their time in summer browsing through open forested areas, where they can find the salmonberries, blueberries, and other shrubs they like to eat. You are not likely to see one unless you happen to be in the forest, too. In late summer and fall, they turn to fishing for spawning salmon along shallow rivers and streams. In winter, when food is scarce, they enter a state of semihibernation characterized by a drop in metabolic rate. They are easily awakened, however, and may even leave their dens for short periods.

Spring may be the best time to spot black bears as they feed on tender new growth along beaches and in open meadows and hillsides. Look for clearings on the mountainsides (such as slide or avalanche scars) where the new vegetation has grown. The dark-colored animals are visible against the bright green cover or as they cross lingering patches of snow. The Anan Creek Bear Observatory near Wrangell provides an excellent opportunity to view both black and brown bears.

Brown, or Grizzly, Bear

The large brown bear, known also as the coastal brown bear and grizzly, lives throughout the Southeast mainland and on the northern islands, especially Admiralty, Baranof, and Chichagof. Small populations occur on Wrangell and Etolin Islands in the southern Panhandle. The concentration of brown bears on Admiralty Island is estimated at approximately one bear per square

Grizzly bear

mile, one of the highest in the world. In summer some of these Admiralty Island bears can be viewed from an observatory at the Stan Price Bear Sanctuary at Pack Creek.

Brown bears and grizzlies used to be considered separate species, but biologists now believe them to be the same. Nevertheless, bears living inland with primarily a vegetable diet (usually called grizzlies) tend to be smaller than coastal bears that feed on protein-rich salmon during summer and fall.

Color is not a good test for distinguishing a brown bear from a black bear, since both species vary in color. Brown bears range from dark black-brown to blond. Size is a better indicator. Mature males weigh from 500 to 900 pounds, and larger bears can reach 1,400 pounds. The brown bear also has a prominent hump over the shoulders (actually an extension of the powerful front leg muscles) and a round, massive head.

Sitka Black-tailed Deer

This abundant game animal provides winter meat for many Southeast families. The Sitka black-tailed deer is a member of the mule-deer family and is native to the coastal rain forests of Southeast Alaska to northern coastal British Columbia. The Sitka species is small; the average adult buck weighs 120 pounds in fall and the doe about 80 pounds. The reddish-brown summer coat turns dark gray in winter. The name comes from the small flag of a tail, which is black on top and white beneath.

Home for these animals varies with the season. After the fawns are born in May and June, the deer move out of the forest and up to the alpine meadows, where they feed during the summer months (the opposite of the bears, which come down from the mountains in the summer to feed off berries and salmon). When fall frosts limit the available food, the deer return to the forest and remain there throughout the winter and early spring, foraging among leaves and shrubs. In deep snow conditions they may be forced down onto the beach to search for dried grass or, in extreme conditions, seaweed. In spring and early summer, they move to the beach to nibble new grass and other succulent plants. You may see them there with their new spotted fawns, especially in the early morning, as you glide by in your ship.

Moose

Moose are found generally in the mainland river valleys of Southeast Alaska. The largest herd is located at the northern end of the Panhandle around Yakutat. Smaller herds roam near Haines, Berners Bay (on the mainland between Haines and Juneau), and in the drainages of the Taku, Stikine, and Unuk Rivers. You stand a good chance of encountering the large animals if you explore these rivers by small boat; otherwise, you can only hope to spot them from the air or see them grazing on the flats at the river mouths as you pass by on your ship. Ferry passengers occasionally sight them on the large sandy flats at the entrance to the Katzehin River in Chilkoot Inlet, on the way to Haines and Skagway.

Moose weigh up to 1,600 pounds. They spend much of their time knee-deep in swamps or shallow ponds, where they munch on willow twigs, weeds, and grass. Although somewhat ludicrous in appearance, with a mule-shaped body, small ears, and an improbably long nose, the animals are greatly respected for their strength and ferocity, especially in defense of their young, and for their excellent meat. Many local hunters set off resolutely every fall to "get their moose" to fill the freezer.

Mountain Goat

If you have sharp eyes or binoculars, you may be able to pick out a group of mountain goats in the high rocky outcrops that border the Inside Passage. The goats are mighty small to the naked eye—you have to look for small white dots that appear about half an inch high against the gray rock. You may be lucky and see them closer up, especially in Glacier Bay or Tracy Arm Fjord near Juneau.

Mountain goats make their home in the most rugged and inaccessible parts of the Coast Mountains. Their hooves are fitted with cushioned pads that allow them to clamber up and down the sheer rock walls. They have all-white shaggy coats, long chin whiskers, and short black horns—in contrast to the light-colored and curved horns of Dall sheep, with which they are frequently confused (Dall sheep are not native to

Mountain goat

Southeast, anyway). Mountain goats spend summer in high meadows, where they feed off grasses and alpine shrubs. In winter they forage along the wind-blown ridges that are free from snow. Some may climb down to tree line and nibble at the hemlock trees.

Red Squirrel

You are likely to catch sight of red squirrels whisking along the spruce branches above your picnic table or hear them scolding you for some imagined transgression. This forest native measures only 11 to 13 inches long to the tip of its bottlebrush tail. The belly is white, and the back and tail are brown to rust. A white ring around each eye enhances an already bright countenance.

True to their reputation, red squirrels spend the summer months storing food, collecting spruce cones and piling them in heaps for winter use. They make their nests in the trunks of trees and sometimes in dense foliage, but once the young are raised, the squirrels live a solitary existence, each within a prescribed territory.

The red squirrel is Alaska's most common squirrel. The only other species in the state are the Arctic ground squirrel of the tundra and the northern flying squirrel that inhabits the spruce/hemlock forests throughout Alaska. The latter species is nocturnal, however, and you are unlikely to see one.

Gray Wolf

The gray wolf population is thriving in Alaska. The densest accumulations occur in Southeast, where they inhabit the mainland and major islands except for Admiralty, Baranof, and Chichagof. The animals range in color from black to near white, with those in Southeast usually somewhat darker than those in the north. The wolf is a good deal larger than the average dog or coyote, the adult male weighing 85 to 118 pounds (the coyote weighs 25 to 40 pounds). In the north wolves feed primarily on moose and caribou. In Southeast Alaska their diet consists of deer and goats as well as small animals, such as squirrels and an occasional bird or fish.

Historically the wolf has been trapped and hunted in Alaska for different reasons. The thick pelt, used for parka ruffs, can bring good money to the hunter. In northern and interior parts of Alaska, wolves have been considered a threat to game animals (especially moose and caribou) sought by sport hunters and depended upon by resident subsistence hunters, including Alaska Natives, for food. Until the early 1970s, in fact, the state paid a $50 bounty for wolves to protect declining game species from the predators. In the past the state had sanctioned aerial wolf hunting, but that practice is no longer allowed. The controversy over game management policy has heightened in recent years and spilled into the national arena as wildlife organizations and other groups have come to the defense of the wolf.

Unless you venture into the remote areas of Southeast, you are not likely to see a wolf. But it is not uncommon for kayakers and other independent boaters to spot an occasional animal prowling the shoreline in search of a meal, or to hear its captivating howl in the night.

Coyote

The coyote is a relative newcomer to Alaska, having migrated out of Canada's interior. First noted at the beginning of the twentieth century, their numbers now range as far north as the Brooks Range. In Southeast Alaska they appear to exist on the mainland only and are not especially prevalent. The coyote is about one-third the size of a wolf, averaging 30 pounds, with a coat that varies from tan to gray.

The coyote's appetite for sheep and chickens has given it a bad reputation in the Lower 48. In Alaska, where there are few sheep or chickens to prey upon, the coyote is forced to eat birds, squirrels, and the like. There was a $25 bounty in the state until 1969 that resulted in some hunting. Presently coyotes are only occasionally trapped for their pelts and are otherwise not much bothered.

Other Animals

A raft of other animals inhabit the coastal forest. The porcupine is much in evidence in Southeast, as dog owners will testify. Although nocturnal, the porky often can be glimpsed plodding along forest trails and even on the highway. The forest provides both shelter and sustenance, spruce bark (the inner layer) being a principal food. In the woods you will see vertical bare patches on the trunks of trees where a porcupine has dined off the bark. In summer porcupines augment their diet with leaves, tender branches, and buds.

Beaver pelts have been prized since the days of the Russian occupation and were used as a trade medium for many years. So many beavers were taken after the U.S. purchase of Alaska that they became a protected species in 1910. Beavers are still trapped, but under state regulation. In Southeast beavers are most abundant near Yakutat and Juneau, but they live on other river drainages on the mainland, too, where they dam streams to satisfy their requirements for 2 to 3 feet of water year-round. This depth provides the beavers with a hiding place from predators, and a way to transport logs and food.

Of the other fur-bearing animals, the versatile land, or river, otter is at home on land as well as in both salt and fresh water. You can distinguish the river otter from the sea otter by the muscular tail, which makes up one-third of the animal's total body length of 40 to

60 inches. The dark brown fur includes some gray on the chin and throat. River otters are wonderful swimmers and can dive to at least 60 feet. In winter they seem equally suited for snow and ice, where they run and slide and slip and tunnel just like human children. They eat fish, supplementing their diet with shellfish and occasional birds. They might show up anywhere. I once watched a pair frolicking among the boats in the Wrangell harbor.

Southeast's other fur-bearing animals include the wolverine, marten, mink, and ermine, which dresses in brown for summer but switches to white in winter. The sea otter, whose luxurious fur brought Russian traders to Alaska in the first place, has begun to reappear in Alaska waters after years of protection. These creatures at one time occupied the entire Pacific coast from northern Japan through the Aleutian Islands and along North America to Baja California. Reintroduced in Southeast Alaska during the late 1970s, they may be a familiar sight again one day. Your best chance of seeing them is probably around the northwest Chichagof and Yakobi Islands area, near Elfin Cove, or during a day cruise to Salisbury Sound, 25 miles north of Sitka.

River otter

Mammals not found in Southeast Alaska include the caribou and the Arctic fox, which frequent the Arctic tundra in the northern part of the state; the polar bear, which lives near the edge of the Arctic ice; and the big-horned Dall sheep, whose territory is the high mountains of Alaska's Interior and northern British Columbia.

MARINE MAMMALS

Many species of whale inhabit the waters off the Alaska coast. Some are year-round residents, whereas others arrive for the summer months after wintering in the more temperate waters off Hawaii or Baja California. Some whales are toothed, meaning they have large teeth that they use to catch—but not to chew—sizable prey that they then swallow whole. The others are baleen whales, which feed primarily on tiny shrimplike organisms called krill. The krill is strained from the water by strips of bonelike material hanging from the whale's upper jaw. It was this baleen, or whalebone, that was so essential for ladies' undergarments and, along with whale oil, caused the creatures to be pursued by whalers in the nineteenth century. Ironically, baleen whales, the giants of the deep, feed on krill and microorganisms, whereas the smaller whales, porpoises, and dolphins feed on meaty sea mammals and fish.

Since they are mammals, all whales must surface frequently to breathe air. They exhale through blowholes on their backs. Accompanied by a great deal of water vapor, the exhalations look like small geysers and are commonly known as spouting or blowing, hence the traditional lookout's cry, "Thar she blows!" Often you will see the spout first, which will be your clue to look for the whale.

Humpback Whale

The humpback, a baleen whale, returns to Inside Passage waters every spring after wintering off Mexico or Hawaii. Unlike most other whales, humpbacks come in close to shore to feed in the bays and fjords that outline the coast. They are a familiar and beloved sight in Southeast, and you are almost certain to see some of these elegant creatures as you cruise along the Inside Passage. One group of approximately forty whales feeds around Frederick Sound, the large east-west chan-

Humpback whale

nel at the south end of Admiralty Island, which is rich in krill from late July through early August. Other concentrations occur near the north end of Chichagof Island and in Glacier Bay. The humpbacks also follow the herring runs in Auke Bay and Lynn Canal north of Juneau and in Seymour Canal on the east side of Admiralty Island. When fall comes the humpbacks turn south for warmer waters to breed and bear their young.

The humpback reaches 45 to 50 feet in length and is dark-colored except for the grooved belly. Three characteristics distinguish this acrobatic whale: long pectoral fins, or flippers, which measure up to 14 feet; the huge lobed tail that lifts completely out of the water on a dive; and the hump that lies in front of the small dorsal fin.

In recent years biologists have focused considerable attention on characteristic humpback behavior such as breaching, when the whale leaps clear out of the water. Some scientists think breaching may be a warning behavior or territorial display, but its significance is not yet fully understood. Humpbacks also practice a sophisticated feeding technique known as bubblenet feeding, which, experts believe, helps the whales herd together small prey, such as herring. A whale (sometimes a pair of whales or more) dives beneath the prey and swims around them in an upward spiral while exhaling through its blowhole. This creates a "net" of bubbles in the water that contains the confused fish. The whale dives again and surfaces through the center of the bubble ring with open jaws, scooping in the feed. Scientists have documented other cooperative feeding techniques and recorded a specific humpback song believed to aid in this process. Researchers identify specific whales by the distinguishing patterns on their tail flukes.

Gray Whale

Whale watchers tend to associate the gray whale, a baleen, with the California coast. Great numbers of gray whales are observed every winter as they migrate southward along the coast to their winter breeding grounds in the lagoons of Baja California. But in spring they reverse the journey and spend June through October off northern Alaska, where they feed on small shrimplike crustaceans that live near the ocean floor. That makes a round-trip journey of 12,000 miles. Gray whales do not stay around Southeast Alaska as the humpbacks do, but they are frequently spotted as they pass through inside waters in early summer and late fall.

You probably can distinguish the gray whale by the pointed head that is usually covered with barnacles. There is no dorsal fin, and the flippers are much smaller than the humpback's. This whale is equal to the humpback in size, reaching a maximum length of 50 feet, but it is colored mottled gray instead of black.

Minke Whale

The only other baleen whale common to Southeast is the minke, or piked, whale. The minke is the smallest baleen whale in the Northern Hemisphere, occasionally reaching 33 feet in length. These whales are grayish black on the top side, with a white stomach. Look for a large sickle-shaped dorsal fin placed far back on the body.

Minkes are migrating whales and are found in many oceans from southern California to the Bering and Chukchi Seas, where they spend their summers. When they are in southern waters, they feed on krill, but their northern diet shifts to mackerel, cod, and herring.

Killer Whale

The killer whale, or orca, is unmistakable. In the first place, this whale has striking black and white markings, including a sparkling white chin, white flanks, and a white patch on either side of the head. Then, the male has an enormous triangular-shaped dorsal fin that stands out of the water like a shark's. In adults the dorsal measures up to 6 feet. Whereas other whales may be traveling solo, killer whales are almost always seen in

Killer whale

groups, or pods, containing as many as twenty-five or thirty whales. Herds of 150 have been observed.

A toothed species, orca feed on almost anything that moves in the ocean. Little is safe from this swiftest of whales that can swim at 25 knots and more. These "wolves of the sea" habitually go after seals, porpoises, squid, and many varieties of fish. They have even been observed attacking a swimming moose. Like land-based wolves, they are also capable of organizing their numbers to hunt down whales larger than themselves. Orcas themselves have no natural predators.

Killer whales average 23 feet in length and weigh eight to nine tons. They range all over the world and are frequently seen in the inside waters of Southeast Alaska. Chatham Strait and Stephens Passage are likely places to spot them.

Dall Porpoise

Dall porpoise, another black-and-white sea creature commonly seen in Southeast, seems to delight in cavorting in the bow waves of fishing boats and pleasure craft. The Dall porpoise has a black body with white underside markings that extend halfway up the sides and sometimes the tip of the tail and dorsal fin. How can you tell them from killer whales? First, the killer whale averages three times the size of the Dall porpoise, which reaches a maximum length of 7 feet. Second, the porpoise's dorsal fin is insignificant compared to the large upright triangle of the orca. Finally, the porpoise delights in swimming close to the bow of your boat, but you are more apt to spot the killer whale off in the distance, chasing after something to eat.

Harbor Porpoise

Harbor porpoises frequent coastal bays and river mouths from the Arctic coast of Alaska to southern California. The smallest of the whale, dolphin, and porpoise family, they reach no more than 5 or 6 feet in length. They are colored dark brown to gray and sport a triangular dorsal fin toward the center of the back.

Usually this porpoise is seen alone, in pairs, or in small groups, but it sometimes travels in larger company. You may see harbor porpoises swimming near the surface of the water, but probably not near your ship.

Harbor Seal

The resident species of seal in Southeast is the harbor, or spotted, seal, which is at home in both the North Atlantic and Pacific Oceans. It is a hair seal, as opposed to either a fur seal or sea lion, and the only such seal in Southeast. Like all hair seals, harbor seals are true seals: They have no ears and cannot rotate their hind flippers forward, making them clumsy on land. They are thus primarily water creatures, touching down on land to rest and bear their young. The harbor seal averages 5 to 6 feet in length and varies in color from yellowish gray to blue-gray with dark spots. The coat of stiff hair is used for parkas, moccasins, purses, and the like, which are available in the curio shops of every town.

Harbor seals feed on fish and shellfish—everything from herring to crab. They curry great disfavor within the commercial fishing industry by damaging or stealing salmon caught in nets or on trolling gear. A $2.00 bounty was in effect from 1927 and raised to $3.00 in 1939, but it was removed south of Bristol Bay in 1967. The Federal Marine Mammal Protection Act of 1972 limited seal hunting (and that of all marine mammals) to Alaskan Indians and Eskimos.

You might spot harbor seals anywhere—in the open water, in a protected harbor, on rocky offshore outcrops, or on sandy beaches. They rest with their pups on icebergs in such places as Tracy Arm and Le Conte Glacier.

Steller's Sea Lion

The brownish-black sea lion is the largest of the eared seals—bulls reach 13 feet in length and weigh up to 2,400 pounds. They have tiny, visible ears and, unlike the true seals, can rotate their back flippers forward, making them more mobile on land.

The sea lions' province is the coastal waters from the southern end of the Panhandle to the Bering Sea. They favor remote areas with shallow, rocky bottoms where they can find the herring, rockfish, octopus, and shellfish that make up their diet. Like the smaller harbor seals, Steller's sea lions are fond of salmon and are a nuisance to the commercial fishing industry. Like seals, sea lions have been protected from indiscriminate hunting since 1972 and can be harvested only by Indians and Eskimos.

Although the Steller's sea lion population has declined drastically in other parts of Alaska and worldwide since the 1960s, their numbers appear stable in Southeast. They congregate at rookeries and haul-out spots at various periods of the year. (The Alaska ferries pass right by one haul-out spot, Benjamin Island, at the entrance to Lynn Canal north of Juneau, en route to Skagway and Haines.) I have seen them gamboling in the Juneau harbor in winter.

FISH AND SHELLFISH

Salmon

All five species of salmon exist in Southeast waters: the king salmon, known also as the chinook; the coho, or silver; the sockeye, or red; the chum, or dog; and the pink, or humpback or "humpie." The species differ from one another in several respects, including size, color, shape, anatomical details, and spawning season. They share one of the most dramatic life cycles in nature.

All species of salmon are anadromous, meaning that they spend part of their lives in freshwater and part in the sea. After hatching in the gravel stream beds, the salmon pass the next segment of their lives feeding and growing in the freshwater stream. The amount of time varies according to the species, from almost none in the case of pink and chum salmon to up to three years in the case of cohos. They then migrate downstream to salt water where they spend, again according to the species, from two to three years or more roaming the North Pacific. When they reach maturity, they migrate back to the stream in which they were hatched to spawn. Before reaching freshwater they eat voraciously because they will eat little once they start their upstream dash. It is at this point, while they are moving toward the stream mouth, that they become the targets for commercial and sport fishing.

The salmon spend as much as a few weeks at the entrance to the stream while their bodies readjust to freshwater. Then they begin the exhausting uphill battle to the spawning grounds. When their instincts tell them that they have reached the place, the once-beautiful salmon—now battered, torn, and mortally weary—carry out the spawning ritual. The females scrape a series of shallow nests, called redds, in the gravel with their broad tails and deposit several thousand eggs. The males spill their milt over the eggs, and the females brush gravel over the top. That is the end. Both males and females will die, usually within two weeks.

The fertilized eggs remain in their gravel incubators, developing into embryos, called alevins, and then baby salmon, called fry. When the fry are mature enough to swim downstream, they are known as smolt. The smolt head out for the few good years in the great Pacific; then the cycle begins again.

The king salmon, Alaska's official state fish, is considerably larger than the other four species, commonly exceeding 30 pounds and frequently exceeding 50 pounds. The largest king salmon on record, taken in a fish trap off Prince of Wales Island in 1939, weighed approximately 126.5 pounds. (The salmon was not weighed until after it had been cleaned, so the weight is only an estimate.) This giant salmon is on display at the Clausen Museum in Petersburg. A sport-caught king (93 pounds) was caught at Kelp Bay on the northeast coast of Baranof Island in 1977, establishing a state record at the time. In 1985, however, an even bigger king (97 pounds, 4 ounces) was sport-caught in the Kenai River on Alaska's Kenai Peninsula.

In Southeast the king salmon runs extend from May through July. The major spawning runs are up the Stikine River near Wrangell, the Taku south of Juneau, and the Alsek south of Yakutat. Kings are capable of extremely long freshwater migrations. The northern kings that spawn in the headwaters of the Yukon River travel more than 2,000 miles to their spawning grounds.

King salmon are commercial favorites because of their large size and good flavor, and they retail for several dollars per pound. Their flesh may be either red or white—no one knows why—but there is little difference in its flavor. Local residents fish for kings year-round. A winter-caught king is considered a delicacy because of the flavorful fat that builds up over the winter months.

Next in size to the king is the coho, which reaches thirty-five pounds. Appreciated by anglers for its aggressive response to the hook, the coho is also valuable on the commercial market. The cohos enter the spawning systems from August through November, and sportfishing is good from July through September.

Sockeye salmon are nicknamed "red salmon" because of their spectacular spawning colors. Their bodies turn a brilliant red, and their heads change to an olive green. The sockeye is small compared with the king or coho, weighing only four to eight pounds in maturity.

Sockeye salmon prefer a diet of marine plankton, chiefly small crustaceans. This makes the sockeye an elusive target for anglers, who rarely hook the fish in salt water and almost never on bait. The fly fisherman sometimes succeeds and comes away with a good prize because the sockeye is extremely desirable for eating fresh, home canning, and smoking.

The chum, or dog, salmon is the widest-ranging of any Pacific salmon. This species is found from the Sacramento River in California to the Mackenzie River in Canada, and in Japan. The fish takes its other name from the large doglike teeth that develop during the spawning season.

Chums weigh up to eighteen pounds in maturity (some grow to thirty) but are not sportfishing favorites. Most commercially caught chum are netted. Unlike kings, cohos, or sockeyes, the young chum salmon do not spend a long time in freshwater; they feed in the estuary for a few months and then go out to sea.

Pink salmon are the smallest of the Pacific salmon, averaging only three and one-half to four pounds. They are also the shortest-lived, maturing at two years. They set off for the spawning grounds from late June to mid-October. Most pinks spawn within a few miles of the coast; some even spawn within the intertidal zone of the stream mouth. Like chums, the pinks spend no time in freshwater after they emerge from their gravel incubators. The fry swim up out of the gravel and head immediately downstream to salt water.

Despite such spunk, the pinks were not well regarded by either sport or commercial fisheries until recent years, when the lack of availability of other species tempted some commercial fishermen to concentrate on the increasingly plentiful pinks (reared very successfully in hatcheries). Pink salmon now constitute 80 to 90 percent of the commercial salmon harvest in Southeast Alaska. They are netted, for the most part. Their flesh is softer and less flavorful than coho or king, making them most suitable for canning. The nickname "humpy" comes from the spawning males, which develop a pronounced hump on their backs after they enter freshwater.

Pacific Halibut

Like the salmon, the halibut has traditionally been an important fish in Southeast Alaska. The Tlingit and Haida Indians elevated halibut fishing to an art. Their beautiful carved wooden halibut hooks were proportioned to catch only halibut of the desired size, and their fishing skills were the envy of the early European explorers. Like so many things in Alaska, halibut come in exaggerated proportions. Sport-caught halibut weighing

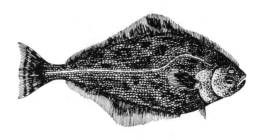

Halibut

more than 300 pounds are brought in by sport fishers every year. The largest on record is a 495-pounder caught near Petersburg.

Halibut are flounder, or bottomfish, which accounts for their flat and generally goofy appearance. The fish starts out looking perfectly normal, but after about six months, the left eye migrates across to join the right, and the halibut spends the rest of its days with both eyes on one side of its head. Then the fish turns over so that the two eyes are uppermost, and what seems to be the top (the dark side) is actually the right side . . . very fishy, indeed. Left to their own devices, halibut live many years—one specimen was estimated to be forty-two years old.

Halibut is an excellent eating fish. The flesh is firm, beautifully white, and mild tasting, and it freezes well. If you are lucky enough to catch a halibut for your table, here are two typically Alaskan things to do with it. Get some Krusteaz buttermilk pancake mix, add enough beer to make a batter that will not slide off your chunks of halibut, and deep-fry it. Or cut your fresh, filleted halibut into small serving pieces and cover with white wine for up to two hours. Drain and roll in dry bread crumbs (preferably from homemade bread). Place in one layer in a buttered baking dish. Mix together two parts sour cream to one part mayonnaise and one part finely chopped onion and spread over the top, reaching clear out to the edges. Sprinkle with paprika and bake at 500 degrees for fifteen to twenty minutes or until light brown on top and bubbling. This dish, called "Halibut Caddy Ganty," was made famous by the kitchen of the Gustavus Inn (near Glacier Bay). I pass it on with the kind permission of the chefs.

Trout

There are two important kinds of trout in the Southeast region. The cutthroat, which takes its name from two red stripes below the mouth, is found from Southeast Alaska north to Prince William Sound in sizes up to seventeen pounds. In freshwater the trout, like others of the family, frequently follow the salmon runs and feed on the new eggs. The cutthroats also are found in salt water.

Rainbow trout live in the river drainages as well as in freshwater lakes where they have been introduced. Some rainbows are seagoing, in which case they are known as steelheads. There is no difference between the two except that one lives in salt water and the other in fresh. The rainbow or steelhead is closely related to the Atlantic salmon and weighs up to twenty pounds. The state-record steelhead, however, was caught off Bell Island near Ketchikan in 1970 and weighed forty-two pounds, three ounces.

Dolly Varden

Silver-green Dolly Varden are members of the char family. Many anglers contend that they are in fact Arctic char, but the scientific community says not. Although closely related, they differ anatomically in certain respects. (The true Arctic char does not exist in Southeast. Its realm is to the north in the coastal regions of the Alaska Peninsula, Bering Strait, and the Arctic.)

Dollies have an unusual life cycle. Like salmon, they spawn in freshwater and migrate downstream to salt water in their third or fourth year. Once at sea, however, they return every winter to a freshwater lake. Those that were spawned in a lake system return there. Those that were not have to find themselves a suitable lake. When mature, at five to six years, the Dollies return to their original streams to spawn. Many survive the spawn, however—perhaps as many as 50 percent—and return to sea.

Fully grown Dolly Varden reach up to 22 inches and weigh three pounds. When fresh out of the water, they have a pattern of small red spots on their sides, which fade with time. They are easy to catch on spinning gear and well worth taking home for the frying pan or smoker. Their flesh is a delicate pink in color, like salmon, but trout-like in texture; the flavor falls nicely in between.

Arctic Grayling

The Arctic grayling is a true Alaskan, dependent upon clear, cold streams and lakes that exist only in the north. The greatest concentrations are found in rivers on the north side of the Brooks Range. Other populations exist in the Cook Inlet region and parts of the Interior. In Southeast Alaska grayling have been introduced successfully in some lakes, among them Antler Lake in the Juneau area; Big Goat, Tyee, and Manzoni Lakes in the Ketchikan vicinity; and several on Prince of Wales Island.

Grayling grow slowly, reaching only 12 inches in six or seven years. Fully mature grayling might reach 20 inches, and some larger ones have been reported. Their diet consists of insects and the like, which makes them a fly-caster's delight. If all these things did not make the grayling special, appearance would. The troutlike body has a dark purple back and silvery green sides. On top is an enormous fanlike dorsal fin, with reddish purple spots on a green background.

Pacific Herring

This productive little fish has been an important contributor to the Southeast economy. The original Indian inhabitants of Southeast harvested both herring and herring roe for food. Herring roe are sticky, and the female herring deposits them—usually in late March to early April—on grass, kelp, or other surfaces in the intertidal area. The Tlingit learned to place spruce boughs in the water at the spawning grounds, and the herring obligingly covered the branches with their sticky eggs. The laden boughs were then removed from the water and hung out to dry. Natives still gather herring roe in this manner.

The commercial herring fishery was launched in 1882 when the first herring reduction plant was built at Killisnoo on Admiralty Island. The products were fish meal, used as a fertilizer and food additive for livestock, and oil, which was used as an industrial lubricant and detergent. The herring industry peaked in 1937, when seventeen plants processed more than 251 million pounds of herring in

Alaska. Salted and pickled herring was also produced in Southeast, especially during World War I. Both industries gradually declined, the last reduction plant closing in 1966. Presently herring are harvested for bait and for roe, which is frozen and exported to Japan.

The Japanese specialty market made the herring sack-roe fishery lucrative—fetching $600 per ton in 1997. Sitka's sack-roe fishery, the most important in Southeast and third largest in Alaska, received national media attention for the intense, derbylike atmosphere that prevailed a few years ago. The Alaska Department of Fish and Game regulates the fishery a little differently now; the 1993 season lasted eight days and took the quota of 9,700 tons. The fishery openings can be as short as a few frantic hours or—as happened in 1996, when the fishermen opted to simply share the total catch with one another—more than a week. The roe fishery does not waste the rest of the fish. Since 1983 it has been illegal to discard the herring carcasses; they are sold for fertilizer and the like.

Blue-green Pacific herring average 9 or 10 inches in length. They run in schools of up to a million fish, which are in turn pursued by salmon and other predators. One stretch of coastline north of Juneau has been dubbed the "milk run" by local fishermen who drag the area for the salmon that habitually chase after the herring that frequent that stretch of water every spring.

There are many other species of fish in the fresh- and saltwater systems of Southeast Alaska, from the tiny eulachon, which was an important source of oil for Southeast Natives, to rockfish, sculpin, cod, and other bottomfish. The U.S. Forest Service publishes a small pamphlet, *Common Fresh and Saltwater Fishes of Southeastern Alaska,* that is a handy reference guide to the many local species.

Crab

If you own a boat and a crab pot in Southeast Alaska, all that remains is to find just the right place to set it down. Toss in a few fish heads, set the pot on the way to your favorite fishing grounds, and pick it up at the end of the day. Dinner that night might include any of the three varieties of crab that inhabit the Southeast coast: king, Dungeness, and tanner.

The famous Alaska king crab is not a true crab at all, as evidenced by the fact that the spiny, spiderlike legs fold backward behind the body instead of forward and in front, like the Dungeness. Regardless, the king crab is a fine prize for the table. By far the largest of the crabs, kings can grow to twenty-four pounds, although seven or eight pounds is the average commercial size. At that they measure 3 feet from leg tip to leg tip. The meat is sweet and firm, not unlike lobster. Besides having excellent flavor, king crab is easy to eat. No messy cracking, picking, and sucking—you just snip open the shell of the leg with kitchen shears and slide out the meat. The small body is usually ignored.

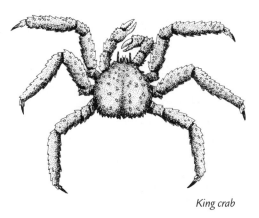

King crab

Dungeness crab is the familiar Cancer shape, a true crab, with eight forward-folding legs and two short claws. Compared with the king, the Dungeness has a large body, but is full of good meat. Locals disagree about which of the crabs is better eating, but I vote for the rich and succulent Dungeness.

Tanner crab, usually marketed as "snow crab," looks something like a cross between the king and the Dungeness. This true crab has long, spindly legs. You frequently see the bulbous claws sold separately in the frozen-food section of the supermarket. The leg meat is delicious but tends to flake into small bits as you remove it from the shell.

Abalone

It takes a hardy diver to brave the frigid waters to harvest abalone. Abalone are abundant, though, the length of the Alexander Archipelago. Occasionally they can be plucked from the bottom at very low tides. The species of abalone that inhabits Southeast rarely grows larger than 5½ inches. The meat is sweet and tender.

Bivalves and Paralytic Shellfish Poisoning

In addition to crab and abalone, the Inside Passage yields several varieties of shrimp (including the tiny Petersburg species), cockles, scallops, octopuses, sea cucumbers, sea urchins, mussels, and at least four varieties of clam. A word of warning here, however: *No bivalves (clams, mussels, cockles, scallops) in Southeast Alaska can be considered safe from the deadly paralytic shellfish poisoning, at any time of year, unless they are sold commercially, in which case they will have been tested and certified safe.* Paralytic shellfish poisoning (PSP) is caused by a toxin produced by a tiny organism known as a dinoflagellate (a similar dinoflagellate causes the sea condition known as the red tide). This organism is ingested by the shellfish, which absorb and store the PSP toxin in their bodies. The toxin does not harm the shellfish but is poisonous to humans. Some shellfish retain the toxin longer than others; clams and mussels are the worst.

Symptoms of PSP show up only *after* the shellfish has entered the digestive tract, so do not try to "see if the clams are poisonous" by holding one to your mouth and waiting for your lip to go numb. The symptoms usually occur within thirty minutes of eating the infected shellfish. They can include a tingling or burning sensation on lips, gums, tongue, or face that gradually spreads to other parts of the body; dryness of mouth, nausea, vomiting; and, in later stages, shortness of breath, choking sensation, slurred speech, lack of coordination. If death occurs, which is seldom the case but does happen, the direct cause will be respiratory paralysis. There is *no antidote* to paralytic shellfish poisoning. If you experience any of these symptoms after eating shellfish, induce vomiting immediately and call a doctor.

Many longtime residents of Southeast Alaska eat clams every year from beaches that they consider safe. I do not. I used to, occasionally, but I found that worrying about PSP took all the pleasure out of eating the clams. Now I save clam and mussel eating for places where I know they are safe, and, in Southeast Alaska, I console myself with crab, shrimp, halibut, trout, and five kinds of salmon.

BIRDS

Some 278 species of bird are found in Southeast Alaska. Many are year-round residents, whereas others stop off on their way to or from nesting grounds and winter homes that may be 10,000 miles apart. Robert Armstrong's *Guide to the Birds of Alaska* (Alaska Northwest Books), illustrated with color photographs, can help with identification. Another good reference source is *Birds of Southeast Alaska, A Checklist,* a pamphlet prepared by the U.S. Forest Service in conjunction with the Alaska Department of Fish and Game and the Juneau Audubon Society. A complete list of birds commonly appearing in Southeast Alaska during at least two seasons of the year appears on pages 141–44. Here are some of the birds that you may encounter during your trip through the Inside Passage.

Bald Eagle

No matter how many times you hear about the bald eagle population in Southeast Alaska, you will not believe the number of eagles you will see until you actually get there and start counting. Bald eagles are in the treetops, on the beach, soaring close over the water, wheeling high in the sky—perhaps 25,000 altogether.

Adult males and females look identical, with pure white head and tail, yellow hooked beak, deep-brown body, and a wingspan of up to 8 feet. Females are slightly larger. The young birds are a mottled brown and white with a dark beak to match. They acquire their adult plumage in their third or fourth year.

There is no other bird that you could mistake for the adult bald eagle. You will soon learn to pick out their white heads glistening in the tops of the spruce and hemlock trees that line the shore of the Inside Passage. The narrow passageway from Sergius Narrows through Neva Strait on the approach to Sitka is one of the best places to view eagles. The Forest Service interpreters onboard the Alaska ferries are apt to initiate an eagle count to see how many eagles can be spotted along this 30-mile stretch. The number has been as high as ninety-four.

You will probably see eagles launch themselves into the sky and glide above the surface of the water, using their keen eyes to spot a meal. Bald eagles feed on herring, smelt, and spawned-out salmon, and they turn to birds and small mammals when they cannot find fish. Basically, they are scavengers.

One of their favorite meals is spawned-out salmon that clog the upper reaches of many Southeast rivers, among them the Chilkat River, near Haines. Natural warm springs keep this river flowing long into the winter when other waters are frozen. The eagles—some 3,500 of them—congregate in the tall cottonwoods along the Chilkat River flats below the village of Klukwan to gorge on the dead and dying salmon from October through January. This incredible sight is the largest gathering of bald eagles anywhere in the world. The best viewing is from mile 18 to mile 22 on the Haines Highway (west out of Haines toward the Alaska Highway). The state of Alaska has established the 49,000-acre Chilkat Bald Eagle Preserve to protect this gathering of eagles and their habitat. Other concentrations of eagles occur along the shoreline of Admiralty Island, where there is an average of two nests per mile around the 678-mile shore, and on the Stikine River, especially in spring.

Bald eagles build their nests in the tops of large, old spruce or hemlock trees that grow close to salt water or mainland rivers. The nests are constructed of branches, small sticks, and moss. Since the birds add to the nests every year rather than build anew, the structures can reach 8 feet in diameter and 7 feet in depth. You can see an eagle nest at the "eagle tree" exhibit at the Alaska State Museum in Juneau.

Eagles are protected by law in Alaska as elsewhere. In places where logging threatens to interfere with their nesting habitat, the U.S. Forest Service and U.S. Fish and Wildlife Service have identified known nesting trees so that logging crews can give them a wide berth. Eagles have not always been treated so carefully in Alaska. The territorial legislature placed a 50-cent bounty (later raised to $2.00) on the birds in 1917 because they were considered a threat to spawning salmon and to the young foxes that were being raised on fox farms. The bounty was lifted in 1953 but not before an estimated 128,000 birds had been killed.

The cry of the bald eagle is the only incongruous thing about this bird. From its size and stature, you might expect a mighty scream, but the eagle communicates in a series of dainty cheeps that build to a high-pitched "kleek keek-eek-eek-eek-eek."

Common Raven

The ink-black raven has been winging through the dripping spruce forests for as long as human memory can recall. The ancestors of present-day Tlingit and Haida Indians awarded the bird a central role in their mythology and celebrated its character in songs, dances, and artistic designs.

Until you see one up close, you could confuse the raven with the Northwestern crow, which also lives in Southeast year-round. Both are black all over. The raven is much larger—measuring more than 2 feet in length, against the crow's 17 inches. The raven also has a much larger bill than the crow's and a pronounced brow. And the raven produces a throaty, melodious "klok" or "kla-wock" that is entirely different from the raucous "caw-caw" of the crow.

Steller's Jay

The saucy Steller's jay, dressed in an electric blue and black plaid coat and black head crest, stays in Southeast year-round. It is not uncommon to see two or three Steller's jays taunting a bald eagle. While the eagle rests stoically on a spruce limb, the jays flap about from branch to branch, chattering imperiously. Eventually the eagle gives up in disgust and flies away. Despite their bickering and bullying ways, I like these handsome birds.

Steller's jay

The Steller's jay takes its name from the Bering expedition of 1741. When Vitus Bering set out to explore the uncharted sea to the east of Russia, he took with him the naturalist Georg Wilhelm Steller. With the ship anchored off Kayak Island near Yakutat in order to replenish the water supply, Steller went ashore to collect specimens of plants and birds not found in Asia or Europe. Among his finds was a brilliant blue, high-crested jay that he recognized as native to North America. The Steller's jay was proof that Bering had found a land that was separate from Russia.

Blue Grouse

The blue grouse, another year-round resident, dwells in mature forest stands and among the dwarf trees dotting the muskeg in alpine areas. Also called the spruce hen, this grouse has a brown-to-gray and white speckled body shaped like a small chicken, a black tail with a band of pale gray at the top, and the feathered legs common to the grouse and ptarmigan family.

The females build their nests on the ground, and it is not unusual to come upon a hen with her clutch of chicks as you are walking through the woods or grassy openings in early summer. In winter the grouse are up in the trees. During the mating season the woods echo with the muffled "huh-huh-huh" of the courtship call. The sound is produced by air sacs on each side of the male's neck and is responsible for the grouse's other nickname, "the hooter."

The blue grouse is the most common species in Southeast (others include the spruce grouse and ruffed grouse). It is the largest of the grouse and a popular game bird, with the males often reaching three and one-half pounds.

Rock Ptarmigan

Ptarmigan are closely related to grouse and similar in appearance but are smaller (two-thirds to one and one-half pounds) and have feathered feet. Of the three species of ptarmigan in Alaska, only the rock ptarmigan lives in Southeast. (The willow ptarmigan, the state bird, inhabits most of the rest of the state.) In summer the ptarmigan is a mottled brown with white wings, but winter brings out an all-white coat except for a bit of black on the tail and (in the male) a band of black through the eye. Ptarmigan are nomadic in winter, wandering from slope to slope in search of a meal of birch buds or willow.

Canada Goose

The Vancouver Canada goose is the largest of the several subspecies that frequent Alaska, weighing as much as sixteen pounds in fall. Many are year-round residents of the Southeast tide flats. One of the largest congregations frequents the Mendenhall Wetlands State Game Refuge in Juneau, where you can often observe them feeding, long necks curved down to the ground. The Canada goose is

Canada goose

unmistakable: a large bird with brownish-gray back and wings, a long black neck, and a black head with white cheeks.

Canada geese mate for life. The Vancouver variety nests in shore grass, under conifers, or in muskegs. They are rare among geese in that they have even been known to nest in trees to protect their young from predators.

Duck

Several varieties of duck brave the Southeast winters. Among the year-round residents are the ubiquitous mallard, the fancy-dress harlequin, the common merganser, and the red-breasted merganser. The white-winged scoter and surf scoter are familiar sights in Southeast. They raft upon the salt water in large groups.

Rufous Hummingbird

In spring the rufous hummingbirds arrive from their warm winter home in Mexico. Decked out in his orange coat and irridescent red throat, the male is a cheery sight after the drab, dull days of winter's end. The female wears green and lacks the brilliant red throat. They haunt Southeast gardens, impatiently awaiting the bright blossoms of summer. In late fall the hummingbirds, which measure no more than 3½ inches long, depart on their long journey south.

PESTS

Unfortunately the winged creatures of Southeast Alaska are not limited to the bird family. Most of the stories you have heard about insects in Alaska are not true—at least about Southeast Alaska. The gigantic mosquitoes that swarm around your head and drive even four-footed animals loco are creatures of the northern tundra, with its inviting pools of freestanding water. Southeastern insects are more apt to be too small to swat.

Usually there is enough breeze along the Inside Passage to keep insects at bay. If not, and the bugs are pesty, your best bet is to roll down your sleeves, button your collar, put on a hat, smear yourself with whatever brand of repellent is popular this year, and try to relax. Nothing seems to draw biting or stinging insects more readily than an overheated, sweaty, enraged human being.

Basically the pests fall into three categories. Mosquitoes really are not that troublesome in most parts of Southeast Alaska and especially urban areas. Those that are around seem to be slow-moving and somewhat dim. In your hotel room at night, for instance, they are easy to hunt down and kill. Campers get the worst of them, and bug netting on your tent is certainly in order.

White-sox, on the other hand, are vicious, tiny, black, biting flies that swarm about your body and try to crawl under your clothes. Failing that, they are happy to bite through your clothes. White-sox (the name comes from their silvery legs) can produce a nasty bite; on some people the raised red spots can itch for days. You do not necessarily feel the bite at the time, though.

The bite you *do* feel at the time—a prolonged prick—comes from the no-see-um. Your skin swells up immediately, and the itch comes and goes for days. These gnatlike insects like the damp—a nice sweaty forehead sends them into ecstasy. They will light on any exposed piece of skin—ears are an especially favorite meal. More than other pests, no-see-ums seem tuned to your state of mind. If you can stay calm and go about your business, they may not be a bother; but start getting anxious about them, perspiring and breathing heavily, and they will fulfill your worst fantasies.

Scientists now think these biting beasts may be attracted to the carbon dioxide that humans expel. Hold your breath!

COMMON BIRDS OF SOUTHEAST ALASKA
(PRESENT DURING AT LEAST TWO SEASONS)

- ☐ Common loon, *Gavia immer* *
- ☐ Arctic loon, *Gavia arctica*
- ☐ Red-throated loon, *Gavia stellata*
- ☐ Red-necked grebe, *Podiceps grisegena*
- ☐ Homed grebe, *Podiceps auritus*
- ☐ Black-footed albatross, *Diomedea nigripes* †
- ☐ Sooty shearwater, *Puffinus griseus* †
- ☐ Fork-tailed storm-petrel, *Oceanodroma furcata* †
- ☐ Leach's storm-petrel, *Oceanodroma leucorhoa* †
- ☐ Pelagic cormorant, *Phalacrocorax pelagicus*
- ☐ Great blue heron, *Ardea herodias*
- ☐ Whistling swan, *Olor columbianus*
- ☐ Canada goose, Vancouver, *Branta canadensis fulva* *
- ☐ White-fronted goose, *Anser albifrons*
- ☐ Snow goose, *Chen caerulescens caerulescens*
- ☐ Mallard, *Anas platyrhynchos* *
- ☐ Pintail, *Anas acuta*
- ☐ American green-winged teal, *Anas crecca carolinensis*
- ☐ American widgeon, *Anas americana*
- ☐ Greater scaup, *Aythya marila*
- ☐ Lesser scaup, *Aythya affinis*
- ☐ Common goldeneye, *Bucephala clangula*
- ☐ Barrow's goldeneye, *Bucephala islandica*
- ☐ Bufflehead, *Bucephala albeola*
- ☐ Oldsquaw, *Clangula hyemalis*
- ☐ Harlequin duck, *Histrionicus histrionicus* *
- ☐ Common eider, *Somateria mollissima*
- ☐ White-winged scoter, *Melanitta fusca deglandi* *
- ☐ Surf scoter, *Melanitta perspicillata* *
- ☐ Black scoter, *Melanitta nigra*

- [ ] Common merganser, *Mergus merganser* *
- [ ] Red-breasted merganser, *Mergus serrator* *
- [ ] Sharp-shinned hawk, *Accipiter striatus*
- [ ] Bald eagle, *Haliaeetus leucocephalus* *
- [ ] Marsh hawk, *Circus cyaneus*
- [ ] American kestrel, *Falco sparverius*
- [ ] Blue grouse, *Dendragapus obscurus* *
- [ ] Rock ptarmigan, *Lagopus mutus* *
- [ ] Sandhill crane, *Grus canadensis*
- [ ] Black oystercatcher, *Haematopus bachmani*
- [ ] Semipalmated plover, *Charadrius semipalmatus*
- [ ] Black-bellied plover, *Pluvialis squatarola*
- [ ] Greater yellowlegs, *Tringa melanoleuca*
- [ ] Lesser yellowlegs, *Tringa flavipes*
- [ ] Spotted sandpiper, *Actitis macularia*
- [ ] Black turnstone, *Arenaria melanocephala*
- [ ] Northern phalarope, *Phalaropus lobatus*
- [ ] Common snipe, *Capella gallinago*
- [ ] Short-billed dowitcher, *Limnodromus griseus*
- [ ] Western sandpiper, *Calidris mauri*
- [ ] Least sandpiper, *Calidris minutilla*
- [ ] Pectoral sandpiper, *Calidris melanotos*
- [ ] Rock sandpiper, *Calidris ptilocnemis*
- [ ] Dunlin, *Calidris alpina*
- [ ] Glaucous-winged gull, *Larus glaucescens* *
- [ ] Herring gull, *Larus argentatus* *
- [ ] Thayer's gull, *Larus thayeri*
- [ ] Mew gull, *Larus canus* *
- [ ] Bonaparte's gull, *Larus philadelphia*
- [ ] Arctic tern, *Sterna paradisaea*
- [ ] Common murre, *Uria aalge* *
- [ ] Pigeon guillemot, *Cepphus columba* *

- ☐ Marbled murrelet, *Brachyramphus marmoratus* *
- ☐ Rock dove, *Columba livia* *
- ☐ Great horned owl, *Bubo virginianus* *
- ☐ Short-eared owl, *Asio flammeus*
- ☐ Rufous hummingbird, *Selasphorus rufus*
- ☐ Belted kingfisher, *Megaceryle alcyon* *
- ☐ Western flycatcher, *Empidonax difficilis*
- ☐ Violet-green swallow, *Tachycineta thalassina*
- ☐ Tree swallow, *Iridoprocne bicolor*
- ☐ Barn swallow, *Hirundo rustica*
- ☐ Steller's jay, *Cyanocitta stelleri* *
- ☐ Black-billed magpie, *Pica pica*
- ☐ Common raven, *Corvus corax* *
- ☐ Northwestern crow, *Corvus caurinus* *
- ☐ Chestnut-backed chickadee, *Parus rufescens* *
- ☐ Brown creeper, *Certhia familiaris* *
- ☐ Dipper, *Cinclus mexicanus* *
- ☐ Winter wren, *Troglodytes troglodytes* *
- ☐ American robin, *Turdus migratorius*
- ☐ Varied thrush, *Ixoreus naevius*
- ☐ Hermit thrush, *Catharus guttatus*
- ☐ Swainson's thrush, *Catharus ustulatus*
- ☐ Golden-crowned kinglet, *Regulus satrapa*
- ☐ Ruby-crowned kinglet, *Regulus calendula*
- ☐ Water pipit, *Anthus spinoletta*
- ☐ Bohemian waxwing, *Bombycilla garrulus*
- ☐ Starling, *Sturnus vulgaris* *
- ☐ Orange-crowned warbler, *Vermivora celata*
- ☐ Yellow warbler, *Dendroica petechia*
- ☐ Yellow-rumped warbler, *Dendroica coronata*
- ☐ Wilson's warbler, *Wilsonia pusilla*
- ☐ Pine grosbeak, *Pinicola enucleator*

- [ ] Common redpoll, *Carduelis flammea*
- [ ] Pine siskin, *Carduelis pinus* *
- [ ] Red crossbill, *Loxia curvirostra* *
- [ ] White-winged crossbill, *Loxia leucoptera* *
- [ ] Savannah sparrow, *Passerculus sandwichensis*
- [ ] Dark-eyed junco, *Junco hyemalis* *
- [ ] Tree sparrow, *Spizella arborea*
- [ ] Golden-crowned sparrow, *Zonotrichia atricapilla*
- [ ] Fox sparrow, *Passerella iliaca*
- [ ] Lincoln's sparrow, *Melospiza lincolnii*
- [ ] Song sparrow, *Melospiza melodia* *
- [ ] Lapland longspur, *Calcarius lapponicus*

* Year-round resident
† Outside waters

CHAPTER SEVEN

SIGHTS ALONG THE WATERWAY

As you travel along the Inside Passage, you will observe a variety of wildlife, from seabirds to breaching whales; tall granite mountains; velvety green islands; and blue glaciers tumbling to the sea. But there is much more to Southeast Alaska than breathtakingly beautiful scenery, and your shipboard vantage point will allow you to observe the workings of life in this northern rain-forested land.

For people who inhabit the communities along these waterways, the Inside Passage is a transportation corridor, a lifeline to the outside world. There are few connecting roads along the shore. All day long the narrow passageways hum with activity as vessels work their way north and south. Fishing boats are frequent sights in summer and fall. You will see them with nets spread in the water and unloading the catch at the dock. Cruise ships are another summertime phenomenon. Three dozen or more cruise vessels make scheduled visits to Southeast Alaska from May through September of every year. Alaska Marine Highway ferries and commercial tugs and barges are year-round denizens of the waterway.

You may notice that the water itself is not as empty as it first appears. Southeast Alaska is still relatively free of man-made debris, but nature has strewn the water with old logs and clumps of seaweed. The occasional iceberg passes by on a one-way journey to oblivion. There are interesting navigational aids along the route, especially in the narrow channels, and floats to mark the location of private and commercial crab pots. On the shore clear-cuts indicate where the timber industry has been at work. You may pass staging areas where logs are rafted together for the trip to the mill or see tugs with a raft in tow. Always there are unexpected little scenes that are visible only from your special shipboard view: a homesteader's cabin tucked in the trees at water's edge; a sailboat riding at anchor in a quiet cove; an ancient cemetery with marble monuments poking above the grass; a cluster of abandoned cannery buildings; a glimpse of weathered totem poles guarding their secrets of the past; a derelict boat marooned on the tide; a secret beach, perfect moon of sand—can you ever find it again?

If you travel the Alaska Marine Highway System during the summer months, a U.S. Forest Service shipboard interpreter will be onboard your state ferry to point out and explain sights along the route. The interpreter program is a cooperative arrangement between the state of Alaska and the Forest Service. The Forest Service provides the interpreters as well as maps, books, brochures, and films for their shipboard presentations. The Alaska Marine Highway System provides passage, accommodation, and meals. The Forest Service personnel present films and short, informal talks on such topics as bald eagles, humpback whales, glaciers, and the Tongass National Forest; they also give historical introductions to each Inside Passage community. Through such exercises as "eagle counts" while traveling through some of the especially narrow passages, they involve you in the passing scene.

The interpreters are equipped to answer questions about virtually every facet of life in Southeast Alaska, from where to find a campground to what date the Russians settled in Sitka. They maintain extensive information files onboard and a library of books and pamphlets about Southeast Alaska that they will lend to you during the voyage.

TROLLERS, GILLNETTERS, AND SEINERS

In late spring, when the snow leaves the mountains, the collective thoughts of Southeasterners turn to salmon. Sportfishermen dig favorite rods out from behind the piles of skis, while commercial fishermen begin sharpening hooks and mending nets. Along about May the docks erupt in a frenzy of hull scraping and painting.

Commercial fishing is heavily regulated by the state of Alaska, both as a means of ensuring adequate future runs and as a way to comply with national and international fishing treaties that allocate salmon harvests. The state's Limited Entry Program has restricted the number of commercial fishermen who can participate in different salmon fisheries around the state. The state also licenses fishermen according to the type of gear they use. This all helps to control the amount of gear in the water. Then, during the fishing season, the Alaska Department of Fish and Game determines how long the commercial harvest will last in each location, based on the strength of the runs. Depending on the type of gear, the allowable fishing periods, called "openings," can be as brief as a few hours. The days are long gone when commercial fishing crews could go out in spring and fish until they couldn't stand it any longer.

A troller works its way along the Inside Passage. MICHELLE GURNEY

Three types of boat are used for salmon fishing in Southeast. Two of them use nets to trap the salmon, whereas the third employs hooks. You are likely to see all three as you travel around Southeast in the summer.

Trollers

Trollers fish with baited hooks or lures that are trailed through the water from long poles extended from the side of the boat (sometimes from the front as well). Each pole has a heavy stainless-steel line attached to it with several hooks so that an average-size vessel might drag up to sixty hooks through the water at one time. You can recognize the troller by the long poles, or outriggers, extended horizontally over the water. When the boat is not actively fishing, the poles are pulled up to a vertical position alongside the center mast. Power-trollers are equipped with hydraulically powered winches that haul in the heavy gear. On hand-trollers operators crank in the lines by hand.

Troll-caught salmon, usually kings or cohos, are the highest-quality fish on the market. They are removed from the line as soon as they strike and are immediately killed, gutted, and iced in the hold, where they stay until they are unloaded at a cold-storage facility for further tidying up and freezing. These salmon end up in the fresh or fresh-frozen case in your supermarket or on the menu of the best seafood restaurants across the country. Only a small percentage of salmon leaves Southeast Alaska in an unfrozen or uncanned state. Those that do come from the troll fishery. (A trawler, incidentally, is something else entirely: a large fishing vessel that pulls a net bag through the water. There are no salmon trawlers in Alaska.)

Gillnetters

Gillnetters are the smaller of the two net-fishing salmon boats employed in Southeast Alaska. The net is wound around a large spool-shaped reel on the stern or bow. With the boat in position, the operator lets the net out in a line stretching across the current from the boat. The end of the net is marked with a buoy. The top of the net is supported by floats, and the bottom, fixed with weights, hangs straight down in the water like a curtain. The salmon, heading for their spawning stream, swim into the net headfirst. The size

The spool-shaped reel on the stern labels this boat as a gillnetter. ALASKA DEPARTMENT OF FISH AND GAME

of the mesh prevents them from swimming forward, and when they try to back out, they are caught by the gills, hence the name gill net. After a time the fisherman hauls in the net over the reel and plucks out the salmon (called "picking salmon"). Gill nets are designed to selectively catch fish. Smaller fish escape by swimming through the mesh openings, and larger specimens knock up against the net and swim away undamaged. The nets come in different sizes of mesh in order to target specific species. The salmon are iced onboard and usually sold in the round.

On some gillnetters, known as bow-pickers, the reel is mounted on the bow of the boat instead of the stern. Whether bow-mounted or stern-mounted, the reel is what to look for to identify a gillnetter. Newer boats are made of aluminum or fiberglass and have a long, low profile something like a large riverboat with a cabin. Some boats are outfitted for both trolling and gill-netting, so they have both poles and drum.

The gill-net fishery is very concentrated and intense. Openings may be for only a few days a week, and crews work around the clock. During one of these openings, so many gillnetters may be crowded into one inlet that your ship will be forced to weave through an obstacle course of boats and nets.

Purse Seiners

Purse seiners are the volume vessels of the fleet. They fish by deploying a large circular net, called a seine, and harvest primarily pink and chum salmon (some sockeye) destined for canneries. These 58-foot vessels are the largest of any salmon fishery: Whereas a troller or gill-netter can be operated by a one- or two-person crew, a seiner needs a crew of six.

Seiners are the largest boats in the fleet. Look for the circular power winch. ALASKA DEPARTMENT OF FISH AND GAME

Using a power skiff, the seine crew deploys the net out in a circle from the mother boat. After a suitable period of time (minutes or hours, depending on the circumstances), they tighten the bottom of the net with a drawstring—called "closing the purse"—and haul the net and contents aboard. Some of everything will be inside: seaweed, sea urchins, jellyfish, halibut, sharks, cod, and—they hope—a substantial quantity of salmon. They keep the salmon and return the rest to sea.

Purse seining is at once the most efficient and least discriminating method of harvesting salmon. The fish are iced and off-loaded directly to cannery tenders (large vessels that transport ice and supplies to the fishing grounds and fish to the cannery) or cannery docks for cleaning and processing. The seiners are the major source for canned Alaska salmon.

Seiners are easily identified—look for the boom with a circular power winch at the top that hoists the net onto the large afterdeck. When the vessels are underway, the huge net with its floats will be coiled on the afterdeck, and the power skiff rides upside down on the stern. Should you be sightseeing by plane during a seine opening, you might look down on the delightful sight of seine nets scribing perfect circles on the water.

Longliners

Southeast enjoys good halibut fishing, too. Petersburg is the halibut capital of the region, but you will see the big halibut boats (up to 60 feet) in many Southeast harbors. Commercial halibut fishing involves the use of longlines. A longline is made up of a series of 1,800-foot (approximate) line lengths, called skates, to which leaders with baited hooks are attached. The skates are tied together to form one line several miles long. A large halibut boat might have 15 miles of gear in the water.

The line is laid down on the bottom of the ocean (halibut are bottom feeders), and the ends are marked with floats. When the halibut have had a chance to get on the hooks, the line is reeled in over a drum at the gunwale (side) or stern, and the halibut are lifted off. The fish are iced in the hold and taken to a cold-storage plant, where they are processed and frozen for shipment to the Lower 48.

The halibut harvest in Southeast Alaska is regulated by the North Pacific Fishery Management Council. The allowable harvest has been very small in recent years, and as a result the few halibut openings have been short and intense. During these dangerous derby-style openings, exhausted crews worked around the clock under brutal conditions, and accidents resulted. The local consumer suffered as well, as fresh halibut was available only during a few short periods a year. A new policy, recently adopted, assigns an Individual Fishing Quota, or IFQ, to each qualifying fisherman. The fisherman can now harvest the quota anytime during the mid-March through mid-November season, which eliminates the derby openings and provides fresh halibut to the consumer for a much longer period. The downside: Some fishermen do not qualify for IFQs and have been eliminated from the industry. Also, the IFQs, like Limited Entry Permits, have become marketable commodities. Critics fear the industry will become controlled by larger fishing interests at the expense of the small, independent operator.

Promise of Profits

Commercial fishing has become big business in Alaska, requiring enormous capital investment with only the promise of substantial profits. In 1999 a power-troll permit for Southeast Alaska cost around $14,800. Drift gill-net and seine permits cost $35,000 to nearly $39,000. A new fishing vessel, equipped with modern electronic navigation devices and fish-finding equipment, could cost between $100,000 and $1,000,000, depending on the type. To those payments must be added the cost of fuel, insurance, and supplies.

Thanks to improved management, successful hatcheries, and a series of mild winters, the total annual catch in all of Alaska has exceeded 100 million salmon for the past decade and in 1995 passed the 200-million mark. The 1994 catch in Southeast Alaska of 76.4 million salmon was the largest on record; the average catch in Southeast for 1991 to 1995 was 66 million salmon. In 1998 Southeast fishermen caught 62.8 million salmon. But 1993 illustrated the cyclical and somewhat mysterious nature of fisheries when the pink salmon simply failed to show up in some areas of Southeast. In this economic and regulatory climate, a top seiner (a "highliner") might gross $150,000 a season; a top power-troller or gillnetter might gross around $50,000 to $60,000. The average operator of a commercial fishing vessel may not even meet expenses.

The industry, as you might imagine, is heavily regulated, and prices vary widely from year to year depending on the size of runs, inventories, and the marketplace. Despite the soul-searching and upheaval in the industry, commercial fishing still enjoys an aura of romanticism. Being offshore and independent, living in concert with the natural elements—these aspects of the lifestyle haven't changed. Despite the specter of six-figure boats and batteries of equipment, there is still room in the industry for the small-scale operator who goes out in a small boat with a couple of handlines and brings in a few salmon. For less than $10,000 you can purchase a hand-troll permit and participate in the lifestyle of the commercial fishery. The average hand-troller grosses less than $5,000 all summer—not a living, but enough to make expenses and justify the pleasure of working in Alaska's beautiful outdoors.

CLEAR-CUTTING

As you cruise among the larger islands such as Chichagof and Prince of Wales, you will see bright green, squared-off patches on the hillsides amid the surrounding darker green forest. These are areas that have been clear-cut, evidence of the timber industry at work. The bright green color indicates the new growth taking form where the old trees were cut. The clear-cutting is carried out on both private lands (most owned by Southeast Native village and regional corporations) and National Forest lands.

Clear-cutting is the method most commonly used for harvesting spruce and hemlock stands in the Tongass National Forest. Clear-cutting means cutting down every tree within a specified area, as opposed to removing only selected specimens and leaving the rest. Logging companies favor clear-cutting in the difficult terrain of Southeast Alaska for obvious reasons: They can concentrate all the road building, cutting, and hauling in one area. Selective cutting requires such techniques as helicopter logging, which is dangerous, expensive, and inefficient.

A-frame hoists lower bundles of logs into the water for a trip to a sawmill.

Clear-cutting, according to the timber industry, increases the productivity of the forest by replacing uneven old-growth stands of mixed value with easy-to-harvest trees of uniform size and spacing. And the new stands have a higher percentage of spruce than old-growth forest because clear-cutting makes way for the full sunlight that the more desirable spruce requires. By the time a clear-cut patch has regenerated and matured, the tree mix will be 50 percent hemlock and 50 percent spruce, versus 70 percent hemlock and 30 percent spruce in the old stands. In 90 to 125 years, the patch will be ready to harvest again.

Clear-cutting remains controversial. Critics consider the practice unsightly, wasteful, and damaging to the environment, and they charge logging companies with leaving too much timber and debris on the ground. Clear-cuts, plus the extensive road networks required to support them, risk damaging salmon-spawning streams from erosion and debris, destroy wildlife habitats, and compromise virgin wilderness—forever. Over the years management changes have lessened these effects in the national forest by reducing the maximum allowable size of a clear-cut from more than 2,000 acres to just 100; the average size of a clear-cut in the Tongass today is fewer than eighty acres. The Tongass Timber Reform Act passed by Congress in 1990 stipulated additional changes in industry practices to safeguard salmon streams. Logging companies must now leave 100-foot, no-logging buffer strips along both sides of salmon streams and tributaries. Private land owners such as Native corporations are not bound by federal regulations, however; they fall under state jurisdiction. The Alaska Forest Practices Act requires buffer strips but does not regulate the size of clear-cuts, and some Native corporation logging practices have been greatly criticized.

You may see other signs of the logging industry during your trip through Southeast. A-frame hoists at the water's edge are used to lower bundles of logs into the water, where they are formed into log rafts for the trip to the mill. The logs are corralled by a perimeter of boom logs chained together in the shape of a rectangle. The log rafts are towed to the mill by powerful tugboats, called "bullboats" because they "bull" the logs around.

NAVIGATIONAL MARKERS

You will notice several types of navigational markers along the Inside Passage route. Some are red, some green, some blinking, others not. All these markers are navigational aids that the Coast Guard has positioned to mark safe passageways through difficult channels or harbor entrances. Most of them are buoys that are anchored to the ocean floor. Their color, markings, shape, and number are all clues to how the passage should be navigated.

The color of the buoy indicates where the boat should pass. Red buoys are kept on the right, or starboard, side of the vessel when returning from sea (in other words, inbound, heading upstream, or entering the harbor), as in the the mariner's expression "red right returning." Green buoys are kept to the left, or port, side. When outbound, or heading out to sea, the situation is reversed. Buoys painted with red and white vertical stripes mark the center of the channel and can be passed on either side. Port and starboard buoys are also numbered consecutively from the beginning of the passage to the end. Red buoys are always even-numbered; green buoys always odd-numbered. Mid-channel markers are not numbered but may be lettered. In very shallow or narrow channels, such as Wrangell Narrows between Wrangell and Petersburg, mariners must thread their way from buoy to buoy very carefully to avoid running aground.

Shape provides a further indication of buoy type. Regular red buoys, called nuns, are pointed or cone-shaped on top. Green buoys, called cans, are can-shaped or cylindrical. Lighted buoys are topped with battery-powered red, green, or white lights that flash intermittently at night to give mariners their position. They are also identified with reflective markers called daymarks—square-shaped, green, and odd-numbered for port; triangular, red, and even-numbered for starboard.

Groups of small, round floats that you see bobbing on the surface of the water, usually red, are not navigational aids but buoys marking the location of commercial crab pots.

LIGHTHOUSES

With their tall white towers and red roofs, lighthouses are among the most picturesque sights along the Inside Passage. There are several on the route from Prince Rupert to Skagway. Congress provided for the building and maintenance of lighthouses in U.S. waters as early as 1789, but none was constructed in Alaska until 1900. Before then the only navigational warning light on the entire Alaska coast was the seal-oil lantern burning in the cupola atop the governor's residence on Castle Hill in Sitka (replaced by a simple post light after the mansion burned in 1894). Eventually twelve lighthouses stood watch over the Inside Passage. Originally all the lighthouses were manned by a lighthouse keeper (sometimes a family) who lived in splendid isolation from the usual cares of the world.

At present the lights are automated. The last manned light station in Alaska was Five Fingers, which was fully automated in the summer of 1984. From south to north the lighthouses you will pass along the Inside Passage include Tree Point, Dixon Entrance (lighted

The Cape Decision lighthouse is one of twelve that stood sentry over the Inside Passage.
U.S. COAST GUARD

April 30, 1904); Mary Island, Revillagigedo Channel (lighted July 15, 1903); Cape Decision, Sumner Strait (lighted March 15, 1932); Five Fingers, Stephens Passage (lighted March 1, 1902); Point Retreat, Lynn Canal (lighted September 15, 1904); Sentinel Island, Lynn Canal (lighted March 1, 1902); Eldred Rock, Lynn Canal (lighted June 1, 1906); and Cape Spencer, Cross Sound (lighted December 11, 1925). You will also pass the Canadian Green Island and Lucy Island lighthouses just out of Prince Rupert.

The original lenses from some of these lighthouses are displayed in museums around Southeast. Check the Tongass Historical Society Museum in Ketchikan, the Juneau-Douglas City Museum in Juneau, and the Sheldon Museum in Haines.

THE NARROWS

The Inside Passage contains two very narrow stretches of water: Wrangell Narrows and the connecting passages of Peril Strait

A Place for Light Sleepers

Visitors looking for a unique place to spend the night might want to bunk at one of Southeast Alaska's lighthouses. Several of the lighthouses, first erected to warn mariners of navigational hazards, now serve as bed-and-breakfasts or lodges.

The U.S. Coast Guard leased several lighthouses to non-profit organizations that agreed to maintain the facilities for public use. Under the deal the Coast Guard still works the lights, but the leaseholders take care of the property. The most accessible of those could be the Point Retreat Lighthouse on the northeast tip of Admiralty Island, about 17 miles from Juneau, and the Sentinel Island Light, which is not far from the Juneau road system just off Benjamin Island.

The Alaska Lighthouse Association plans to open up a bed-and-breakfast at the **Point Retreat Light,** which is about a half-hour boat ride from Juneau. Dave Benton, an association founder, said there will be rustic lodging available in the first year of the operation, and things will grow more polished as the project matures. The idea behind the Point Retreat site is not to create a huge resort. "We want to keep the place intimate and maintain the character of the place," Benton said. To contact the Alaska Lighthouse Association, visit www.aklighthouse.org or write Benton at P.O. Box 240149, Douglas, AK 99824-0419.

The Gastineau Channel Historical Society runs the **Sentinel Island Light,** which can be reached by boat or helicopter and is open to the public by appointment only. You can stay overnight at the lighthouse by special arrangement for $50 per person per night during certain times of the year. To visit the 6.5-acre island, contact the society at (907) 586-5338 or glrrlg@alaska.net.

The **Five Fingers Light,** about 64 miles south of Juneau in Stephens Passage, is run by the Juneau Lighthouse Association. Jennifer Klein, one of the members, said the lighthouse has four rooms available for lodging. The daily price for a stay is expected to be around $350 a person, not including transportation. The three-acre island is one of the best whale-watching sites in Southeast. Steller's sea lions hang out nearby, and trails run through the island's forest. For information visit their Web site at www.5fingerlighthouse.com or call (907) 364-3632 or (907) 790-3339.

Karen Johnson of Sitka is leading an effort to restore the **Cape Decision Light** on Sumner Strait near Petersburg. It may take a couple more years before it is ready for visitors, but anyone wanting information can call (907) 747-7803 or write her at 224 Katlian, Sitka, AK 99835.

On Rockwell Island, a tiny spot of land just a few minutes across the water from downtown Sitka, sits the **Rockwell Lighthouse,** built by local veterinarian Burgess Bauder. Bauder rents the lighthouse at the winter rate of $125 per night for two people, $150 for four, $175 for six, and $200 for eight. Summer rates are $150 for two, $200 for four, and $35 for each additional person. Each level of the lighthouse sleeps at least two people, and eight is the largest group Bauder rents to. To reach Bauder call (907) 747-3056 or write P.O. Box 277, Sitka, AK 99835.

challenge navigators and prove greatly interesting to passengers. You have ample opportunity to study the navigational aids marking your passage as your ship negotiates the twists and turns between looming shores. Few cruise ships travel these constricted waterways, but Alaska ferries pass through them on their scheduled runs between Wrangell and Petersburg, and to Sitka. If possible, schedule your trip so that you make the passage in daylight. If you must make the trip at night, it is worth getting out of bed to watch as your ship glides between the red, green, and white blinking lights that mark the route.

Wrangell Narrows

Winding like a slender ribbon for 21 miles between Mitkof and Kupreanof Islands, Wrangell Narrows terminates at Petersburg and

Frederick Sound. At one point this chute of rushing ɔ 100 yards. More than seventy navigational markers ɪsman through the passage. Passing through Wrangell s you so close to shore that you can almost reach out evergreen. Darkness transforms the waterway into a maze of winking colored lights that Alaskans have dubbed "Christmas Tree Lane." Your ship glides silently between them as dark cliffs loom overhead.

The passage is so squeezed—an average ½-mile wide at high tide—that the current rips through the narrows at up to 8 miles an hour with every tidal change. The tide enters and exits from both ends. The channel was dredged to an average low-tide depth of 26 feet in the 1940s, but has since silted in another 4 feet. The shallowest point is currently 19 feet. Large ships, such as the Alaska ferries, do not attempt Wrangell Narrows unless the water measures at least 2 feet above average low tide.

Wrangell Narrows is the preferred route between Wrangell and Petersburg for all types of vessel—fishing boats, tugboats with log rafts, state ferries, and private cruisers. There is ample room for small craft to pass, but large ships remain in radio contact with one another and pass at prearranged wide spots in the road. Fog is the helmsman's worst enemy in Wrangell Narrows. Even with radar, ship captains delay passage until the next tide, if possible, rather than grope their way through the maze of markers. If thick fog descends en route, the best choice is to anchor well off to the side and wait for it to lift.

Peril Strait

Peril Strait is a diagonal cut between Baranof and Chichagof Islands formed by an ancient fault. The waterway, which serves as an inside route to Sitka, takes its name not from hidden rocks in the water, but from an incident that occurred during the time of the Russian occupation in 1799. That year a party of Aleut hunters on their way from Sitka to Russian headquarters at Kodiak stopped to camp on a beach, where they found quantities of mussels. More than one hundred Aleuts died from the debilitating illness that we now know as paralytic shellfish poisoning. The Russians named the waterway *Pogibshii*, meaning deadly, which has come down to us in English as Peril Strait. The passage narrows at Poison Cove, where the fateful mussels were collected, and Deadman Reach, where the hunters ate their last meal.

From there Peril Strait closes to almost a ditch in a series of zigzagging passages leading to Sitka. The first is Sergius Narrows. There are only 300 feet from buoys to shore, and the tide rushes through at speeds close to 9½ miles an hour. Large ships can pass only at slack tide. The next passage is Kakul Narrows, which emerges into Salisbury Sound. Beyond some jewel-like islands in the distance, you can see the ocean, and you probably can feel the Pacific swell. The passage narrows again into Neva Strait and constricts still further to Whitestone Narrows before opening again to Olga Strait and Sitka Sound.

Bald eagles often concentrate along the 30-mile stretch encompassing Sergius Narrows and Whitestone Narrows. As your ship glides between the forested islands, the eagles virtually line up in the treetops to greet you. You might also see deer at the water's edge. Most of the big cruise ships do not take the Sergius Narrows route, but all sorts of other vessels, including state ferries, use these waterways.

AN INTERNATIONAL BOUNDARY

The boundary between the United States and Canada extends from the southern point of Prince of Wales Island to the mainland at the entrance to the Portland Canal. Traveling northbound by ship, you pass over the line while crossing Dixon Entrance en route to Ketchikan. The border follows the Portland Canal inland to the Coast Mountains and continues along the range from peak to peak to the vicinity of Skagway. From Skagway the line turns abruptly westward and stretches almost to the sea again but stops at Mount Fairweather, parallels the Saint Elias Mountains to Mount St. Elias, and then jumps onto the 141st meridian for a straight run northward to the Arctic Ocean.

The boundary was fixed in a treaty between Britain and Russia in

Bald eagles are especially prevalent along Sergius and Whitestone Narrows approaching Sitka. JOHN SCHOEN

1825. The southern line was established at latitude 54°40' north, but Britain's Hudson's Bay Company retained the right to use navigable rivers in Russian Alaska to reach their inland posts in Canada. When the United States purchased Alaska from Russia in 1867, the old boundaries were retained with only minor adjustments.

PART TWO

EXPLORING ALASKA'S SOUTHEAST

CHAPTER EIGHT

MAIN-LINE PORTS OF THE INSIDE PASSAGE

The towns and villages that border the Inside Passage are as ruggedly individualistic as Alaskans themselves. Some, like Juneau and Skagway, were born out of the gold rush, whereas others, Sitka and Wrangell for example, date from earlier periods in Alaska's history. Petersburg has retained the atmosphere of a busy fishing depot, whereas Ketchikan balances fishing, timber, and tourism, and Juneau is a white-collar government town.

Despite substantial differences in character, all Southeast communities have this in common: a working waterfront. No matter where you visit, you will find docks and harbors busy with fishing boats, tugboats, pleasure craft, ferries, floatplanes, tour boats, and cruise ships. In this island region you will find much of the action down at the docks.

OF SPECIAL INTEREST

Southeast communities share a deep appreciation for their roots, even though the roots may extend back fewer than one hundred years. All the larger towns have excellent **local history museums.** History buffs will discover relics from the gold rush, the steamship era, or the heyday of the salmon canneries. Local museums also contain fine displays of Tlingit and Haida artifacts.

Ketchikan's busy harbor is crowded with fishing boats, pleasure craft, and exotic cruise ships.

Several communities mount **summer theatrical productions.** Usually these lighthearted melodramas spoof the town's history or gold rush events or play heavily on familiar verses of the Bard of the Yukon, Robert Service. Some of the plays have been running for years, with periodic variations in the script. They're quite well done and provide good family fun. In some communities—Haines, Juneau, and Ketchikan for sure—you may have the opportunity to attend a

Tlingit or Haida dance performance. Don't miss this opportunity. The dance brings to life the language, colorful blankets, and elaborate masks and headdresses otherwise relegated to museums.

If you want to see Alaska, it's not enough to visit the towns and communities—you have to get out in the wilderness. Touring activities are available from every major community to accomplish this. **Flightseeing** by plane or helicopter, though costly (around $100 to $130 per person for a forty-five-minute tour), is a rewarding and uniquely Alaskan experience. Popular excursions include tours over the ice fields straddling the Coast Mountains, trips to nearby glaciers (helicopter glacier tours land right on the ice), and flights into Misty Fjords and Glacier Bay national monuments.

Likewise, it is important to experience Southeast from the water. **Cruise options** abound. Depending on the community, you can make a day or overnight cruise to glacier-filled fjords, travel up mainland rivers, or take wildlife-viewing excursions among coastal islands. Any of these options will give you the opportunity to observe the Southeast inhabited not by humans but by whales, porpoises, bears, and other wild creatures. The ferries of the Alaska Marine Highway System offer many alternatives for inexpensive day cruises. You can also get out on the water by arranging a **fishing charter.** Consult local visitor information centers for a list of excursions and charter operators.

You will find developed **trail systems** in every town. Consult the local visitor center and U.S. Forest Service office for brochures and other information about nearby trails. Advance reading for serious trekkers might include Margaret Piggott's *Discover Southeast Alaska with Pack and Paddle* (The Mountaineers), which outlines trails in all the major towns (including the historic Chilkoot Trail from Dyea near Skagway to Lake Bennett).

SHOPPING FOR LOCAL ART

If the heart of Southeast is down at the docks, the soul can be found in the many galleries displaying the work of local artists. One of the singular aspects of Southeast Alaska is the high caliber of local artwork, which includes traditional Native crafts such as wood and

Art items for sale in a Sitka shop are contemporary versions of Southeast Native themes.

silver carving as well as graphic arts, painting, sculpture, pottery, and weaving. You will find Southeast artwork on sale in galleries, bookshops, and private studios in all the larger communities and featured aboard Alaska state ferries. For less than $100 you can find a lot of high-quality local art that will remind you of your trip and give you pleasure for years to come.

Several Southeast artists have achieved national repute. For example, the colorful, folksy prints by Juneau artist Rie Muñoz sell in galleries across the United States. A frequent traveler to "bush" regions of Alaska, Muñoz has made a concerted effort to record Alaska Native cultural traditions and scenes from daily Alaska life. Original Muñoz paintings, should you find one, sell for thousands of dollars, but a signed Muñoz print, framed notecard, or poster makes an affordable souvenir.

Another well-known artist, Dale DeArmond of Sitka, produces very small editions of handmade woodblock prints and fine wood engravings of a variety of local subjects, such as animals, birds, and figures from Alaska Native legend. Her exquisite, bold prints are very reasonably priced.

William Spear's enameled art pins—collected, worn, and traded throughout Alaska—can also be spotted in classy museum shops from Seattle to New York City. Most of the wearable treasures designed by this Juneau artist retail for less than $15. And anglers from one end of the Pacific coast to the other delight in the humorous fish-art T-shirts created by Ketchikan artist Ray Troll.

KETCHIKAN
Population 17,922

Ketchikan has a habit of collecting nicknames: "Alaska's First City," because it is the first stop for ferries and cruise ships threading north through the Inside Passage; "Salmon Capital of the World," for the tremendous fishing industry that founded the town; and, more dubiously, the "Rain Capital." Technically Ketchikan is not the rainiest place in Southeast (that distinction goes to the community of Little Port Walter on the southern tip of Baranof Island, where there is measurable precipitation approximately 239 days of the year), but the average yearly rainfall of 162 inches has led local wags to comment: "If you can't see Deer Mountain, it's raining; and if you can see it, it's about to rain."

The rain does not dampen spirits, though. Ketchikan is a robust, fun-filled town with a restless energy that is almost palpable. On a given summer day, there might be two or three—and some days as many as seven—cruise ships moored along the wharf, the seine fleet getting ready to put to sea, and salmon milling below the Creek Street Bridge. The scene in Tongass Narrows will include floatplanes departing for Misty Fjords flightseeing, Alaska state ferries, airport ferries, tugs and barges and fishing boats all maneuvering for space, with a few dozen kayaks and skiffs thrown in for good measure.

In years past Ketchikan projected something of a rough-and-tumble mill-town image, but the rough edges are wearing away. Ketchikan presently offers first-class lodging, fine galleries, trendy cafes, and such grace notes as **Whale Park,** a small downtown oasis

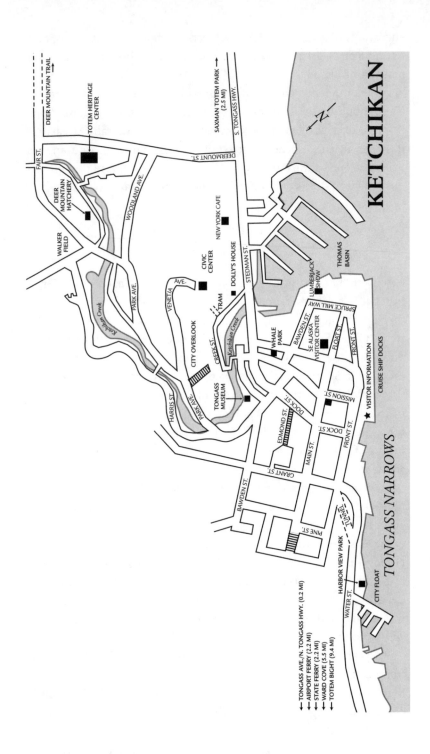

KETCHIKAN

N

Deer Mountain Trail
Totem Heritage Center
Deer Mountain Hatchery
Walker Field
Woodland Ave.
Fair St.
Park Ave.
Harris St.
Ketchikan Creek
Venetia Ave.
City Overlook
Tongass Museum
Creek St.
Tram
Civic Center
Dolly's House
New York Cafe
Stedman St.
Deermount St.
Saxman Totem Park
(2.5 mi)
S. Tongass Hwy.

Whale Park
Bawden St.
SE Alaska
Visitor Center
Lumberjack Show
Spruce Mill Way
Thomas Basin
Mission St.
Dock St.
Grant St.
Edmond St.
Main St.
Dock St.
Front St.
Float St.
Front St.
Visitor Information
Cruise Ship Docks

Bawden St.
Pine St.
Tunnel
Harbor View Park
Water St.
City Float

TONGASS NARROWS

Tongass Ave./N. Tongass Hwy. (0.2 mi)
Airport Ferry (2.2 mi)
State Ferry (2.2 mi)
Ward Cove (5.5 mi)
Totem Bight (9.4 mi)

of lush gardens, hanging flower baskets, and a newly commissioned totem pole. You'll enjoy your stay in this lively waterfront city.

Background

Ketchikan lies on the western coast of Revillagigedo Island, 90 miles north of Prince Rupert, British Columbia, via the Marine Highway. Revillagigedo is a Spanish name, the island having been named in honor of the Count of Revilla Gigedo, who was viceroy of Mexico in the late 1700s. The correct Spanish pronunciation is Rheh-vee-ya-hee-*hay*-tho. Local residents, however, shorten the name to Revilla, which, Anglicized or "Alaskacized," then becomes Ruh-*vil*-la. The name Ketchikan is thought to have been derived from a Tlingit word meaning "the thundering wings of an eagle," or the sound of the eagle's wings in flight.

A Tlingit fishing camp—"Kitschkhin" or "Kitskan"—had been well established in the area when settlers built a small saltery at the mouth of Ketchikan Creek in 1883. Within two years canneries had sprouted at the nearby communities of Quadra on the mainland and Loring on Revillagigedo Island. In 1887 the Quadra cannery was moved to Ketchikan, and the present-day settlement was born. The Tongass Packing Company packed 5,500 cases of salmon that first year, the beginning of an industry that grew to more than a dozen canneries producing more than two million cases of salmon a year, earning Ketchikan the title "Salmon Capital of the World."

Mining contributed to the growth of the settlement when gold was discovered in the area in 1897. Prospectors located good copper deposits on Prince of Wales Island the same year, and the community was launched on another tack. Lumber production started at about the same time. The Ketchikan Spruce Mill began operations in Ketchikan in 1904, providing lumber for many needs including packing boxes for the canneries. The mill remained the focal point of downtown Ketchikan for several decades, in more recent years producing cants (sawed logs) for export to Japan. It shut down in 1985. Ketchikan's timber industry suffered again in March 1997, when Louisiana-Pacific shut down its Ward Cove pulp mill, the town's biggest private employer. The mill was built in 1954 to produce a dissolving pulp used to manufacture plastics and other synthetics.

The company's small-log sawmill is still operating, and plans are in the works to open a veneer plant.

The salmon fisheries declined in the 1940s and nearly collapsed in the 1970s, mostly from overfishing, but the industry gradually recovered. Commercial fishing and fish processing remain a vital part of the economy and lifestyle of the community. Like all Southeast towns, Ketchikan relies on both tourism and government to flesh out the economy.

Getting There

You can reach Ketchikan by air or by water. Alaska Airlines provides daily jet service from Seattle and Juneau. The airport is located on Gravina Island, across Tongass Narrows from the city of Ketchikan. A small ferry shuttles passengers and automobiles between the airport and the airport ferry terminal, a little more than 2 miles north of the Ketchikan city center (0.5 mile north of the Alaska state ferry terminal). Ketchikan is a port of call for both main-line ferries traveling north and south along the Inside Passage and for smaller vessels serving Metlakatla, Prince of Wales Island, and Hyder. The many cruise ships that visit the port tie up at the city dock on the downtown waterfront or anchor just offshore.

To See and Do

Like other communities along the Inside Passage, Ketchikan is squeezed onto a narrow ribbon of land between the mountains and the sea. Much of the business district hangs over the water on pilings. A number of attractions near the city center can be reached on foot, whereas others require a bus or automobile trip "out the road." A two-hour **waterfront cruise,** available from Alaska Cruises (907-225-6044) and other operators, is a good way to get your bearings.

The central sights can be viewed on the **walking tour** developed by Historic Ketchikan. Pick up a map at the dockside visitor center. The full tour requires about two hours' walking time and takes in the major attractions of Creek Street, the Totem Heritage Center, Deer Mountain Hatchery and Eagle Center, and the Tongass Museum: all relatively flat terrain. Along the way you will glimpse some of

Ketchikan's famous staircases leading to residential neighborhoods high in the clouds. If you can muster the strength to climb the stairs to the **overlooks** above Upland Way and Front Street, you will be rewarded with spectacular views of the waterfront and ship activity on Tongass Narrows.

Front Street, where cruise ships dock, bustles with hotels, eating establishments, and jewelry, gift, and souvenir shops. **Annabelle's Famous Keg & Chowder House** in the historic Gilmore Hotel (326 Front Street) is a nice place to stop for seafood. Mission Street offers targets for gallery shopping: Among others, try **Scanlon Gallery** (318 Mission Street).

Front Street turns inland just past the visitor center and becomes Mill Street. On the right the U.S. Forest Service's **Southeast Alaska Visitor Center** rises from the site of a former spruce mill. The 22,000-square-foot center features elaborate interpretive exhibits about public lands, resources, and recreational opportunities throughout Alaska, particularly the Tongass National Forest.

Catercorner to the visitor center on Spruce Mill Way and Bawden Street is the **Great Alaskan Lumberjack Show.** In the early 1900s Alaska's timber industry was in full swing, and lumberjacks harvested timber in one of North America's most grueling environments. Each summer hardy lumberjacks from the Southeast would gather in Ketchikan to compete for bragging rights as "King of the Woods." Today rugged woodsmen compete in chopping, sawing, climbing, and logrolling competitions three times a day—rain or shine. Call (888) 320-9049 for show times.

Few sights in Southeast Alaska so delight the eye as **Creek Street,** built on pilings above Ketchikan Creek. The wooden boardwalk, rimmed with galleries and shops, was the red-light district of Ketchikan during the rowdier days when loggers and fishermen came to town looking for entertainment. The city closed the twenty-odd houses in 1953. Creek Street, local wags used to say, was the spot where "both fish and fishermen went upstream to spawn," a concept that greatly influences the plot of Ketchikan's own rip-roaring, homegrown summer musical melodrama, *The Fish Pirate's Daughter.*

At number 24 on the right, painted peppermint green with a red door, you'll find **Dolly's House.** Big Dolly Arthur arrived in Alaska in

Creek Street, built on pilings above Ketchikan Creek, was known as the red-light district in the early days of the gold rush. Today it is rimmed with galleries and shops. MICHELLE GURNEY

1914 at age twenty-six and exercised her considerable charms until Creek Street closed. Dolly's House has been restored as a small museum that offers a glimpse into her life and times. A photo of Dolly in the front room shows a spirited "Big Blonde" type of generous proportions. At five-foot-eight, she was not called Big Dolly for nothing, and her weight ballooned to 240 pounds in later years. The dining-room table is set for company, and the bottle of bootleg whiskey stands at the ready in a tiny wet bar positioned strategically over the creek. A quick toss through the trapdoor took care of any incriminating evidence. Dolly's clothes hang in the upstairs boudoir, and her chunky pink and red costume jewelry sprawls on the dressing table. Also on Creek Street is **Parnassus,** a delightful bookstore (new and used), a gift shop, and an espresso bar. You'll also find Ray Troll's **Soho Coho** art gallery, featuring his own and other artists' work.

If you carry on down Stedman Street, you'll bump into the **New York Cafe and Ketchikan Coffee Company.** Housed in the historic **New York Hotel** (established in 1925), this quaint cafe offers healthy Alaskan fare, including homemade soups, salads, and sandwiches, as well as a variety of delightful desserts. Because they are open late—until 10:00 P.M. on weekdays and 11:00 P.M. on weekends—this is a great venue to visit for a latte and a piece of pie after dinner.

Back on Creek Street, a red funicular climbs to the attractive seventy-two-room **WestCoast Cape Fox Lodge/Heen Kahidi Restaurant and Lounge** and adjacent **Ted Ferry Civic Center,** 130 feet above the city center and Tongass Narrows. Hotel guests ride free to this great view; other visitors pay a nominal fee.

Follow the wooden boardwalk and the signs to the **Totem Heritage Center** (601 Deermount Street), a repository for original, unrestored totem poles that have been retrieved from the deserted Tlingit communities of Tongass and Village Islands and the Haida village of Old Kasaan. There is a central gallery where five of the massive poles

Guests can ride a red funicular to the WestCoast Cape Fox Lodge. MICHELLE GURNEY

are displayed, plus exhibit cases of Native art and artifacts, including a beautiful set of traditional wood-carving tools made by Tsimshian carver Jack Hudson. Each implement, decorated and shaped to fit the carver's hand, is itself a work of art. The Totem Heritage Center is also used for workshops in Native crafts such as wood carving, beading, basketry, and silver engraving. You may see young artists sorting and stringing beads or working on dance blankets or other projects. In the beading room notice the handsome copper-and-wood screen depicting Raven with the sun and moon.

Outside the Totem Heritage Center stands a contemporary totem pole carved by Tlingit master carver Nathan Jackson. This pole, **Raven–Fog Woman,** recalls the story of the mythical hero Raven and Fog Woman, his wife, who created the first salmon. According to this legend, Raven went fishing with his two slaves to gather the winter's food supply but managed to catch nothing but bullheads. As they were returning to camp, a heavy fog engulfed their canoe, and they lost their way. Suddenly a woman appeared in the canoe. She asked Raven for his spruce-root hat, which she took in her left hand. All the fog disappeared into the hat, and Raven was able to find the way home. Fog Woman became Raven's wife and produced sockeye salmon for him out of baskets of spring water like rabbits out of a hat. When she had produced enough salmon to fill many smokehouses, Raven forgot his former hunger and began to mistreat her. She left him to return to her father's house, and as she walked into the sea, all of the salmon followed, leaving Raven nothing to eat but the bullhead.

The pole depicts Raven at the top, easily recognized by his wings and straight beak. He is holding a bullhead on a line. Beneath him his two slaves, Gitsanuk and Gitsanqeq, also hold bullheads. At the bottom of the pole, Fog Woman holds the spruce-root hat in her left hand and a salmon in her right.

From the Totem Heritage Center, cross the footbridge over Ketchikan Creek to reach the **Deer Mountain Hatchery and Eagle Center.** This facility can produce 400,000 salmon and 35,000 steelhead annually. Released into Ketchikan Creek, they migrate downstream into Thomas Basin and salt water. After a hazardous life at sea, the surviving adults return to the hatchery to spawn. Depending upon the

month, you may see young fish in rearing pens or adult fish returning through the white water to reach the hatchery. The kings normally spawn from the end of July through August, and coho from
the end of November through December. The adjacent **City Park**
has creekside picnic tables.

The **Tongass Historical Museum,** at 629 Dock Street, occupies
one of the nicest sites in the city. The building, which also houses the
public library, practically straddles Ketchikan Creek. Inside you can
hear the sound of water rushing beneath your feet. The museum
embraces all the themes that thread through Ketchikan's history:
Native cultures, mining, timber, and fishing, with permanent and

*Salmon climb these rapids on Ketchikan Creek as they make their way toward the Deer
Mountain Hatchery to spawn in July.* MICHELLE GURNEY

changing exhibits. You can walk through the exhibits in an hour.

"This Is Our Life" focuses on the changing cultures of Southeast Native peoples. Showcases reveal a lifestyle rich with creativity. You will see beautiful and functional spruce-root and cedar-bark baskets, bentwood boxes and elaborate feast dishes, a shaman's necklace and rattle, and a large Chilkat blanket. A carved wooden crest hat in the shape of a salmon comes from the Dog Salmon clan on Prince of Wales Island. Elders of the Tlingit, Haida, and Tsimshian peoples guided the preparation of the display and explained how the artifacts were made and used.

The museum also exhibits the original lens from the Tree Point light station at Dixon Entrance. Originally illuminated by a kerosene vapor lamp, the light was replaced by a rotating beacon in 1963.

The totem pole outside the museum, **Raven Stealing the Sun,** was commissioned by the City of Ketchikan to honor the Tongass Tlingit who originally inhabited the area. The figures recall the story of Raven, who brought light to the world by stealing the box of daylight from a chief on the Nass River (see page 74). The pole was designed and carved by Tlingit artist Dempsey Bob and raised in 1983. **Chief Johnson's pole,** at Mission and Stedman Streets across from Whale Park, portrays the mythical bird Kadjuk, the crest of the Johnson clan. Israel Shotridge carved this replica of the 1901 original. The same artist created the **Chief Kyan totem** raised in Whale Park in 1993.

Two and one-half miles south of Ketchikan on the South Tongass Highway, another vast collection of totem poles stands sentry duty at **Saxman Totem Park.** Tlingit from Cape Fox and Tongass villages formed the village of Saxman in the late 1800s. It is named for Samuel Saxman, a schoolteacher lost with two other men in the winter of 1886 while they were hunting for a new village site. The twenty-four totems were brought to the site from abandoned villages on Tongass, Cat, Pennock, and Village Islands and from the old Cape Fox Village at Kirk Point under a U.S. Forest Service and Civilian Conservation Corps project in the 1930s. Some were repaired and restored, and others completely replicated—a process that continues today.

The park is on the uphill, or left, side of the highway as you proceed south. **Sun and Raven** stands at the entrance. Originally carved in 1902 as a memorial column, the pole recalls several Raven myths. You can identify Raven at the top, with his characteristic straight beak. The corona around his head represents the Sun, who entertained Raven during the Deluge. The eye-shaped designs on his wings, with small faces inside, symbolize the power of flight and Raven's ability to change form. The three small figures between Raven's wings represent the Children of the Sun. Below them is Fog Woman, Raven's wife, who produced salmon out of spring water. Next is Raven again, diving after Frog to the bottom of the ocean to visit the creatures of the sea.

The **Tired Wolf house posts,** uphill from Sun and Raven, were carved in approximately 1827 for members of the Wolf phratry who had once crossed paths with a particular wolf. According to their story, the men of Forest Island House were out fishing one day in their canoe when they came upon a wolf swimming for shore. He was so exhausted that his tongue lolled out of his mouth. They rescued the wolf and took him to live with them, and the animal became a faithful companion and helped them to hunt. In the carvings the wolves' tongues are hanging out of their mouths. The long tail up the back of each post distinguishes Wolf from Bear. Notice the small face that forms the pupil of the eye in one of the wolves, a carver's device to symbolize the life force.

The majority of the totem poles are arranged in a wide grassy area at the top of the street. Look to the right to see the **Lincoln pole.** This is a replica. You can see the original pole in the Alaska State Museum in Juneau. The precise history of this famous totem has been lost to the past, but the carving was erected on Tongass Island in 1883 to commemorate the clan's first sighting of a white man many years prior. The carver evidently used a picture of President Lincoln as a model for the figure, wearing a stovepipe hat, at the top of the column. Raven, the clan crest, appeared at the base, and the pole was known as the Proud Raven pole.

The plain shaft with the single lonely figure at the top wearing a potlatch hat is the **Seward pole,** which was carved around 1885 to commemorate Secretary of State William Seward's tour of Tongass Island in 1869. During his visit Seward was entertained by the clan chief. He was given a ceremonial spruce-root hat, furs, and a carved and painted chest. On the pole the secretary is shown seated on the chest and wearing the potlatch hat. Some say the Seward pole is actually a ridicule pole that was erected because Seward did not reciprocate the hospitality shown him by the people of Tongass Village.

There are several Frog totems in the park. Besides the Frog figure on the Sun and Raven pole, there is a mortuary column showing Raven poised for flight on top and Frog midway down the shaft, and **Frog Tree,** with two Frog totems atop a crosspiece on an upright support.

A small face within an eye usually represents the life force. This is one of the Tired Wolf house posts at Saxman.

Some say the Seward pole, carved around 1885 to commemorate Secretary of State William Seward's visit, is actually a ridicule pole.

The latter pole was erected in memory of a woman whose name was Two Frogs on a Drifting Log. The legend tells of a young Tlingit woman, a chief's daughter, who went to live with a tribe of frogs in a lake near their village. The father was eventually able to rescue her and bring her home, but she was unable to eat human food and soon died.

Many visitors photograph **Loon Tree,** the pole with the three bear cubs. The top figure, Loon represents the crest figure of a particular Tlingit clan. Below Loon, three bear cubs make their way headfirst to the base of the pole. The cubs represent the story of Kats, who married a she-bear that appeared to him in human form

The community house at Totem Bight overlooks Tongass Narrows. The spot was formerly a Tlingit campsite.

and was ultimately killed by their cub-children. Kats's bear wife is at the bottom of the pole, holding the human figure of Kats between her front paws. You will see many other carvings representing the popular legend of Kats, his wife, and their cub-children.

For more information about the poles in Saxman and other totem collections, the standard reference book is *The Wolf and the Raven* (University of Washington Press) by Dr. Viola Garfield of the University of Washington Department of Anthropology, and Linn Forrest, who was the U.S. Forest Service architect in charge of the Civilian Conservation Corps totem restoration project. The authors were actively involved in the restoration project and have tried to document the history of each totem at Saxman as well as those at Totem Bight and Klawock totem parks. The book is available in most Southeast bookstores.

Saxman Native Village includes a gift shop, a carving shed where you may see new poles being carved, and **Beaver Tribal House,** with a beautiful carved house screen and house posts. In summer the community hosts scheduled performances of the **Cape Fox Dancers,** Saxman's traditional Tlingit dance group.

The road northward from the city center takes you to the terminals for the airport ferry and the Alaska state ferry. Just north of the downtown tunnel, you'll find small, flower-hung **Harbor View Park,** with tables and benches overlooking the commercial fishing float. At Ward Cove, midway along the 18.4-mile North Tongass Highway, is the former Louisiana-Pacific pulp-mill site. Roads lead inland to the **Ward Lake Recreation Area,** with several attractive national forest campgrounds and picnic shelters. An easy, mile-long trail circles the lake.

At mile 10 you reach **Totem Bight State Historic Park.** A broad path leads through the forest to fourteen totem poles and an elaborately decorated clan house on a point overlooking Tongass Narrows. The site, with its gentle beach and salmon stream, was formerly used by the Tlingit as a summer campsite. Two Haida mortuary columns, Eagle and Thunderbird, guard the trailhead.

The community house was constructed by the Civilian Conservation Corps as a replication of an early-nineteenth-century clan house with painted housefront, carved corner posts, and a tall totem pole at the entrance. An oval hole in the bottom of the pole frames the doorway into the house. The interior is fashioned in typical style, with a central fire pit for cooking and heating and a wooden platform around the perimeter where the inhabitants sat, slept, and stowed their belongings.

The other totems in the park are arranged along a path overlooking the water. Some are Haida in origin; others are Tlingit. You can pick up a brochure explaining the history and significance of each pole at the park entrance.

No fires, food, or camping are allowed at Totem Bight, but you can enjoy a picnic at the U.S. Forest Service campground at **Settlers' Cove** at the northern end of the road system. You will find a boat launch, campsites, and picnic tables. A path leads along the beach to the right. You duck into the mossy forest, following the trail and the sound of rushing water, and come to a bridge that fords the stream.

Other "out-the-road" opportunities include two full-service fishing resorts: locally popular **Clover Pass Resort and R.V. Park** (mile 15), a casual complex with cabins, rental boats, and a good restaurant

The 2.2-million-acre Misty Fjords National Monument is a brief floatplane ride from Ketchikan. U.S. FOREST SERVICE

lounge, and the tonier **Salmon Falls Resort** on Behm Canal (mile 17). The restaurants of both resorts are open to the public.

Ketchikan is the nearest departure point for plane or boat excursions into **Misty Fjords National Monument,** a 2.2-million-acre coastal ecosystem encompassing the east side of Revillagigedo Island and a portion of the mainland between Behm and Portland Canals. "Misty" was designated a national monument in 1978 and given wilderness status in 1980. Within the monument the deep fjords of Walker Cove and Rudyerd Bay penetrate the wilderness with sheer rock walls rising to 3,000 feet. As the name implies, it's a moody and immensely beautiful environment of veiled peaks and waterfalls nourished by 150 inches of rain and snow annually. Wildlife is prevalent, and the bays and coves offer good fishing, camping, photography, and wilderness exploration. The Forest Service maintains fourteen recreational cabins within the monument (available for $25 per night), several mooring buoys, and hiking trails.

The untouched wilderness of Misty Fjords can be accessed by floatplane or boat only. Several air taxi services offer Misty Fjords flightseeing from Ketchikan. On a typical flight the pilot will set down in the upper reaches of the monument and shut off the engine so that you can enjoy the peace and solitude of the setting. **Alaska Cruises** (P.O. Box 7815, Ketchikan, AK 99901; telephone 907-225-8636; www.goldbelttours.com) offers combination cruise/fly tours into Misty Fjords plus kayak drop-offs. Kayaking in Misty Fjords is increasingly popular. **Southeast Exposure** (P.O. Box 9143, Ketchikan, AK 99901; telephone 907-225-8829) and **Southeast Sea Kayaks** (1430 Millar Street, Ketchikan, AK 99901; telephone 800-287-1607 or 907-225-1258; www.ktn.net/seakayaks) provide kayak instruction and rental and guided kayak trips into the monument. For more information about Misty Fjords, contact the U.S. Forest Service, Southeast Alaska Visitor Center, 50 Main Street, Ketchikan, AK 99901; telephone (907) 228-6220. If you don't have a car with you and are interested in cycling around Ketchikan and its surrounding sites, mountain bikes are available through Southeast Exposure. They are located across from the tunnel at 515 Water Street. Prices range from $6.00 an hour to $22.00 for a full day.

Special Events

In addition to the usual parade, Ketchikan puts on a ripsnorting **Timber Carnival** on the Fourth of July with such events as ax throwing, choker setting, power-saw bucking, ax chopping, and pole climbing. The contests are held on Walker Field off Park Avenue in town, and they guarantee splendid entertainment for everyone. The combination of parade, Timber Carnival, and evening fireworks display over Tongass Narrows recommends Ketchikan as a destination over the Fourth. Other annual Ketchikan celebrations include a **Beer Festival** that takes place toward the end of July; the **Blueberry Arts Festival** in August; the **Great Alaska Sport Fishing Championship** in September; and the **Winter Arts Fair** in November, which is followed by the **Winter Art Walk** in early December. February hosts two celebrations, the **Wearable-Art Show** and the **Festival of the North,** a winter arts and music gala. A grueling **Double Ironman Triathlon** is held in March; the **Alaska Hummingbird Festival** takes place in April; a **Sea Art Walk** is held in early May; and the renowned **King Salmon Derby** takes place toward the end of May and early June.

The ripsnorting Ketchikan Timber Carnival draws an enthusiastic Fourth of July crowd.

WRANGELL

Population 2,308

Wrangell is a solid frontier town with a strong spirit of independence. The false-fronted buildings on Front Street all exhibit different shapes and designs. Each stands alone, aloof from the next. The streets are broad and paved. There are wide sidewalks—room to pass without jostling your neighbor.

Although Wrangell boasts a number of major-league visitor attractions—a beach scattered with petroglyphs, an important Tlingit clan house and totem poles, the magnificent scenery of the Stikine River—the tourism industry is still in the formative stages. On the one hand, you'll see a "real" Alaska town—before the prettying up (hanging flower baskets, colorful banners, strategically placed

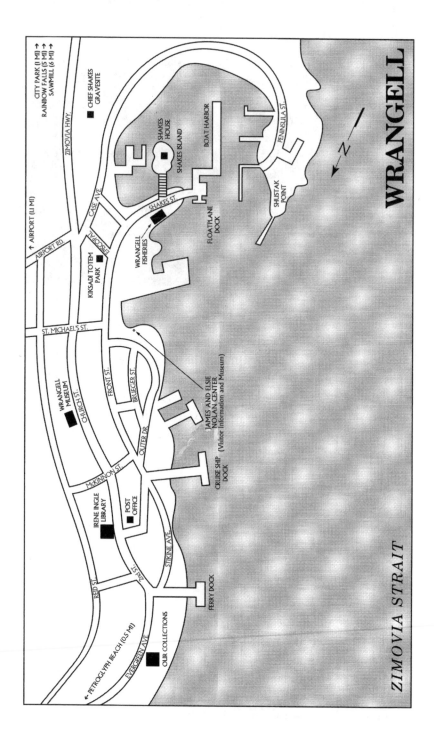

WRANGELL

ZIMOVIA STRAIT

City Park (1 MI) →
Rainbow Falls (5 MI) →
Sawmill (6 MI) →

Airport (1.1 MI) ↑

Zimovia Hwy.

Airport Rd.

Chief Shakes Gravesite

Case Ave.

Shakes House

Shakes Island

Boat Harbor

Shakes St.

Wrangell Fisheries

Floatplane Dock

Peninsula St.

Shustak Point

N

Kiksadi Totem Park

Front St.

St. Michael's St.

James and Elsie Nolan Center
(Visitor Information and Museum)

Wrangell Museum

Church St.

Brueger St.

Outer Dr.

Cruise Ship Dock

McKinnon St.

Irene Ingle Library

Post Office

Stikine Ave.

Ferry Dock

2nd St.

Red St.

Petroglyph Beach (0.5 MI) ←

Evergreen Ave.

Our Collections

Tugboats in Wrangell Harbor await the next assignment.

benches . . .) that an aggressive tourism industry usually brings; on the other hand, facilities such as the museum and visitor center operate on limited hours and with limited staff. For instance, the visitor center is not open at all on weekends, and the town is extremely quiet on Sundays. Visitors need to show some initiative and independence: Walk around, ask questions, and enjoy the frontier spirit that still exists in Wrangell.

Background

Wrangell's multinational history has been the direct result of the town's proximity to the swift-flowing Stikine River, which reaches 330 miles from the Southeast mainland into British Columbia. Located on the northern tip of Wrangell Island, just 7 miles from the river delta, Wrangell has been a terminus for river activity since the Tlingit Indians first used the Stikine to trade with the Athapaskans in the Interior.

At the time of the Russian occupation of Alaska, the Stikine delta and neighboring islands were the home of a powerful group of Tlingit Indian clans that came to be known as the Stikines. The chief of the Stikines was Shakes, the fourth in a succession of chiefs of that name. (The seventh and last Chief Shakes to assume the title died in 1944.)

His village, known as Kots-lit-na, was situated on Wrangell Island, approximately 20 miles to the south of the present town of Wrangell. Around 1811 the Russians began trading with the Tlingit for the valuable furs such as beaver and land otter that were obtained up the Stikine. The story of the modern settlement of Wrangell begins not with the Russians, however, but the British. In the early 1800s, when the Russians were busy relocating their headquarters from Kodiak to Sitka, the British Hudson's Bay Company controlled the fur trade in Canada. The British moved their posts farther and farther west until they reached the Pacific, where they ran smack up against the Russian-American Company in their bid for the Native fur trade. In 1825 the two countries signed treaties fixing the boundaries between Russian-America and Canada. The agreements gave the Hudson's Bay Company the right to use navigable Southeast streams to reach its posts in Canada, provided that no Russian settlement stood in the way. Increasingly desirous of reaching the fur supply on the mainland just beyond the Russian coast, the Hudson's Bay Company decided to establish a post on the Stikine, which would give them easy access to the Interior and an easy exit to move the furs to market.

Before the British could set this plan in motion, the Russian-American Company got wind of the scheme. The Russians sent their own expedition, commanded by Captain-Lieutenant Dionysius Zarembo, to cut off the British from the Stikine trade by establishing their own fort at the river mouth. In 1833 they began building Redoubt Saint Dionysius (redoubt meaning "fort") on the shore of a sheltered bay (now Wrangell Harbor) on the northern tip of Wrangell Island. The fort, the second non-Native settlement in Southeast Alaska, was named for Zarembo's patron saint. When the British arrived—too late—to build their own fort, they were met with a show of force and made to back down. The Russian flag was raised over Redoubt Saint Dionysius on August 26, 1834.

Once the crisis had passed, the British managed to get what they wanted anyway. In 1839 the Russian-American Company agreed to lease to the Hudson's Bay Company all of the mainland coast from Portland Canal at the southern border of Russian territory to Cape Spencer west of Glacier Bay for ten years. The price was 2,000 land-otter skins annually, plus a quantity of provisions such as wheat and salt beef, which were always in short supply. Under this arrangement Redoubt Saint Dionysius passed into British hands and assumed the name Fort Stikine. Under the British flag the Stikine settlement became a major trading center for the neighboring Tlingit Indians. Chief Shakes had already moved his community from Kots-lit-na to the small harbor area now known as Shakes Island. Other clans lived nearby on Wrangell Island and on the mainland. In exchange for valuable furs, the Indians were given manufactured items that they wanted such as cloth and the rich wool Hudson's Bay Point blankets.

Fort Stikine was abandoned in 1849. When Alaska was sold to the United States in 1867, the trading settlement was received by the U.S. Army. Once again the name was changed, this time to Fort Wrangell for Baron Ferdinand von Wrangell, who had been the chief manager for the Russian-American Company from 1830 to 1836 when Redoubt Saint Dionysius was founded. The U.S. Army built new quarters on a rise near the site of the old fort. Fort Wrangell closed in the 1870s with all of the other army posts in Alaska except Sitka. Some of the buildings were purchased by a retired army supply officer who opened a trading post.

Wrangell was the jumping-off point for three different gold rushes to the Interior. In 1861 the Stikine strike, the first gold strike to affect Alaska, took prospectors upriver to a spot called Buck's Bar. Captain William Moore transported the prospectors from Wrangell to Buck's Bar aboard his steamer the *Flying Dutchman*. By the time the second wave of prospectors arrived in 1873 on their way to the new strikes in the Canadian Cassiar district, the population of Wrangell had dwindled. Once again the quiet outpost was transformed into a boomtown as fortune seekers geared up for the trip into the wilderness, then spent their hard-won diggings on the way back out again. Wrangell was suddenly the busiest spot in the territory. An estimated 3,000 people went up the Stikine and packed into the Cassiar in 1874. Three years later the first mission school in Alaska was opened at Wrangell. By 1880 steamers ran directly to Wrangell from Portland and Victoria, British Columbia.

When the Cassiar rush ended, Wrangell subsided into inactivity once more. Historian Hubert Howe Bancroft reported in 1886 that the fort was deserted and the town "nearly so, except by Indians. . . .

The main street is choked with decaying logs and stumps and is passable only by a narrow plank sidewalk."

The town rebounded with the rush to the Klondike in 1898, as prospectors scrambled to get to Dawson in the shortest possible time. Some of them elected to follow the Stikine to Telegraph Creek and hike 160 miles overland to the headwaters of the Yukon. But by the time this strike had run its course, Wrangell had gained an economic toehold with two canneries and a sawmill.

These industries continue to dominate the economy. The timber industry, although no longer embodied in a single, large sawmill (which closed in 1994), is still a major element of the economy. The downtown harbor houses a sizable fleet of trollers, gillnetters, and seiners, plus a large cannery and several smaller seafood processors. Besides salmon, they package halibut, crab, and the prized local shrimp, from salad size to beefy prawns. The recent development of major mines across the border in Canada finds Wrangell once again serving as a gold rush depot as well. Enormous Hovercraft transport gold concentrate down the Stikine while supplies and crews move in the other direction. The surge of activity has turned the Wrangell airport into one of the busiest in Alaska for international traffic.

Wrangell is a scrappy town. The community has stuck it out for more than a century, through good times and bad. Consider the *Wrangell Sentinel*. The newspaper started publication on November 20, 1902, and continues today—the oldest continuously published newspaper in Alaska.

Getting There

So far, Wrangell has not been a regular stop on most cruise-ship itineraries, although a few small and medium-size vessels now call there. Wrangell will undoubtedly become more popular as cruise companies search for undiscovered destinations and less crowded ports. Alaska state ferries call at Wrangell on their normal route between Bellingham/Prince Rupert and Skagway, and the ferry terminal is right in the center of town. The airport, with daily jet service to cities along the Seattle-to-Juneau route, is 1.5 miles north of town. Wrangell can also accommodate private yachts, sailboats, and charter or private airplanes.

You can find comfortable accommodations both in town and out the road, including an increasing number of bed-and-breakfasts. The waterfront **Stikine Inn** remains unmatched for convenience and its spectacular view out to Zimovia Strait. Harding's **Old Sourdough Lodge** (1 mile from town) and **Roadhouse Lodge** (mile 4 Zimovia Highway) are good alternatives. (See the Wrangell lodging directory, pages 344 to 345, for a complete listing.)

To See and Do

Wrangell is so small that you can walk to all the major attractions. In fact, most visitors come to Wrangell to take a trip on the Stikine River or to visit places like the Anan Creek Bear Observatory. This small community, however, also boasts the only USGA-rated golf course in Southeast Alaska. Since the state ferry docks downtown, you view much of the community even if you are in port for only an hour or two. The visitor center is located near the waterfront in the downtown area just off Outer Drive in the new **James and Elsie Nolan Center,** but keep in mind that hours are limited. The center is typically only open from 10:00 A.M. to 4:00 P.M. from Monday through Friday. If you know you will be arriving on a weekend, it may be a good idea to call Wrangell's Convention and Visitors Bureau at (800) 367–9745 or visit www.wrangell.com in advance of your trip. They will send you a complete package with all the information you will need to make the most of your visit. If the visitor center is open, you can pick up a guide, brochures, and any other information you need.

The area toward the water is what is known as the "downtown fill area." This is the part of town that was filled in after the 1952 fire destroyed the waterfront side of Front Street that had been built on wooden pilings. Front Street continues southward toward the boat harbor. You will pass old false-fronted wooden buildings, each painted a different color and design. Some show the founding date: **Biehl's, 1898,** for example. At the intersection with Episcopal Street, you come to Wrangell's pocket-sized **Kiksadi Totem Park.** Four new totem poles, replicas of historic Wrangell-area carvings, stand in the park surrounded by plantings of shrubs and trees. The **One-Legged Fisherman pole,** at the upper left of the park, represents a Tlingit myth about a supernatural being of the Eagle clan known as the one-

The Kiksadi Totem Park is surrounded by shrubs and trees. MICHELLE GURNEY

Shakes House is a replicated Tlingit community house of hand-adzed lumber and no nails. The house is typically open when the cruise ships are docked. MICHELLE GURNEY

legged fisherman (in the pole, however, he is given two legs). The one-legged fisherman used a magic harpoon to catch salmon, which he strung up on ropes, as shown in the carving. The original version of the tall pole at the front, the **Kiksadi pole,** was carved in the 1890s to honor a chief of the Kiksadi clan, whose crest figure, the Frog, appears near the top.

When you reach the end of Front Street, Shakes Street continues around to **Shakes Island,** a grassy compound with a replica of the Shakes community house and several totem poles, and the **boat harbor,** with its seafood-processing plants and berths of commercial fishing boats and tugs. There are few signs—you have to proceed on faith. On the way you pass the **Marine Bar,** which is the site of the original Russian fort, Saint Dionysius.

Shakes House, like the community house at Ketchikan's Totem Bight, was constructed as part of the Civilian Conservation Corps's totem restoration project in the 1930s. The building was meant to be a replica of the house where the various Chiefs Shakes lived after the clan moved from Kots-lit-na. All the lumber and support poles were hand-adzed to give the house an authentic look, and, like the original dwellings, no nails were used in the construction. The green and black Bear totem framing the entrance was painted and carved on the interior screen in the original Shakes House.

The interior of the house is open to view by appointment but is often open while cruise ships are in town. Call (907) 874-3747 to arrange a visit between 10:00 A.M. and 5:30 P.M. The house is arranged in the traditional style with a central fire pit for cooking surrounded by two tiers of wooden platforms for sitting, sleeping, and storage, and has a smoke hole in the roof. A carved and painted wooden screen separates the chief's private quarters from the common room. Instead of the original Bear design, the screen is decorated with the design from a Chilkat blanket that belonged to the Shakes family. The interior house posts were originals brought from the old village in the 1800s. Now more than 200 years old, they have been removed for protection and display in the Wrangell Museum. Carved replicas replace the originals in Shakes House. The Shakes Island house was dedicated in 1940 at a great potlatch that was attended by Indian leaders and other dignitaries from Southeast Alaska. On this occasion the next chief in the Shakes line, Kudanake, age seventy-six, formally assumed the title of Shakes VII.

Shakes Island holds several totem poles from the Wrangell area. Some of the poles belonged to the Shakes clan, whereas others were copied from poles owned by neighboring clans. The two short poles directly in front of the house at the left are replicas of memorial poles. If you go around behind them, you can see the carved niches where the ashes of the deceased would have been placed.

The **Bear-up-the-Mountain pole,** with bear prints leading to the Bear figure at the top, is similar to the Kats pole at Totem Bight but recalls a different story. This pole commemorates the ancestors of the Shakes family who were led up the highest peak in the area by a grizzly bear to escape the great flood. The clan took Bear as their crest, and the pole symbolizes their tracks up the mountain to safety. The original version of this pole was a memorial to the younger brother of Chief Shakes VI.

To the left of the Bear-up-the-Mountain pole stands the **Double Whale Crest Hat,** or **Gonakadet pole.** The original version of this pole contained the ashes of Chief Shakes VI's father and mother. The carving recalls the story of a young man who slew a legendary lake monster called Gonakadet. The youth found that by putting on the monster's skin he could swim under the lake waters indefinitely and catch salmon and halibut for his family to eat. He had to return each morning, however, before the ravens called. One morning he failed to come home, and his wife found him dead on the beach, still inside the monster's skin. From that day on the village people called the youth by the name of Gonakadet. One night Gonakadet's wife heard him calling out to her to climb onto his back and hold on tight. She did as he bid, and he took her to his home beneath the water. Gonakadet and his wife are seen only occasionally, but the sighting is always considered good luck.

Stories of some of the other poles on Shakes Island are contained in a pamphlet entitled *The Authentic History of Shakes Island and Clan,* by E. L. Keithahn (Wrangell Historical Society). You can obtain a copy at the Wrangell Museum.

Chief Shakes's grave site is across the boat harbor from Shakes Island on the uphill side of Case Avenue. The plot is enclosed within a Russian-style picket fence with two Killer Whale totems on top. This is the grave site of Shakes V, who was head of the clan when the British occupied Wrangell and at the time of the American purchase.

Back in the center of town, the **First Presbyterian Church** on Church Street is known for the large, red, neon cross that shines for miles out to sea at night. Local mariners use the cross, erected in 1939, as a navigational light. The church is the oldest American protestant church in Alaska, dating from the time of the first mission school in Wrangell. The building, which was founded in 1879, was severely damaged by fire on two occasions and has been extensively renovated. The **Saint Rose of Lima Catholic Church** next door is the oldest Roman Catholic parish in Alaska.

The **Wrangell Museum,** which is temporarily located at 318 Church Street, will be relocated to the new James and Elsie Nolan Center in the summer of 2004. Summer hours are 10:00 A.M. to 5:00 P.M. Monday through Friday and 1:00 to 4:00 P.M. on Saturday (907–874–3770). The museum collection includes petroglyphs, which are rock carvings of undetermined age. They have been found on several beaches in Southeast Alaska. Archaeologists do not know

Detail of ceremonial Tlingit dance blanket in the Wrangell Museum shows beads and abalone-shell buttons.

their significance; some speculate they were a type of boundary marker. Some of the etched designs are clearly shaped like animals, others like human faces. Some just look like abstract scribbles. The most extensive known collection of petroglyphs in Southeast Alaska is at Wrangell's Petroglyph Beach north of town.

The museum, operated by the City of Wrangell, is devoted to local Wrangell history. Of the Native artifacts, one of the most interesting pieces is a ceremonial Tlingit dance blanket depicting a Bear design sewn by a Wrangell woman more than thirty years ago. The Bear totem is outlined in abalone-shell buttons and thousands of tiny beads. There are 232 buttons in the border alone. The collection includes carved wooden halibut hooks, cedar-bark and spruce-root baskets, and the original Chief Shakes House corner posts. The museum also exhibits a Tlingit spruce canoe, thought to be the only one left in existence.

The exhibit room also contains an assortment of items connected with Wrangell's rich and varied past: for example, small, lidded copper kettles of a type that the Hudson's Bay Company first sent to Canada around 1782, a Russian iron float used to suspend fishing nets, old cameras, and a collapsible wooden crate from Chas. Benjamin's store in Wrangell.

To get to **Petroglyph Beach,** a fifteen-minute walk from the ferry terminal or city dock, walk north on Evergreen Avenue. After a few minutes you will come to a barnlike building on the left with a sign that reads OUR COLLECTIONS. **Our Collections** is a hodgepodge of miscellanea that was lovingly gathered and protected over a lifetime in Wrangell by Elva Bigelow and her late husband, Bolly. Whether you should visit Elva's private museum is a matter of personal inclination. Some people find the Bigelow barn distressingly reminiscent of a garage in need of a cleaning. Others—the types who enjoy rooting around at garage sales—will wax poetic over the treadle and hand-crank sewing machines, old trapping gear, lanterns and binnacles, waffle irons, copper wash kettles, or cooperage tools. You may get a charge out of the old costume jewelry or the valve off the *Matanuska.* Our Collections is memorabilia, curiosities, and old things, in no particular rhyme or order. Much of the pleasure in viewing them comes from meeting the collector and hearing her stories about her things.

Petroglyph Beach lies another 0.3 mile beyond the Bigelow house. Start looking for the trail marker and sign just after you have passed a mobile-home park on the right. A wooden boardwalk leads from the road to the beach. There are perhaps forty different petroglyphs carved onto the rocks at this important site. You need a tide below the 12-foot level to find them. There are no directional signs, so locating them is something like an Easter egg hunt. Here are some hints: Turn right at the end of the boardwalk and walk along the beach, keeping your eyes on the rocks between you and the water. You will see strange images looking back at you. When you come to a large rock outcropping in front of a small building, walk straight toward the water. You should see a spiral on a nearby rock. Look to the right and you should see a big face.

Hunting for petroglyphs makes a pleasurable family expedition. The mysterious images, depicting birds, fish, sea mammals, and faces, appear and disappear according to the light and whether the rocks are wet or dry. In years past it has been something of a Wrangell tradition to make souvenir rubbings from the petroglyphs, using rice paper and a crayon. Archaeologists now frown on rubbings, however, for fear the carvings will be damaged. They recommend photographing the images instead, but this is tricky business. Local experts recommend using a polarizing filter to reduce glare and shooting in the late afternoon or evening, when maximum shadows enhance the design. Wetting the surface will help provide definition. The Forest Service sells souvenir rubber stamps with rock-art designs, including some from Wrangell glyphs.

Wrangell offers the usual complement of hiking trails, picnic spots, and other opportunities "out the road." **City Park,** about 1 mile south of town on Zimovia Highway, has waterfront picnic tables and shelters. At approximately mile 4.5, across from Shoemaker Harbor and Shoemaker Bay Recreational and RV Park, a short, easy trail leads through the rain forest to **Rainbow Falls,** a local favorite. For other destinations, contact the Forest Service (907–874–2323). In

Rock carvings have been found in many locations in Southeast Alaska. They may have been used as boundary markers.

addition to a host of interpretive programs offered on Saturday mornings, they have a pamphlet on hiking trails and recreational facilities in Wrangell.

The Stikine River is the backyard playground for Wrangell residents. Since 1980 the waterway has been protected as part of the 443,000-acre **Stikine–Le Conte Wilderness** that encompasses much of the mainland territory between Wrangell and Petersburg. The internationally navigable and historic waterway offers something for everyone: river and mountain scenery, glaciers, wildlife, fishing, boating, and camping. The broad, braided delta serves as a stopover for several hundred thousand migrating shorebirds, such as the western sandpiper. Snow geese, sandhill cranes, mergansers, and whistling (tundra) swans rest and feed on the river flats as well. During the April run of eulachon (a type of smelt), the delta hosts more than 1,500 bald eagles—the second-largest known concentration of bald eagles in the world (after the Chilkat River near Haines).

The arms and side sloughs of the Stikine nurture all five species of salmon and provide habitats for moose, brown bears, wolves, and many other creatures. The upper reaches of the river include some very enticing spots, such as Shakes Glacier and Chief Shakes Hot Springs, a Forest Service recreation facility with an enclosed wooden bathhouse in a forest glade and an outdoor tub overlooking a meadow of lupine and a distant mountain range (heavily, and sometimes rowdily, used by locals, especially on summer weekends). The mosquitoes can be fierce, but oh, the setting. . . .

A garnet ledge on the river delta is the site of a historic garnet mine. The ledge was deeded to the children of Wrangell and the Boy Scouts of America by one of Wrangell's civic leaders many years ago. Digging your own garnets is not necessary, though, as they are sold in local shops and by Wrangell children who greet ferry and cruise-ship passengers with muffin tins full of purple stones. Priced according to size (usually $1.00 to $5.00 each), they make inexpensive and unusual souvenirs.

Several local charter operators provide jet-boat service up the Stikine and will tailor the trip to your interests. Todd Harding of **Stickeen Wilderness Adventures** (P.O. Box 934, Wrangell, AK 99929; telephone 907–874–2085 or 800–874–2085) operates a variety of vessels, including the 50-foot, twenty-three-passenger *Stikine Princess,* built expressly to sightsee the Stikine.

Boat and floatplane charter operators can also take you to the **Le Conte Glacier,** 25 miles north of Wrangell, and to the **Anan Creek Bear and Wildlife Observatory,** 30 miles south on the mainland. During July and August the salmon spawning in Anan Creek attract a high concentration of black and brown bears, as well as eagles and harbor seals. The Forest Service has constructed a roofed observatory on a bluff overlooking a set of falls where the bears habitually fish. You can reach the observatory by a moderate 0.5-mile trail from the boat or floatplane anchorage.

Anan offers a unique opportunity to view and photograph bears in their natural habitat. This is not a game park or a zoo; the bears are not contained or restrained, so certain rules must be followed to maximize safety for both animals and humans. Please follow the instructions given by your guide or the Forest Service personnel on site.

There is also a Forest Service recreation cabin on Anan Bay, a mile from the observatory via a planked trail, but it is heavily used so make your reservations well in advance. The cabin costs $25 per night. For more information contact the U.S. Forest Service, Wrangell Ranger District, P.O. Box 51, Wrangell, AK 99929; telephone (907) 874-2323.

Alaskan Hidden Treasure Charters (907-874-3999) operates tours of the Stikine River; in addition, they offer excursions to Telegraph Creek, fishing charters, and a tour to the Anan Creek Bear and Wildlife Observatory.

The visitor center can provide you with a complete list of charter companies. When booking with some of the smaller charters, it is recommended that you make your reservations six to seven months in advance, as this will guarantee that your tour actually goes out that day (walk-ins the day of an excursion are not always guaranteed a spot).

One new addition to the Wrangell recreation scene is a nine-hole golf course named **Muskeg Meadows,** which is located near the airport. This regulation course, which includes a 250-yard driving range, is carved into a beautiful rain forest. With its ocean and mountain views, it promises a truly memorable experience. This is a challenging course for all golfers, as there are many unique hazards to deal with, including the Raven Rule, which states that a ball stolen by a raven can be replaced with no penalty—as long as there's a witness. Local stores rent clubs and can provide transportation to the course. More information is available from Muskeg Meadows at (907) 874-4654 or visit www.wrangellalaskagolf.com.

Special Events

Like other small towns, Wrangell puts on a rousing down-home **Fourth of July celebration** with fireworks, a loggers' rodeo, and a parade. Local residents contend that Wrangell's loggers' contests are better than those of other communities because real loggers compete instead of professional contestants drawn by the prize money offered elsewhere. Wrangellites also host a **Polar Bear Swim** in January and the **Tent City Winter Festival** on the first weekend in February to celebrate the role that Wrangell played in three gold rushes and to give residents some relief from the winter wearies. There is a food-and-craft fair and lighthearted contests such as beard-growing and tall tales. The **Garnet Festival,** celebrating the history of garnet mining, is held in April. The Wrangell **King Salmon Derby** and **Muskeg Meadows Annual Golf Tournament** take place in May. Like many other Southeast communities, Wrangell also hosts a **Bear and Beer Festival** to toast local brews and honor the bears of Anan. And there is a **Festival of Lights** and **Christmas Tree Ceremony** in early December.

PETERSBURG
Population 3,224

Petersburg stands out from the other Southeast communities by virtue of its Norwegian heritage. The townspeople celebrate their Scandinavian origins during the renowned Little Norway Festival that takes place annually on Norwegian Independence Day (the third weekend in May) and in the attractive *rosemaling* (traditional Norwegian tole painting in floral design) that garnishes shopfronts and homes. It is a neat community with prim houses and careful yards.

Along with the Norwegian heritage comes fishing. This is a cannery town. With four seafood-processing plants and the largest

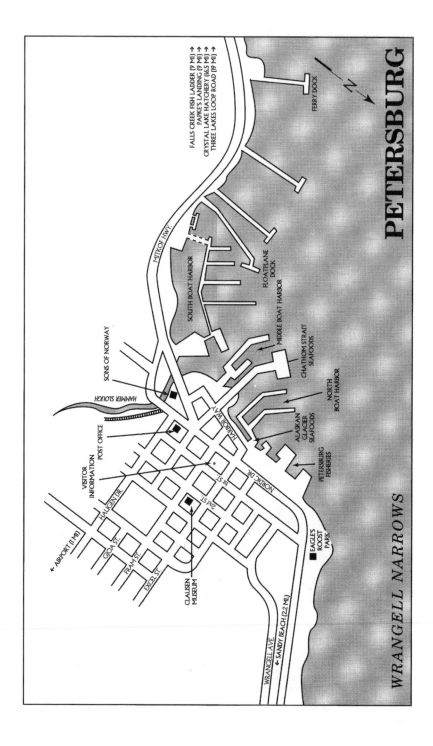

PETERSBURG

Falls Creek Fish Ladder (9 MI) →
Papke's Landing (9 MI) →
Crystal Lake Hatchery (16.5 MI) →
Three Lakes Loop Road (19 MI) →

FERRY DOCK

N

MITKOF HWY.

SOUTH BOAT HARBOR

SONS OF NORWAY

HAMMER SLOUGH

POST OFFICE

VISITOR
INFORMATION

HALGEN DR.

AIRPORT (1 MI) ←

GJOA ST.

FRAM ST.

EXCEL ST.

1st ST.

2nd ST.

CLAUSEN
MUSEUM

WRANGELL AVE.

SANDY BEACH (2.2 MI) ←

NORDIC DR.

HARBOR WAY

FLOATPLANE
DOCK

MIDDLE BOAT HARBOR

CHATHAM STRAIT
SEAFOODS

NORTH
BOAT HARBOR

ALASKAN
GLACIER
SEAFOODS

PETERSBURG
FISHERIES

EAGLE'S
ROOST PARK

WRANGELL NARROWS

home-based halibut fleet in Southeast, fish and fishing are the dominant themes. Even the streets are named for famous old boats of the commercial fishing fleet.

Except for the Little Norway Festival, there is little organized activity planned around tourists in Petersburg. The streets are refreshingly bare of curio and T-shirt shops. But there is plenty to see and do in this town of friendly, hardworking Norwegians.

Background

Petersburg is situated on the northern tip of Mitkof Island. It is the last stop for most northbound ferries before reaching Juneau and is the prize that awaits mariners who have navigated the 21-mile Wrangell Narrows.

The town was founded by Peter Buschmann, who emigrated from Norway to Tacoma, Washington, with his wife and eight children in 1891. Six years later he was homesteading a site along Wrangell Narrows that showed potential for a year-round fish-processing industry. Not only were both salmon and halibut in abundance, but there was a natural harbor, timber with which to build, and a ready supply of ice from the Le Conte Glacier just 25 miles away.

The Petersburg harbor affords a fantastic view of the snowcapped peaks that guard the Wrangell Narrows. MICHELLE GURNEY

Other Norwegians followed Buschmann to his spot on Wrangell Narrows, and they set to work developing a neat, well-planned, Scandinavian-style community. By 1900 the Icy Straits Packing Company, with Buschmann as manager, had constructed a sawmill, wharf, warehouses, bunkhouses, and store and had packed 32,750 cases of salmon. The fishermen brought in salmon for the cannery in summer and fall and harvested halibut in winter. Peter Buschmann's new community, called Petersburg, grew into a stable, year-round enterprise, in contrast to the mining towns that were subject to cycles of boom-and-bust.

The salmon industry proved successful, but it was halibut that put Petersburg on the map. Packed in glacier ice, the fine white fish was shipped by steamer to Seattle and forwarded directly to eager East Coast markets. Petersburg emerged as the halibut capital of Alaska and remains so today.

At the height of the cannery era, as many as eight seafood-processing plants operated simultaneously in Petersburg. The town remains the major fish-processing community in Southeast, with three processing plants and a reduction plant that produces fish meal from scraps. Petersburg Fisheries, Buschmann's old company (now a subsidiary of Icicle Seafoods), has operated continuously since its founding. Besides salmon and halibut, the town processes crab, herring, prawns, and the tiny, delectable Petersburg shrimp that are fished within a 25-mile radius of town. Petersburg ships 150,000 pounds of shrimp to market annually.

Getting There

As with nearly all Inside Passage communities, access is by water or air only. The trip between Wrangell and Petersburg via the 21-mile Wrangell Narrows is among the most exciting legs of the Marine Highway. Alaska state ferries make the trip on the regular north/south run. The ferry terminal is about 1 mile south of town. Few cruise ships currently include Petersburg in their Southeast itineraries. Those that do—mostly the smaller "exploration class" vessels—dock right downtown at one of the boat harbors. There is daily jet service on Alaska Airlines between Petersburg and other Southeast communities, with connections to the rest of Alaska and the

Lower 48, and scheduled commuter airline service to Juneau on Wings of Alaska and LAB Flying Service.

To See and Do

Petersburg is an artist's delight, whether the medium is oils, watercolors, or color film. So many images leap to the eye, from kerchiefed cannery workers in tall rubber boots to old wooden buildings reflected in Hammer Slough. A walk around town rewards you with scenes of three boat harbors and the halibut fleet, canneries, rosemalinged storefronts and housefronts, and the natural scenery of Wrangell Narrows. Make your first stop the **Petersburg Visitors Information Center**—a joint effort of the Chamber of Commerce and the U.S. Forest Service—at First and Fram Streets, where you can acquire a town map and Mitkof Island road guide. It is also a good idea to pick up a copy of the **Viking Visitor Guide,** which includes a lengthy listing of things to do in Petersburg, and a copy of the hiking trails booklet, as well as an Alaska tide table. The folks at this information center are extremely knowledgeable about the area and are able to answer any questions you throw their way.

The seafood plants of **Petersburg Fisheries** (Buschmann's old company) and **Norquest Seafoods Inc.** lie at the north end of town. You can take a half-hour tour of the latter with lifelong Petersburg resident Patti Norheim, whose father started the shrimp cannery in 1916. Call **Tongass Traveler Tours,** (907) 772-4837. Depending on the season, you'll see shrimp, crab, salmon, or halibut being processed. **Tonka Seafoods,** a small specialty processor, also offers tours. Call (907) 772-3662. Tours of the other processors are not available, but there's plenty of activity visible from the docks.

Continuing past Petersburg Fisheries on Nordic Drive, you'll round a bend to the north and see Wrangell Narrows opening up into Frederick Sound. **Eagle's Roost Park,** on the left, captures the view with a hilltop garden, picnic tables, benches, and stairs leading down to the beach. Bald eagles perch in the trees at this site overlooking their prime fishing grounds. The road continues about a mile north of town to **Sandy Beach Recreation Area,** where you can see petroglyphs at low tide (fifty minutes earlier every day). The carvings adorn a rock at the north end of the beach on the water side

A boatload of Dungeness crab arrives at the Petersburg Fisheries dock. Petersburg is still a major fish-processing community.

(check your Alaska tide table to ensure a visit at low tide). Although these carvings have not been dated, scientists believe they are related to fish traps and reflect Tlingit religious or spiritual beliefs.The Frederick Point Boardwalk has been replaced by Cabin Creek Road, which leads to the city's new reservoir. A 1-mile walk on the new dirt road will bring visitors to a set of stairs that lead to the **City Creek walking bridge,** where salmon can sometimes be seen.

Back in town on Nordic Drive, look in at any of the local galleries for silver jewelry and paintings by local and regional artists and **Lee's Clothing** for imported Icelandic and Norwegian sweaters or any other gear you may need to replace. In the vicinity are galleries where local artists display their work, **Sing Lee Alley Books,** and **Helse** restaurant and natural foods store, patronized for homemade soup and bread, muffins, sandwiches, and brownies—which disappear fast. **Alaskafe** (306B Nordic Drive) is also worth a stop. They have a nice selection of paninis, coffees, and pastries, as well as an Internet connection.

At the south end of town, stilt houses line the narrow, wood-planked street above **Hammer Slough.** The barnlike **Sons of Norway Hall,** begun by founder Peter Buschmann in 1897 and completed in 1912, stands on pilings at the entrance to the saltwater inlet. The oft-photographed hall, painted white with red rosemalinged shutters, still hosts the local chapter of the International Sons of Norway, who work to preserve the town's Norwegian heritage.

Beside the Sons of Norway Hall you will see the **Bojerwikan Fishermen's Memorial Park.** Dedicated May 20, 2000, the park is sponsored and maintained by the Sons of Norway and the City of Petersburg. Its purpose is to commemorate and acknowledge the members of the community who have been lost at sea or who have spent much of their lives working in the fishing industry for their families and the Petersburg community.

The **Clausen Memorial Museum** (Second and Fram Streets) focuses on local history and community life, especially commercial fishing. Exhibits include the world's largest king salmon (estimated weight 126.5 pounds), captured in a fish trap off Prince of Wales Island in 1939, and the record chum salmon (36 pounds). Interest-

Weathered houses on stilts line the shore of Hammer Slough, where the street is still planked with wood.

ing displays illustrate the operation of different types of commercial fishing gear. You will also find a model fish trap, old cotton and linen fishing nets, early canning equipment and outboard engines, the lens from the Cape Decision lighthouse, and relics from fox farming and whaling.

Exhibits pertaining to early Petersburg include photos and belongings of founder Peter Buschmann and his wife, Petra, and household objects of the period, such as a wooden hat stretcher and high-top shoes. Persons familiar with Norwegian custom will know of the traditional dress, the *bunad,* which differs from region to region. The museum has on display the bright blue Petersburg bunad, embroidered with Alaskan wildflowers.

Outside the museum stands the ***Fisk*** (Norwegian for "fish"), a bronze fountain sculpture of halibut, salmon, and herring. Former Petersburg artist Carson Boysen created the work for the 1967 Alaska Centennial as a celebration of all Southeast fish. A similar theme inspired the wood-and-copper mural on the outside wall of the museum, a community project organized by the Petersburg Arts and Crafts Guild in 1977.

With a free afternoon in Petersburg, you may want to visit **Viking Travel** (101 North Nordic Drive; 907-772-3818) to find out about any interesting excursions they have planned, or call **Tongass Kayak Adventures** (907-772-4600) and explore Peterburg's shoreline. You might also rent a bicycle or a car and explore the **Mitkof Highway.** The road passes the Alaska state ferry terminal and extends southward along Wrangell Narrows to mile 34.

At approximately mile 10 you come to the **Falls Creek Fish Ladder.** Stairs lead from the parking area to a bridge from which you can watch migrating coho and pink salmon maneuver upstream in late summer and fall. Just past the sign to the fish ladder, look for another road on the right to **Papke's Landing,** a favorite recreation spot overlooking Wrangell Narrows. There is a state float and boat-launch ramp, and the entrance road is a riot of fireweed and other wildflowers in July. Kupreanof Island is only a few yards away. The site is named for Herman Papke, who homesteaded the area in 1903. "Ol' Man Papke" lived alone in his log cabin, raised a bountiful garden, and observed the happenings around him, which he recorded every day in his diary for some sixty years. He died in 1964—among the most beloved of area residents and definitely not forgotten.

At approximately mile 14 a planked Forest Service trail (barrier-free) takes you a third of a mile across the muskeg to **Blind River Rapids,** a beautiful spot with excellent king salmon fishing in July, coho in late August and September, and cutthroat and Dolly Varden in late summer and fall. Two miles farther south a sign points to the **Trumpeter Swan Observatory,** a simple blind positioned to overlook Blind Slough. One of the northernmost wintering areas for trumpeter swans, Blind Slough attracts fifty to one hundred birds between late October and April. Several hundred additional swans stop over during their southward migration to other wintering grounds along the northwest coast. The **Crystal Lake Hatchery** at mile 17.5 is worth a stop. It produces more than a million king salmon and hundreds of thousands of coho and steelhead annually in the outdoor rearing pens. Visitors are welcome to have a look around. Walk past the adult holding pen and onto the viewing bridge where you will spot a stream filled with adult salmon in July. Because of the abundance of fish, this is also an excellent viewing site for bald eagles. The adjacent **Blind Slough Recreation Area** has picnic shelters and grills and is a popular swimming hole for locals.

At mile 22 you come to **Ohmer Creek Campground**—with just ten spots, it is nice and quiet. The **Ohmer Creek Trail** (barrier-free), located just next to the campsite, follows the creek through a mature rain forest. This interpretive trail leads anglers to good fishing spots along the creek. On your way back to town, consider the **Three Lakes Loop Road,** an old logging road that leaves Mitkof Highway to the north at mile 20 and loops through hills and forest to rejoin the highway near Papke's Landing. The road winds through some beautiful country with vistas of trees, wildflowers, and water. Short trails (less than 0.5 mile) give access to three large freshwater lakes (Sand, Hill, and Crane) that harbor small populations of cutthroat trout. The Three Lakes area was once the site of considerable logging activity but is now used primarily for recreation. Enjoy a picnic or hike; take some photographs and watch the wildlife. In winter Petersburg residents frequent the area for ice fishing, snowmobiling, and Nordic skiing.

Still have time to spare in Petersburg? Head down to the south harbor at high tide and watch for the Steller's sea lions, who occasionally follow fish into the harbor to feed. This community also has a swimming pool, **Melvin Roundtree Memorial Pool,** and a gym. Schedules are available at the visitor center, where you will also find information on the local movie theater. And if you happen to see any yellow-and-black bicycles around town, the Parks and Recreation Department sponsors those. Use of the bikes is free, but please park them at Tent City, just up the road from Sandy Beach, once you are finished.

Excursions from Petersburg center on the **Le Conte Glacier,** 25 miles to the east. The southernmost tidewater glacier in North America, the Le Conte flows into Frederick Sound from the Stikine Ice Field in the Coast Mountains. This glacier has remained relatively stable since the mid-1960s, although it did retreat about 0.5 mile between winter 1994 and spring 1996. The terminus is very active and produces a continuous crop of icebergs along the mile-wide face. Some 2,000 harbor seals live in Le Conte Bay and rear their pups on the glacier icebergs. Boat, floatplane, and helicopter excursions to the glacier are readily available from Petersburg. Check in with **TEMSCO Helicopters** (located at the airport; 907-772-4780) or at **Viking Travel** (101 North Nordic Drive; 907-772-3818). For a truly tailored trip, contact **Petersburg Vacations** (877-442-4010), a new company offering custom vacation packages.

Special Events

The full glory of Petersburg's Norwegian heritage erupts the third weekend of May during the **Little Norway Festival.** Folk dancing, costumes, halibut-filleting contests, and Viking raids characterize this annual celebration of Norwegian Independence Day. Tables groan under the weight of fish cakes and puddings, gravad lox, lutefisk, and an array of Norwegian desserts—all prepared by the good Norwegian cooks in town. There is also a salmon bake at Sandy Beach. The **Petersburg Salmon Derby** takes place on Memorial Day weekend, and the community salutes U.S. **Independence Day** with an old-fashioned Fourth of July. Other annual festivities: **Octoberfest,** featuring an arts and crafts fair, and a **Festival of Lights** to kick off the Christmas season.

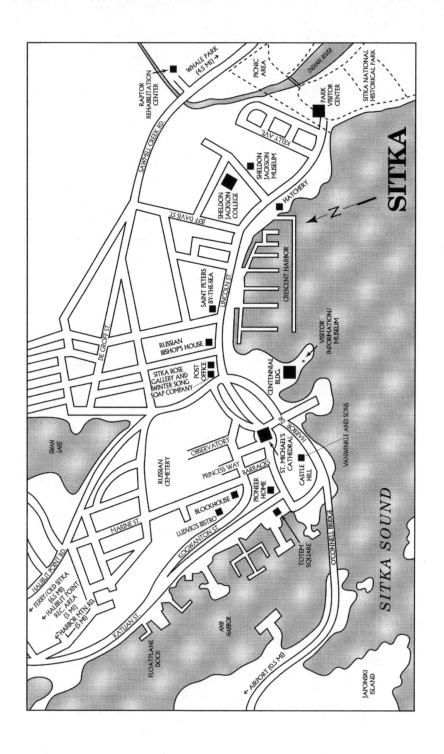

SITKA
Population 8,835

As a visitor destination, Sitka enjoys an unfair advantage over other Southeast cities. The setting is unbelievably spectacular, from the countless forested islands that bob and weave upon Sitka Sound to the perfectly symmetrical cone of Mount Edgecumbe that rises to the west. Add to that the exotic Russian heritage, the fabulous totem park, and the attractive city center that corrals all the important sights within easy walking distance of the harbor. Even the lodgings have a touch of the extraordinary: In Sitka can you book a stay in a faux lighthouse on a private island.

The Sitkans have put their Russian pedigree to good advantage, from their widely acclaimed Russian dance troupe to bus drivers in tunics who meet the ferries. Saint Michael's Russian Orthodox Cathedral dominates the heart of town. Orthodox crosses in the old Russian graveyard and blackened cannons on Castle Hill are other relics of a foreign heritage.

Sitka takes pride in being a cultural center and college town. The community supports two colleges, two libraries, two museums, and a national historical park containing one of the largest exhibitions of Tlingit and Haida totem poles in existence. The annual Sitka Summer Music Festival unites outstanding musicians from all corners of the United States and abroad, while the Sitka Symposium, held concurrently, draws guest writers of an equally high caliber.

Big changes have occurred in the Sitka economy in recent years. In 1993 the Japanese-owned Sitka pulp mill—the city's largest employer—closed; however, tourism and major health facilities with a regionwide constituency have done an amazing job of picking up the slack. Prospects for the future look bright.

Background

Sitka is situated on the west coast of Baranof Island on Sitka Sound, a body of water that faces the open Pacific. The site of the Russian capital after 1804, the town is the oldest non-Native settlement in Southeast. Sitka was home to a community of Tlingit Indians prior to the Russian arrival. When Alexander Baranof, chief manager of the Russian-American Company, decided to move the Russian headquarters from Kodiak in 1799, he bargained with the local Tlingit chief for ground for a fort. The completed post, consisting of various outbuildings enclosed within a wooden stockade, was located 6 miles north of the present town and called Saint Archangel Michael.

The Tlingit grew increasingly hostile toward the Russians and the Aleut hunters they brought with them from Kodiak. Armed with guns and ammunition received from English and American traders in the area, they attacked the fort on a Sunday in June of 1802, burned the buildings, and killed all the occupants except the few who managed to escape into the woods to take refuge aboard foreign trading vessels in Sitka Sound.

Baranof, who was away at Kodiak at the time of the massacre, immediately began making plans to retake Saint Archangel Michael. The battle was joined in September 1804, the Tlingit making their stand from a wooden stronghold near the beach at Indian River (the site of the present-day historical park), and the Russians bombarding with cannons. After several days of negotiations, interspersed with shelling, the Tlingit abandoned the site and retreated northward to Chichagof Island. The Russians built a new settlement where Sitka is located today, calling it New Archangel. By the following spring they had completed eight buildings within a wooden stockade and cleared land for gardens and livestock. Shipyards were established two years later.

The Tlingit Indians were allowed to return to Baranof Island in 1821. They rebuilt their homes around the Russian encampment, outnumbering the colonists about three to one. The Russians were in constant fear of another uprising, but their food supplies were low, and they depended upon the Tlingits' superior hunting skills to provide meat to be purchased for the table.

New Archangel reached the height of activity and stability in the 1840s and 1850s. Besides the fur business, the settlement bustled with shipbuilding and repair facilities, sawmills, a forge and foundry, a salmon saltery, and even an ice industry that shipped blocks of lake ice to California markets. The colony expanded to include schools, a hospital, a library, a clubhouse, and Saint Michael's Cathedral. The crowning jewel was the governor's residence, built at the top of a hill overlooking the harbor. A seal-oil beacon was kept burning in the cupola window, and a 3-foot-diameter reflector projected the light 6 miles out to sea to guide mariners into the harbor. This was the first lighthouse on the Alaska coast. The interior, furnished with fine European furniture, rugs, paintings, and a library, was considered a haven of culture and enlightenment for European traders who plied the lonely waters of the North Pacific coast. Although rebuilt many times, the structure came to be known as Baranof's Castle and the hilltop site as Castle Hill. Today Castle Hill remains a monument to the Russian colony, but the last castle burned down in 1894.

When the fur trade declined, the Alaska colonies became expensive to maintain. With both British and American traders threatening the Russian prerogative, the political situation was uncomfortable, and renewal of the Russian-American Company charter was in question besides. Russia decided to give up Alaska, and in October of 1867 the Russian flag was lowered from Castle Hill and the American flag raised in its place. The Americans changed the name of the community to Sitka, a derivation of the Tlingit word for their forested island by the sea.

The years following the Russian departure were lean ones for Sitka. Employment centered on the sawmill, which operated intermittently, and fishing. Sitka was the site of one of the first two salmon canneries built in Alaska in 1878 (the other was at Klawock on Prince of Wales Island). The plant folded after two years, however, and Sitka did not become a successful fish-processing center until after 1900.

The gold rush caught up to the community at about the same time. Prospectors had been poking around Baranof Island, like other places, and there were attempts at lode mining in the vicinity as early as 1871. A rush to Sitka followed the discovery of gold-bearing quartz at Stewart Ledge on Silver Bay, slightly southeast of Sitka. In 1879 George Pilz built Alaska's first stamp mill on the Stewart claim. (Pilz would also finance the two vagabond prospectors who located the Juneau lode the following year.) In the years that followed, other mining efforts were made on nearby Chichagof Island. The two biggest Chichagof gold mines produced consistently until World War II closed them down. Gypsum was also mined on Chichagof for a seventeen-year period beginning in 1906.

A mission school opened in 1878 under the auspices of the United Presbyterian church and evolved into an industrial trade school for Native students. The school continues at present as Sheldon Jackson College, a private four-year institution specializing in fisheries management, forestry, wildlife management, and other Alaska fields of interest. The college is named for Dr. Sheldon Jackson who, as general agent for education in Alaska's infancy, is credited with establishing the state's school system. With the founding of Sheldon Jackson College, Sitka was on the way to reestablishing itself as a cultural center, but in 1906 the capital of Alaska was transferred to Juneau, where the predominant gold-mining activity had centered.

The whaling industry moved onto Baranof Island in 1912 when the U.S. Whaling Company established a shore station at Port Armstrong on the south end of the island. Using a fleet of three modern "killing boats" with bow-mounted harpoons, the company harvested 314 whales the first year. The station processed the entire carcass, extracting oil and turning leftovers into fertilizer. When the whaling operation ceased in 1923, the Port Armstrong facility continued as a herring-reduction plant.

The next surge of development came with the military in the late 1930s, when a U.S. naval air station was built on Japonski Island, across Sitka Harbor from the city. World War II brought an army fort as well, and suddenly Sitka was host to 30,000 military personnel and 7,000 civilians. It was also at this time that Harbor Mountain Road was built. The 6-mile-long road to the summit would take military personnel to a lookout built to protect army and navy installations in the Sitka area. After the war the naval station was converted to the Bureau of Indian Affairs' Mount Edgecumbe boarding school to accommodate Native high school students from all over Alaska. Harbor Mountain has become a popular summer recreation spot for locals. Since 1972 the facilities on Japonski Island (which also include the Sitka airport), have been brought within easy reach by the 1,225-foot O'Connell Bridge from Sitka. Mount Edgecumbe boarding school continues as a unique high school that attracts students from all ethnic groups and all corners of Alaska to pursue a curriculum focused on Pacific Rim studies. An entrepreneurial pro-

The view as you drive down from the summit of Harbor Mountain. MICHELLE GURNEY

gram provides hands-on experience on the import-export trade, and language requirements specify competence in Japanese or Mandarin Chinese.

Presently Sitka's economy is supported by two colleges (Sheldon Jackson College and the University of Alaska/Southeast), tourism, commercial fishing and fish processing, and health facilities, which provide services for Native patients from throughout Southeast Alaska. Besides housing a sizable commercial fishing fleet, the town has two fish-processing plants, the newest a cold-storage facility built in 1980 to process salmon, black cod, herring, and halibut. The Alaska Pulp Corporation mill, built 6 miles east of town in 1960, closed in 1993.

Getting There

Sitka figures in most cruise-ship itineraries. The vessels usually run down the outside coast of Baranof Island after visiting Glacier Bay and anchor in Sitka harbor opposite town. Alaska state ferries dock at the Marine Highway terminal 7 miles north of town near Old Sitka, the site of the first Russian settlement. In summer buses meet every ferry and offer shuttle service to downtown lodgings and ferry stopover tours of Sitka sights—the service is available twenty-four hours a day and guaranteed to get you back before sailing. Sitka is also serviced by Alaska Airlines on the Seattle-to-Juneau route as well as from Anchorage. The airport is located on Japonski Island, across O'Connell Bridge from the downtown area.

To See and Do

Your first destination should be the **Sitka Convention and Visitors Bureau** at 303 Lincoln Street, on the second floor. An information desk is located at Harrigan Centennial Hall (overlooking Sitka Sound near the cruise-ship embarkation point), where you will find maps, brochures, and other information. Check on the performance schedule of the Sitka **New Archangel Russian Dancers** (907-747-5516), a women's dance troupe that has entranced audiences with authentic Russian, Byelorussian, Moldavian, and Ukranian folk dances since 1969. You should also check in with Tribal Tours (907-747-7290 or 888-270-9697, ext. 13) to find out when the **Naa Kahidi Dancers** are performing. This troupe tells the story of the creation of the Tlingit dance, accompanied by musical recordings from the early 1900s. While you are in Centennial Hall, take a turn through the **Isabel Miller Museum,** devoted to items from local history. An extensive scale model of Sitka shows how the community looked during the Russian era. Exhibits from the Russian tenancy include ice saws that were used to cut blocks of ice from Swan Lake for shipment to San Francisco during the gold rush.

Other displays feature enterprises of later years, including fishing, logging, and gold mining (note the mold for forming gold bricks). Of special interest: copies of documents pertaining to the Alaska Purchase agreement and a copy of the actual warrant for $7.2 million (the original is in the Smithsonian Institution in Washington, D.C.).

During summer at the other end of the Centennial Hall, members of the **Baranof Arts and Crafts Association** proffer a selection of recent work. There is also a small wildlife display of bald eagles, sea otters, fur seals, beavers, Arctic foxes, and other fur-bearing animals and pelts.

Outside the building stands a 50-foot ceremonial canoe carved by local woodworker George Benson for the Alaska Purchase Centennial commemoration in 1967. The canoe was hollowed from a single 70-foot red-cedar log that was towed to Sitka from Port Renfrew, British Columbia, behind a fishing boat. The painted totemic designs represent Eagle and Raven, the two major phratries, or social divisions, in Tlingit and Haida culture. On one side of the canoe, Eagle is on the prow and Raven on the stern. The order is reversed on the opposite side.

Leaving the Centennial Hall with map in hand, take a stroll through town. **Saint Michael's Russian Orthodox Cathedral,** which straddles Lincoln Street, the main thoroughfare, and dominates the skyline, is a replica of the original cathedral that was built on the site between 1844 and 1848. In 1966 the old church was destroyed by a fire that swept through the business district. The townspeople rushed in and managed to save almost all the precious icons and other furnishings that had been brought from Russia in the early days of the church. A National Historic Landmark, the cathedral was rebuilt in 1976 from blueprints that architects had created only shortly before the fire to record the exact measurements of the historic structure.

The architecture, a mixture of bulbous onion dome and delicate spire, reflects a combination of styles that was common around Saint Petersburg at the time of the Russian occupation. Natural-colored canvas (originally sailcloth) covers the interior walls. The dome is painted sky blue on the inside, and the windows set around the top flood this artificial heaven with natural light.

The cathedral is a showcase of icons (sacred images or paintings) brought to Alaska from Russia. The two most prized are *Our Lady of Sitka,* familiarly known as the "Sitka Madonna," and *Christ Pantocrator* (Christ the Judge or Christ Omnipotent) that flank the doors of the altar screen. Both paintings are attributed to Vladimir Borovikovsky, a leading eighteenth-century portrait artist and one of Russia's most revered masters. The Sitka Madonna, the oldest of the icons and thought to have been the gift of the Russian-American Company employees, is regarded by many faithful as a miraculous healer and protectress. At Saturday evening services, letters are read from faithful the world over petitioning the Sitka Madonna to intercede on their behalf. The painting, of a gentle-faced madonna hold-

Sitka's Saint Michael's Cathedral is a prominent reminder of the Russian influence.

ing the Christ Child, is oil on canvas overlaid with a heavy silver-gilt *riza*. (The riza, or metal overlay, often elaborately carved or sculpted, became common in seventeenth-century Russia as a means of honoring and protecting the sacred image.) Another cherished icon, Saint Michael the Archangel, patron saint of the cathedral, was brought to Sitka in 1816 by the first ordained priest.

Other interesting items within the cathedral: the carved and painted doors in the altar screen, saved from the original church; silver-gilt wedding crowns dating from 1866; Bishop Innocent Veniaminov's pearl-encrusted miter; and a 13-inch silver-gilt tabernacle with cloisonné cupola and steeple modeled after the cathedral.

Saint Michael's Cathedral is the seat of the Russian Orthodox church in Alaska; the bishop travels from Sitka to parish churches throughout the state. The cathedral is a working church with an active congregation and regular services, to which visitors are always welcome.

As you walk through Sitka, you may notice small white-and-blue road signs that say TSUNAMI EVACUATION ROUTE. The signs are in place to direct visitors to higher ground in the unlikely event there is ever a threat to human safety. **Lincoln Street** is lined with enticing shops and galleries. **Impressions Gallery, Artists' Cove Gallery, Mojo's Cafe and Lunch Spot,** and **Old Harbor Books** are especially worth your while. Behind the bookshop the inviting **Backdoor Cafe** draws an artsy crowd for espresso, pastries, and sandwiches. On Sunday mornings local performers gather here to play their accordions and guitars and to recite poetry. **Abby's Reflections Apparel & Quiltworks** (231 Lincoln) sells original Alaskan cross-stitch and needlepoint patterns. At **Three Guys by the Church** (235 Lincoln), you'll find unique necklaces of rare beads and polished ivory created by Sitka artist Phil Slattery, and at **Fairweather Prints** (209 Lincoln), you'll drool over colorful hand-silkscreened and hand-painted garments of "wearable art" (lots of fish art) produced in a Sitka studio. At 236 Lincoln Street you'll come across **Pizza Express.** The atmosphere isn't great, but the food is. Originally from Puerta Vallarta, the owners prepare excellent Mexican cuisine, and based on the comments from neighboring tables, the pizza is quite good as well.

Also check out the **Russian-American Company** in the Bayview

Trading Company (407 Lincoln) for Russian imports such as carved wooden toys, wool shawls, and lacquerware. For a substantial meal go to **Van Winkle & Sons** (205 Harbor Drive), a block from the Centennial Hall, for their specialty, Northwestern cuisine. They also have wonderful fresh seafood specials.

A short path leads to the top of **Castle Hill.** Castle Hill was the site of a Tlingit Indian village when Alexander Baranof reestablished the Russian fort in 1804. The Russians destroyed the Indian houses and built their own quarters with the manager's residence at the top. In time the residence came to be known as Baranof's Castle and the hilltop site as Castle Hill. The castle was rebuilt twice before fire destroyed the structure completely in 1894.

On October 18, 1867, Castle Hill was the site of transfer ceremonies between Russia and the United States as the Russian flag came down and the Stars and Stripes was raised in its place. The transfer is reenacted at the site every October 18 as part of the Alaska Day celebration. Several Russian cannons still guard the hilltop (note the double-eagle insignia), and historic markers explain the significance of Castle Hill. Over the past several years, archaeologists have uncovered 40,000 artifacts from Alaska's past. The dig was completed in 1998. The site offers a sweeping view over Sitka Sound and is barrier-free.

The large red-roofed building across Lincoln Street is the **Pioneer Home,** a state-supported residence and medical-care facility for Alaska's longtime residents. There are several Pioneer Homes in the state. Sitka's, built in 1934, was the first. The 13½-foot bronze statue of a prospector in front of the home was created by Alonzo Victor Lewis in 1949. The residents and staff of the Pioneer Home welcome visitors. They are especially proud of their gardens, planted with native Alaska species, and a basement shop, which sells handicrafts made by residents. **Totem Square,** across Katlian Street from the Pioneer Home, contains a Russian cannon and three anchors recovered from the Sitka vicinity, probably lost by early British or American explorers. The totem pole, designed by local carver George Benson in 1940, displays the double-headed eagle of Sitka's Russian heritage.

Continue along to 256 Katlian Avenue to **Ludvig's Bistro.** Opened in fall 2002, the bistro is the expansion of a highly successful catering operation run and owned by Colette Nelson and Lisa Bower. It's a cozy spot with a warm atmosphere—and even better, the food, which they refer to as "rustic Mediterranean fare," is fabulous. To avoid disappointment call (907) 966-3663 to make dinner reservations, or just pop in for a hearty lunch.

To walk off your meal, continue along Katlian Avenue to view dozens of bald eagles. If they're not swooping overhead, they're in the

The prospector stands outside Sitka's Pioneer Home, a state-supported residence and medical-care facility. MICHELLE GURNEY

treetops across the street from the Seafood Producers Co-operative.

Uphill from the Pioneer Home, you'll see the **Russian block-house**—a replica of the type the Russians built to guard their stockade. Three such structures stood sentry along the wall separating the Indian village from the Russian community. Old headstones and Orthodox crosses mark the adjacent **Russian cemetery.** The only original Russian building still standing in Sitka is the **Russian Bishop's House** on Lincoln Street at the opposite end of town from Totem Square. While en route, stop in at the **Sitka Rose Gallery** at 419 Lincoln Street to see a lovely selection of local art, or walk through the gallery into the **WinterSong Soap Company,** which is also inside this beautiful Victorian home. Handcrafted soaps, salves, and bath products will likely be in production as you visit. The bright yellow building on the next block is the Bishop's House. The house—the oldest building in Alaska that has not been significantly altered and one of the few remaining Russian log structures in Alaska—was built in 1842 by the Russian-American Company to house Bishop Innocent Veniaminov, the first bishop of the Russian Orthodox Church. The church continued to use the facility until 1972. Now owned by the National Park Service, the Bishop's House received a $4.5 million restoration as part of Sitka National Historical Park. Visitors can view the bishop's study, private apartments, and chapel, restored to their 1850s appearance. The fee is $3.00 per person. All but one of the icons in the chapel were in the original house.

A grassy esplanade takes you the short distance along Crescent Boat Harbor to Sheldon Jackson College and the main portion of Sitka National Historical Park. Just past the Russian Bishop's House you will come to the stone and brown-shingled **Saint Peters-by-the-Sea Episcopal Church,** built in 1899. A few more steps bring you to the state-owned **Sheldon Jackson Museum.** The octagonal concrete structure was built in 1895 as a repository for the articles that Dr. Sheldon Jackson collected in remote areas of Alaska during his travels as general agent for education. The collection of Alaskan Indian, Eskimo, and Aleut artifacts is one of the most important in the world.

When you walk through the door, look up: On top of the display cases and suspended from the ceiling are examples of all the tradi-

The Sheldon Jackson Museum has a rich collection of Native artifacts, including carved wooden masks.

tional kinds of sleds and boats used in Alaska, from dog and reindeer sleds to kayaks, umiaks, and canoes. Start with the Eskimo and Aleut exhibits. Intriguing items include ceremonial masks, including finger masks that the women used for dancing; fishing flies made of stone, bone, and sinew or baleen; bentwood sunshades for kayaking; waterproof clothing of walrus intestine and salmon skin; and a man's ivory-decorated workbox with a set of tools for making nets.

The Tlingit and Haida exhibits include a collection of argillite carved by the Haida, Tlingit feast dishes, beautiful bentwood boxes, baskets, and a historic Chilkat blanket and pattern board. Don't miss the Raven's-head helmet worn by Sitka Chief Katlean during the battle with the Russians in 1804. If you have time left, open some of the special display drawers, which contain some of the little charmers from this extensive collection, such as ivory sewing implements, jewelry, pipes, and lip labrets.

The eighteen totem poles in **Sitka National Historical Park** are spaced along a forested path beside the sea. The 107-acre park is the site of the Tlingit and Russian battle of 1804. The original collection of totem poles was gathered at the instigation of District of Alaska Governor John Brady, who had a deep and abiding interest in preserving Alaska Native culture. The poles—most from Prince of Wales Island near Ketchikan—were displayed at the 1904 Louisiana Purchase Exposition in Saint Louis. After the fair, they were returned to Alaska for placement in the Sitka park. During the 1930s the poles were repaired by the Civilian Conservation Corps as part of their totem restoration project, and most have since been replicated.

The park visitor center has exhibits on Tlingit culture, including old house posts from the Sitka area, Chilkat blankets, and a brief slide-tape presentation on the history of Sitka and the battle of 1804. One wing is devoted to workshops and demonstrations of Native wood carving, silverwork, bead- and buttonwork, and other crafts. An excellent booklet, *Carved History, The Totem Poles and House Posts of Sitka National Historical Park,* by Marilyn Knapp (Alaska Natural History Association and National Park Service), sold at the visitor center for just $5.00, describes all the totem poles in the park and is an excellent keepsake. You can also borrow this book from the information desk on the honor system. There are more than 2 miles of established trails within the park, although you do not have to walk that far to see the totem poles. If it is a nice day, bring a picnic lunch with you. There is a picnic shelter across Indian River from the totems; a path follows along the riverbank to a Russian memorial.

One of the totem poles in front of the visitor center is a relatively new pole that was created for the nation's bicentennial celebration in 1976. The **Bicentennial pole,** carved by Duane Pasco, depicts new concepts in a traditional style. The topmost figure represents the

The middle figure of the Bicentennial pole depicts the arrival of the white man with his rifle and religion.

Northwest Coast Indian of today holding two staffs, one symbolizing the rich heritage of the past and the other the unknown future. The second figure recalls the arrival of the white man (note beard and dress) with his rifle, religion, and paper treaties. Raven and Eagle are below him, and on the bottom the Coast Indian in pre-contact days, holding a wooden halibut hook and rattle.

Slightly farther afield but still within walking distance (or take a cab), the volunteer-operated **Alaska Raptor Center** (1101 Sawmill Creek Road; 907-747-8662) treats injured bald eagles and other birds of prey and rehabilitates them for release back to the wild. During a tour of the nonprofit medical clinic and education center (available as a walk-in or with Sitka tour operators), you can see several recuperating eagles close at hand.

With such a variety of interesting sights convenient to town, one tends to overlook opportunities for enjoying Sitka's abundant natural scenery. Two special places "out the road" are **Halibut Point State Recreation Site** (approximately mile 5, Halibut Point Road, north of Sitka), a beautiful meeting of forest and sea, with picnic areas, views, and beachcombing; and **Whale Park,** a high overlook off Sawmill Creek Road from which migrating humpback whales can be seen in fall and early spring. The facilities include a large viewing deck with picnic area and interpretive signs. You can also dial in to 88.1 Aqua Radio on your FM dial. This local station has placed an underwater microphone in the bay, and you can hear the distant chirp of the whales as they enter. When you hear the sounds getting distinctly louder, you will know it's a good time to head toward the park, where you'll have a chance to see whales, sea otters, or even sea lions that often hold court on the rocks beside the viewing platform.

The newest adventure on the island is **Sea Life Discovery Tours** (877-966-2301; www.sealifediscoverytours.com), where you can explore Alaska's marine world in the Southeast's only semisubmersible boat. The waters around Sitka are some of the most productive in the world, so you will see lots of sea life, including jellyfish, anemones, crabs, sea urchins, and clams.

Several charter operators offer **sightseeing and naturalist cruises** from Sitka, including trips to the tubs at nearby Goddard Hot Springs. A list of wildlife charters that make the trip is available from the Sitka Convention and Visitors Bureau. **Sitka's Wildlife Quest** is offered by Allen Marine Tours (888-747-8101) for $49 per person. This popular tour provides the opportunity to observe sea otters, whales, bald eagles, and even the special ABC brown bear. The bear is named for the Admiralty, Baranof, and Chichagof Islands—the only place where this bear is found.

If you're more interested in hiking, there are plenty of trails in the area, and they're easily accessible from town and out on the road. You can purchase a Sitka Trails book for about $8.00 at many spots in town, or you can visit the U.S. Forest Service, Sitka Rangers District near the old harbor on Katlian Avenue—they have trail maps as well as a photocopied trail guide. Popular routes include the 3-mile Gavan Hill Trail that takes you to the top of Gavan Hill, where you will gain a great view of Sitka Sound. From here you can also trek across to the summit of Harbor Mountain and its trail system. If you'd rather catch a ride to the summit of Harbor Mountain, **Howard Ulrich** offers tours with the promise of a few great stories you'll want to take home (907-747-8294). Trail Works, a local nonprofit group, is working on the Sitka Cross Trail that will eventually join all of the trails across Sitka, including the popular Indian River, Mt. Verstoria, and Thimble-berry Lake Trails. Call **Sitka Bike and Hike** (877-292-5325) if you would rather take a guided hike or if you'd like to rent a bike to explore the island. Bike rentals are also available through **Yellow Jersey Cycles** (907-747-6317), which is just across from Centennial Hall.

Sitka is also a great spot for kayaking. **Sitka Sound Adventures** (907-747-6375) offers rentals as well as daily and overnight tours. For a true wilderness experience, contact the Forest Service (877-444-6777) to check out the availability of the twenty-four cabins they maintain in the Sitka area. Cabins cost anywhere from $35 to $45 a night and can sleep up to fifteen people.

While you can easily get around on foot, it's interesting to note that cab fares are set at $4.00 in town; there's also a local transit system. Call **North Star Rent-A-Car** (907-966-2552) if you'd like to rent a vehicle. Ryan Fahey, the owner, will even pick you up from your bed-and-breakfast at your convenience.

If you are considering an overnight stay in Sitka, Carol Denkinger's **Alaska Ocean View Bed & Breakfast Inn** (907-747-3440) is quite possibly one of the best choices for accommodation. It's like a five-star hotel in someone's home. There's lots of privacy and a fantastic view of Sitka Sound, and you'll often walk in the door only to be greeted by a sign alerting guests to an assortment of baked goods fresh from the oven. Denkinger also acts as a concierge and is an excellent source of local knowledge.

Special Events

The annual **Sitka Summer Music Festival** is held during three weeks in June. Performing artists from all over the world gather in this seaside setting for daily instructional workshops and twice-weekly evening concerts in the Centennial Hall. The festival dates from 1972, when protégés of Jascha Heifetz and Gregor Piatigorsky put together an informal concert in Sitka. The event has proved so popular that there are standing-room-only crowds for the Tuesday and Friday evening performances (there may be some special Saturday concerts too). Write ahead for reserved seats to Sitka Summer Music Festival, P.O. Box 3333, Sitka, AK 99835; (907) 747-6774. Rehearsals are open to the public without charge. Concurrently with the music festival, the Island Institute hosts the annual **Sitka Symposium,** featuring guest writers and lecturers (examples from past symposiums: Terry Tempest Williams, William Kittredge). For information write P.O. Box 2420, Sitka, AK 99835 or call (907) 747-3794.

Independence Day celebrations feature a parade, dance, food booths, and fireworks. The **Alaska Day Festival,** scheduled for five days around October 18, commemorates the Alaska Purchase with a reenactment of the transfer ceremonies on Castle Hill. A costume ball and parade mark the event. In November, Sitka is overcome by **Whale Fest,** featuring a conference on marine mammals, a concert, and a walk/fun run, as well as many other small events. Contact the information bureau for details. Holiday celebrations begin in December. The month-long **Mayfest** heralds spring with special exhibits, events, and the **Sitka Salmon Derby.** The derby is held during the last weekend in May and the first weekend in June.

JUNEAU
Population 30,700

The most remarkable characteristic of Juneau is that no matter how much it feels like a big city, it still retains its small-town charm. To be sure, it's an alluring place, nestled between steep mountains and salt water. But for those of us who make this city our home, the small-town traits are the most endearing. We still know many of the people we pass on the narrow, hilly streets; we call shopkeepers by their first names; and we commiserate together over the rainy weather. Juneau's cosmopolitan atmosphere comes from being the state capital, and the population, for the most part, is well educated, well traveled, and opinionated.

As Alaska's state capital, Juneau bustles twelve months of the year, but especially during the winter legislative session, when the town fairly explodes with elected officials and their staffs, concerned citizens, lobbyists, and the usual political hangers-on. By the time that lot retreats to their own districts in May, the big tour ships come steaming into port—on some days five and six at a time—to unload thousands of eager tourists into the city streets.

The downtown historic district boasts broad pedestrian walkways outlined with brilliant banners and twin-globe street lamps, renovated shopfronts, a trolley car, and flowers, flowers, flowers. Although portions of South Franklin Street still suffer the ill effects of too many bars, Juneau is a very pleasant place to visit.

Visitors to Juneau will find first-class galleries and shops, a choice of small and large hotels, a selection of passable but expensive restaurants, solid professional theater, and on any given night—summer or winter—a menu of activities from which to choose. The beautiful outdoors, remarkably accessible everywhere in Southeast, calls loudly in Juneau. Anglers, skiers, kayakers—all find their bits of paradise here, but none more so than hikers. Dozens of trails give access to mountains, glaciers, beaches, and river valleys around Juneau. Whatever your interests, Juneau can keep you busy for several days.

Background

What we commonly refer to as Juneau is in reality a number of geographically and historically distinct communities interconnected by

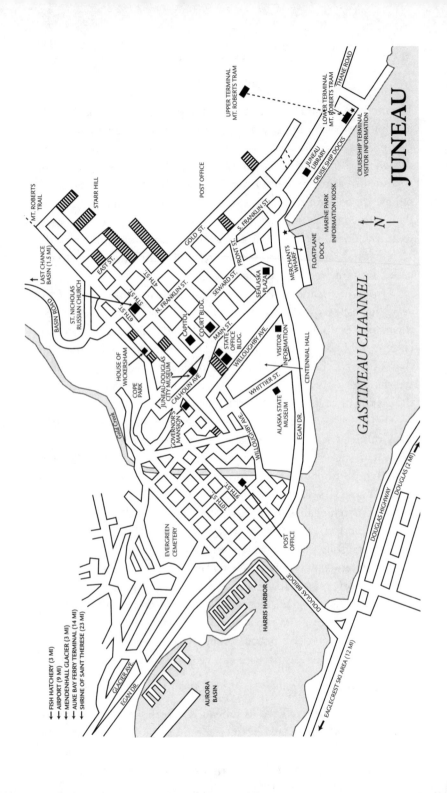

highway and bridge. Juneau proper is snuggled up against the flanks of 3,576-foot Mount Juneau on the Southeast mainland, 900 air miles north of Seattle. The residential communities of Thane, the Mendenhall Valley, Auke Bay, and others stretch north and south of Juneau along the coast. Across Gastineau Channel, by bridge, lies the smaller, formerly independent community of Douglas and neighboring developments on Douglas Island. Together these communities and surrounding lands make up a single municipality—the 3,108-square-mile City and Borough of Juneau.

The story of Juneau and the surrounding communities begins with the discovery of a vast treasure of gold-bearing quartz. The Gastineau Channel area was a fishing ground for local Auke Tlingit in the late 1800s, when prospectors began scouring the hills and gullies of Southeast Alaska and Canada for signs of gold. One man set about locating potential gold-bearing properties more efficiently than the rest. George Pilz, a German-born mining engineer in charge of the Stewart Mine near Sitka, offered a substantial reward ("100 pair of Hudson's Bay blankets and work for the tribe at one dollar per day," he later recalled) to any local Indian chief who could lead him to gold-bearing ore in minable quantities. When samples began coming in from up and down the coast, Pilz sent his men out in teams with Indian guides to investigate the prospects.

Chief Kowee of the Aukes brought samples of ore from Gastineau Channel to Pilz in 1879. To investigate the body of ore, Pilz selected Richard T. Harris and Joseph Juneau, a pair of down-and-out prospectors recently returned from the Cassiar. Harris and Juneau left Sitka in July 1880 and explored several likely looking sites before reaching Gastineau Channel in mid-August. They followed Gold Creek inland, getting good color in their pans and deciding the place was the best prospect so far (which is why they named it Gold Creek), but went back to Sitka without tracing the gold to its source. Pilz was not terribly impressed with their results, and Kowee was extremely put out. The chief carried more samples to Sitka and insisted that Harris and Juneau would have found what Pilz was looking for had they only continued up Gold Creek. When Pilz sent the pair back again, Kowee made sure they reached the mother lode.

On October 3, 1880, Harris and Juneau climbed Snow Slide

Gulch, where they had stopped the first time, and looked down over Silver Bow Basin and Quartz Gulch, which, Harris later recalled, "I named from the fact that it contained the most gold-bearing quartz I had ever seen in one gulch." The quartz outcroppings were shot through with streaks of gold and "little lumps as large as peas or beans." Inspired by this splendid sight, Harris and Juneau fell to work. Harris wrote out a code of local laws governing the staking of claims in the Harris Mining District (this was his legal prerogative according to the Mining Act of 1872, which allowed miners to make regulations concerning claims in their district), and they set out claims throughout Gold Creek Valley for themselves, Pilz, and several creditors and friends. On October 18 they staked a 160-acre town site on the beach along Gastineau Channel, naming it Harrisburgh.

In November the first shiploads of prospectors left Sitka for the new strike location on Gastineau Channel. Forty or so miners spent an uncomfortable winter in Harrisburgh, clearing land to build rough cabins, hacking a pack road to the diggings, and sawing planks to build flumes when the ground thawed in the spring. In February 1881 the miners voted to change the name of the mining camp to Rockwell, for Lieutenant Commander Charles H. Rockwell, who had been sent with a party of men from the naval vessel USS *Jamestown* to keep an eye on developments.

When spring came the banks of Gold Creek crawled with prospectors working their claims while others, recently arrived by steamer from the south, looked for places to drive in their stakes. In May Lieutenant Commander Rockwell returned to Rockwell with a detachment of marines. His instructions were to establish a military post and to preserve order, especially between the miners and the estimated 450 Auke and Taku Tlingit who had taken up residence in the town. The marines put up some small buildings on a ridge over-looking the town, but by December things had simmered down to the extent that the post was closed. Rockwell turned the buildings over to the postmaster, and eventually a federal courthouse was built on the site. Meanwhile the town residents decided to change the name of their community again—to Juneau City after Joe Juneau. The post office dropped the "city" part, and the miners had to be satisfied with just Juneau.

Across the channel on Douglas Island, the ground proved equally rich. The first gold taken out of the entire Gastineau region came from the "Ready Bullion boys," who recovered $1,200 of gold by the spring of 1881 from their claim on Ready Bullion Creek at the southern end of the island. In September 1881 a piece of property close to the Ready Bullion claim passed auspiciously into the hands of John Treadwell, a carpenter-cum-miner who had been sent into the area by a group of San Francisco investors to check out the new strike. After ore samples from Treadwell's claim were tested, Treadwell hastened back to Juneau to acquire more property for the newly established Alaska Mill and Mining Company. Their five-stamp mill, established in May 1882 and replaced by a 120-stamp mill the following year, was the beginning of the great Treadwell mining complex that would produce more than $70 million in gold.

In the ensuing years Gastineau Channel would become a center for large-scale, hard-rock gold mining. Initially lone prospectors took what they could from their claims with shovel and sluice box and then drifted on to other strikes. (Among them was Joe Juneau, who went on to the Klondike and died at Dawson in 1899. Richard Harris mined in Juneau for several years until he lost his claims in a suit brought by one of his original backers. He died in a sanitarium in Oregon in 1907. Both are buried in Evergreen Cemetery in Juneau.) Harvesting the Juneau lode, however, was really a job for organized mining companies with the resources to tunnel deep within the earth and mill thousands of tons of ore per day. Companies formed, consolidated claims, and grew larger. On the Juneau side of the channel, there were the Perseverance and Alaska Juneau mines in Silver Bow Basin, Jualpa at Last Chance Basin, and Ebner Mine on Gold Creek. Across the way were the Ready Bullion, the Mexican, the Seven Hundred Foot Mine, and the Treadwell. Around the mine and mill sites grew the communities of Juneau, Douglas, Treadwell, and Thane, peopled by mine and mill employees and their families. The mines and the businesses that serviced them functioned twenty-four hours a day.

The Treadwell mines reached the peak of production in 1915, with 960 stamps crushing 5,000 tons of ore daily, a world record. Two years later a cave-in at the edge of Gastineau Channel flooded all the Treadwell workings except the Ready Bullion. In 1922 that mine was also shut down for lack of quality ore, bringing to a close one of the greatest mining efforts ever. Over in Juneau the revolutionary Alaska-Gastineau mill at Sheep Creek, patterned after a dry-ore copper mill in Utah, surpassed the Treadwell record by grinding 12,000 tons of ore per day until 1921, when costs became prohibitive. The last of the big mills, the Alaska-Juneau, constructed in 1916, was closed down by the war in 1944, but not before producing $80.8 million in gold. Together these three industrial giants produced $158 million worth of gold at values of $20 to $35 per ounce.

The visible remains of the three great plants are awesomely insignificant. The burned-out shell of the Alaska-Juneau mill is little more than a scar above Gastineau Channel on the approach into town. The Gastineau mill was dismantled and shipped south when the company folded. As for the Treadwell—that wondrous complex of mills, mines, wharves, piers, shops, warehouses, trams, and a town full of people—nothing remains except a few ghostly pilings in the channel and the occasional crumbled foundation that has been spared the advance of the undergrowth.

But by the time the last mine had closed, the surviving communities of Douglas and Juneau had managed to diversify their interests. The governor's office had been transferred from Sitka to the thriving mining town of Juneau in 1906, establishing Juneau as the capital city. The governor's mansion was built in 1912 and the Capitol Building in 1930. When statehood was awarded in 1959, Juneau remained the focal point of state government activity and continues so today, despite repeated campaigns to relocate the capital of Alaska nearer the northern population centers of Anchorage and Fairbanks.

Government—federal, state, and local—employs slightly less than one out of every two workers in Juneau. Tourism plays an integral role in the local economy, the capital city being a destination or transfer point for most cruise ships plying the Inside Passage, and commercial fishing is a significant factor here as elsewhere in Southeast Alaska. The arrival of major merchandisers such as Fred Meyer, JCPenney, Kmart, and Costco has turned Juneau into an important regional retail shopping center in recent years.

Getting There

Access to Juneau is by air and water only. Several flights a day from Seattle, Anchorage, and the communities between land at Juneau International Airport, 9 miles north of the city center. Alaska Airlines services Juneau year-round. Alaska state ferries dock at the Auke Bay Terminal, 14 miles north of Juneau. The three dozen or so cruise ships regularly calling at Juneau during the May through September cruise season tie up at one of the downtown docks or anchor in the Juneau Harbor. If the latter, passengers are lightered ashore, disembarking at Marine Park on the downtown waterfront or at the Intermediate Vessel Float by the Cruiseship Terminal.

To See and Do

Cruise-ship passengers never fail to be awed by their first glimpse of Alaska's capital city. Gliding slowly up the narrow reaches of Gastineau Channel, your ship will pass the remnants of the Treadwell wharves off Douglas Island to the left, while ahead looms the towering profile of Mount Juneau. At the bottom and insignificant in comparison, the buildings of Juneau cling to their shelf between mountains and sea.

Juneau's extensively renovated waterfront facilities extend in one unbroken, flower-festooned walk. At the north end you'll see **Merchants Wharf,** a former seaplane hangar that now houses restaurants and shops, and the **seaplane float,** where flightseeing excursions depart for the Juneau Ice Field. Brightly colored banners mark the location of **Marine Park,** a popular gathering spot and focal point of wharf activity. On sunny days Juneau residents spill out of adjacent office buildings and enjoy their lunches at the outside tables and benches or sprawled on the grass. There is an information kiosk staffed by volunteers who dispense maps, brochures, and answers to questions.

Toward the south end of the waterfront, the wharf continues past the award-winning **Juneau Public Library.** Built on top of the Marine Park Garage, the library affords the best views in town of Mount Juneau, Douglas Island, and the cruise ships parked in Gastineau Channel. Cruise-ship passengers disembarking at the Marine Park wharf near the library will be greeted by a commemorative statue of

A commemorative statue of Patsy Ann, Juneau's official canine greeter, awaits cruise-ship passengers alighting at Marine Park wharf.

Juneau's beloved **Patsy Ann,** an English bull terrier and canine-about-town. Patsy Ann gained her page in local history by her habit of greeting incoming steamships at the Juneau dock. At the south end the wharf terminates at the Cruiseship Terminal and Intermediate Vessel Float.

The **Visitor Information Center,** located inside Centennial Hall (Willoughby Avenue and Egan Drive), contains a reading-and-video area as well as brochures from Juneau and other Southeast communities. Pick up a Juneau Walking Tour map to guide you to the many attractions around town. If the visitor center is closed, self-serve information sites are also maintained at the airport and the Auke Bay Ferry Terminal.

Many downtown buildings have retained their original facades, primarily because Juneau has been spared the sort of major fire that ravaged Douglas and Wrangell. A stroll along South Franklin, Front, and Seward Streets will carry you back to the early twentieth century. South Franklin (all the way to the Cruiseship Terminal) brims with gift and curio shops—and taverns, including the landmark **Red Dog Saloon,** an old-fashioned, sawdust-on-the-floor establishment that draws both residents and visitors. The turreted **Alaska Steam Laundry Building** dates from 1901. At present the building connects with the **Emporium Mall** on Shattuck Way. The interior walls are hung with very interesting photo murals of early-day Juneau. You will find several specialty shops within the mall, including the studio outlet for **William Spear Design** enameled pins. The ground-floor **Heritage Coffee Co.,** a specialty coffee roaster and cafe, serves great sandwiches and desserts.

Recommended art galleries on Franklin Street include the **Decker Gallery,** which carries Rie Muñoz prints, and **Gallery of the North at Warner's Wharf.** Nearby, at 225 Front Street in the newly restored

The Mount Roberts Tramway in Juneau has two cars to whisk passengers about 2,000 feet up the mountain. On the mountain a restaurant, nature center, theater, and gift shops await visitors. DIRK MILLER

Miners Mercantile building, check out **Mt. Juneau Artists** co-op. Only a bit farther, at 217 Seward Street, visit the **R.T. Wallen Gallery** for original stone lithographs and bronzes. Also try **Kaill Fine Crafts** (on Front Street near Franklin) for unusual gift items with or without an Alaska theme. Back on Franklin, the restored **Senate Building** houses several shops (fly-fishing supplies, Irish and Russian imports), as does **Marine View Center** (check out **Taku Smokeries** for local smoked salmon to eat here or on your ship).

South of the library, near the Cruiseship Terminal, you'll come to one of Southeast Alaska's newest visitor attractions: the **Mount Roberts Tramway.** The tram whisks visitors in high-speed gondolas past the 2,000-foot level of Mount Roberts, where they are treated to a spectacular view. The scene that unfolds from the ridge is a stunner, offering panoramic views and photo opportunities of downtown Juneau, Douglas Island, and the forest-rimmed waters of Gastineau Channel. The gondolas began running in 1996. Once at the upper terminal, there's a visitor center, Tlingit Indian interpretive exhibits, shops, and hiker-friendly extensions to existing trails.

If visitors want to ascend the mountain on their own power, the **Mount Roberts Trail** leads about 2.5 miles from the mountain end of Sixth Street to a wooden cross at the 2,500-foot level, near the tram's upper terminal. The trail then continues on to the summits of Mount Gastineau (total distance from Sixth Street, 3 miles) and Mount Roberts (4.5 miles). These trails are not for the casual walker, however, and have in recent years become eroded, rocky, muddy, and potentially hazardous. They are steep at the end.

At Fifth Street between Franklin and Gold, you'll come upon the tiny, octagonal **Saint Nicholas Russian Orthodox Church.** Although constructed in 1894, nearly thirty years after Russia sold the Alaska colony, Saint Nicholas is the oldest original Russian church in Southeast Alaska. The postage-stamp Cathedral Park next door offers a comfortable bench for resting your feet. Continue on Fifth Street 2 blocks toward the mountains, and you will find yourself looking up at a long set of stairs. They lead to **Starr Hill,** one of the oldest and most picturesque residential neighborhoods in Juneau. Many of the houses were built for employees of the nearby mines. Behind Starr Hill, Mount Roberts rises 3,819 feet.

Constructed in 1894, Juneau's Saint Nicholas Russian Orthodox Church is the oldest original Russian church in Southeast Alaska.

Bicycling

In recent years mountain-bike rentals and tours have blossomed in the Panhandle. In nearly every town visitors can find bikes to rent, and in some, guides to lead them on tours. Most of these tours lead bicyclists on roads, dirt paths, and well-traveled routes.

In Juneau there are several trails that bikers might want to try, including the Perseverance Trail in the valley behind town. Other places to ride include the North Douglas Highway, which skirts the edge of Douglas Island by shoreline, and Thane Road, which also hugs the mainland coast.

For a challenging mountain-bike ride, consider the Treadwell Ditch Trail, which follows a trench that was once used to collect water to power mines on Douglas Island near downtown Juneau. For much of its length, the trail is built on a narrow, man-made moraine of debris shoveled out by miners in 1889. Over time, trees have regained a foothold around the trail, and their roots, along with loose rock, debris, windfallen trees, and missing bridges, create considerable challenges for cyclists.

Looking for other options? Mountain Gears, owned by Hans and Tonja Moser (907–586–4327), rents bicycles and is more than happy to recommend trails.

Sockeye Cycles rents bicycles and runs tours in Skagway and Haines (907–766–2869). Sockeye Cycles' tour options include everything from a 1½–hour trip around Haines to a nine-day ride along the historic Dalton Trail and White Pass gold rush routes to the Klondike. In Ketchikan bicycles rentals and tours can be arranged at Southeast Exposure (907–225–8829). Visitors enjoy pedaling on the main road south of town and to Ward Lake, which also has logging roads that can be used by bikers. In many Southeast communities logging roads are obvious mountain-biking routes. But be careful around logging equipment and activities, and check with the local tourism officials before venturing out on the roads.

One other prime biking destination in Southeast is the tiny town of Gustavus. Bicycles seem to be a universal means of getting around in the community, and nearly every place of lodging has its own fleet for guests' use.

The state government complex is centered at Fourth and Main. The six-story **capitol** was built as the Federal and Territorial Building in 1930, when Alaska was not yet a state. Local marble from Tokeen, near Prince of Wales Island, was quarried for the front columns and interior paneling. The Alaska Senate and House of Representatives meet in the building, which houses the governor's office as well. Tours of the capitol are available in summer (check at the tour desk in the lobby or contact the Legislative Information Office, 907–465–4648, to find the time of the next tour departure). During the legislative session (approximately January to May), you can request a special tour by contacting the House of Representatives sergeant-at-arms at (907) 465–3869. Or just look around by yourself. The front doors of the capitol remain open during weekday office hours (8:00 A.M. to 4:30 P.M.). The ground-floor lobby has been restored to the original blue-and-gilt decoration.

The governor has only a short walk from office to home. The **governor's mansion** is a couple of blocks away from the capitol on Calhoun Avenue. The white-pillared colonial, completed in 1912, could just as easily be situated in Massachusetts or Vermont, were it not for the dramatic totem pole in front. The Governor's totem, carved in 1940 by Tlingit Indians from Klukwan and Saxman, represents several Tlingit legends, among them the origin of the mosquito, pictured as the fourth figure from the top. The mansion is not usually open to view. Contact the governor's office in advance (write P.O. Box 110001, Juneau, AK 99811-0001) if yours is a special request, such as for a group of visiting schoolchildren.

More recent additions to the state government complex include the bunkerlike **State Office Building** (which Alaskans quickly dubbed the "S.O.B."), completed in 1974, and the high-rise Alaska **Court Building,** built in 1975. The vast open foyer of the S.O.B. stretches four stories above the lobby floor, and the surrounding tiled terraces offer a marvelous view of Gastineau Channel and Douglas Island. The **Old Witch totem pole** displayed in the foyer came from a Haida village on Prince of Wales Island and was carved in the 1880s. The pole recalls the Haida version of the "old witch," or mother-in-law, story of Gonakadet, who assumes the identity of a lake monster in order to provide fish for his abusive mother-in-law. A **brown-baggers' concert** takes place every Friday at noon on the 1928 Kimball theater organ housed on the lobby floor. There is a small snack bar where you can buy sandwiches and beverages.

The **Friendship pole** displayed in the lobby of the nearby Court Building is one of several large-scale copies of a 28-inch totem pole that has special significance for Chilkat Tlingit of Klukwan, near Haines. In the late 1920s the Indians presented the original pole to Steve Sheldon of Haines, a U.S. deputy marshal who was instrumental in restoring goodwill between conflicting clans. The Friendship totem symbolizes peace by representing both Eagle and Raven moieties on the same pole. From top to bottom, the primary figures represent Eagle, Raven, Hawk, Bear, Frog, Wolf, and (very small) Eagle. This pole was carved by Alaska Indian Arts, in Haines.

Juneau has many treasures tucked here and there about town. The 45-foot **Four-Story totem,** on the corner of Fourth and Main Streets in front of the **Juneau-Douglas City Museum,** was carved in Hydaburg in 1940 and represents four Haida legends. Another pole, beside the museum, was carved for Alaska's Centennial celebration in 1967 by Amos Wallace. This small museum houses a fascinating and artfully displayed collection of equipment and curiosities from Juneau's gold-mining era, such as miners' helmets, carbide lamps, and surveying gadgets, plus a hands-on children's exhibit.

Uphill from the city museum, the **Wickersham State Historic Site** overlooks the city and down-channel view from a part of town known locally as Chicken Ridge. This fine house was built around 1899 for one of the early mine owners. The residence was later owned by Judge James Wickersham, who came to Alaska in 1900 and played a prominent role in shaping Alaska's body politic. As Alaska's voteless delegate to Congress, Judge Wickersham worked tirelessly to achieve territorial status and followed that victory of 1912 with the first statehood bill four years later. He died twenty years before that goal was finally achieved in 1959. The Wickersham House has undergone renovation and restoration. Visitors can view the main-floor rooms, which are furnished as Judge Wickersham enjoyed them, with his 1904 gramophone and his Chickering square concert grand piano, which the Russian government installed in Sitka in the 1850s. Some of Wickersham's vast collection of Alaskan artifacts and mementos spanning his thirty-nine years in Alaska also are on display.

Plan to spend a minimum of one hour at the **Alaska State Museum.** To get there on foot, walk along Egan Drive to Whittier or take a shortcut through the State Office Building: Pass through the foyer and bear right to the rear bank of elevators leading to the parking garage and exit at P2. You will emerge onto Willoughby Avenue, a long block from the museum. (Willoughby follows the original shoreline of Gastineau Channel. The waterfront was extended by tailings from the Alaska-Juneau Mine.)

The ground floor of the museum contains a strong collection of Alaska Native artifacts; for example, Eskimo masks, Aleut waterproof clothing, and carved wooden feast dishes of the Tlingit and Haida. There is a Thunderbird house screen from the northern Panhandle village of Yakutat dating from 1905. The painted and carved screen depicts the mythological Thunderbird, creator of thunder and lightning, emerging from the storm clouds (represented by small faces). The story that inspired the screen concerns a small boy who became lost on a canoe trip down the Alsek River and was subsequently found by Thunderbird. The parents located the boy as he was about to be changed into a bird. Thunderbird agreed to return the child if the family put up a screen in a Yakutat house. Of special interest: the famous Lincoln totem pole carved in the late 1800s to commemorate the clan's first contact with a white man. Needing a model from which to work, the carver apparently used a photograph of Lincoln obtained from an army post that was located on Tongass Island from 1868 to 1870.

Children will enjoy the museum's eagle nesting tree. This unusual exhibit replicates a bald eagle nest in a tall Sitka spruce tree. As you follow the gently spiraling ramp to the museum's second floor, you circle the tree to look down upon the nest and its occupants.

The second floor is devoted to post-contact Alaska. The Russian

Among the Aleut items in the Alaska State Museum is this waterproof gut parka. ALASKA STATE MUSEUM, ALFRED A. BLAKER

heritage corner displays a brass double-headed eagle of the Russian imperial crest. Russian explorers used such crests as territorial markers along the North American coast; this is one of the few known to have been recovered. Another exhibit focuses on gold mining. The museum contains the original French-made lens (circa 1900) from the Cape Spencer lighthouse.

One block from the museum on Egan Drive, the **U.S. Forest Service Information Center** operates out of Centennial Hall, the Juneau convention center. You will find exhibits about the Tongass National Forest, films, books, maps—and plenty of soft chairs. Rest your feet awhile! During summer artists may be demonstrating Native heritage crafts.

All through the year, "Juneauites" pile children, dogs, lunches, and—depending upon the season—fishing rods, berry pails, or cross-country skis into the car and drive "out the road." The destination can be just about anywhere that is pretty to look at and possesses the desired habitat: Twin Lakes for swimming, fishing, or ice-skating; Fritz Cove for blueberry picking; or Eagle Beach for picnicking. Consider renting a car for a day or two to explore the local haunts.

Outside of downtown Juneau, Egan Expressway extends northward along Gastineau Channel past two boat harbors and the bridge to Douglas Island. About 3 miles from downtown, you'll spot the red roof of the **Gastineau Salmon Hatchery,** adjacent to Gastineau Channel. The hatchery raises four species of salmon. You can see the returning adults ascending the fish ladder outside the hatchery throughout summer. Inside, interpretive displays explain the life cycle of the salmon, and a nearly floor-to-ceiling saltwater aquarium showcases local species of marine life. As you drive out the expressway near the airport, look for Canada geese on the **Mendenhall Wetlands State Game Refuge,** the saltwater marsh area that borders Gastineau Channel. These tidelands—green in summer and straw gold in fall—are a feeding station for migrating waterfowl. There is a turnout and viewing platform on the channel side of the highway at mile 6. The Canada geese are present year-round in the Juneau area, but you will see large flocks of them in early summer and fall.

Turn right at Lemon Creek to take a free tour of the **Alaskan**

Brewing Company (5429 Shaune Drive; 907–780–5866), makers of Juneau's award-winning amber beers and pale ale. The tour includes a visit to their hospitality/tasting room and gift shop. Dozens of service enterprises and food outlets are clustered around the airport and nearby shopping malls of the Mendenhall Valley. One shop of note: the **Rie Muñoz Gallery** (211 Jordan Avenue), the headquarters outlet for Rie Muñoz prints, cards, and books.

Thirteen miles north of the city center via the expressway and Mendenhall Loop Road, you come to Juneau's major natural attraction, the **Mendenhall Glacier.** Be prepared for the ever-present hum of helicopter tours. You may see as many as six helicopters hanging over the glacier at any given time. This 12-mile river of ice descends to sea level from a 1,500-square-mile ice field in the Coast Mountains behind Juneau. The glacier was formed during the Little Ice Age, which peaked in the seventeenth and eighteenth centuries, and has retreated 2.5 miles in the last 230 years. The glacier terminates in Mendenhall Lake, which reaches depths of 200 feet. Chunks of ice are continually falling from the glacier with a resounding *crack!*—leaving a deep, blue rent in the 1.5-mile-wide face. There is a newly expanded visitor center and overlook located about 0.5 mile from the face of the glacier where you'll find books, brochures, films, and exhibits pertaining to the glacier and the Juneau Ice Field. Forest Service personnel are

Just 13 miles from Juneau is the Mendenhall Glacier, a 12-mile river of ice that originates in the Coast Mountains.

on hand to answer questions and conduct guided walks. A path leads from the visitor center to an observation point overlooking the glacier and lake. A brochure outlines a self-guided exploration along the "trail of the glacier." You need about forty-five minutes to walk the path and observe the telltale signs of a receding glacier, such as grooved bedrock, kettles or depressions in the soil made by blocks of melting ice, and a glacial moraine. More rigorous trails are mapped out for serious hikers seeking a closer look at the terrain. There is good cross-country skiing near the glacier in winter.

You may be able to see red sockeye salmon in **Steep Creek,** not far from the glacier parking lot. From July through December sockeye, coho, and chum salmon enter the creek from salt water and swim upstream to spawn near Mendenhall Lake. A roadside exhibit on the Mendenhall Loop Road points you in the right direction to observe these spawning salmon.

When you leave the glacier, continue north on the expressway (it becomes Glacier Highway at this point) for **Brotherhood Bridge** over the Mendenhall River, which affords a stupendous view over fields of wildflowers (especially lupine, wild iris, and Alaska cotton) and the glacier beyond. There is a turnout from the highway. The **Kaxdegoowu Heen Dei Trail** starts at this turnout and winds gently along the river for about 2 miles. This wide, level wheelchair-accessible trail makes a good, nonstrenuous family outing. There are several good picnic spots on the river. Another scenic wayside 1.5 miles farther along gives you a view of **Auke Lake.** In summer the lake suggests a quiet paddle in a canoe or kayak, and you will see sockeye salmon there late in the season. In winter the scene turns to ice and glittering snow.

Past a small lily pond at the edge of Auke Lake, there is a turnoff for the lakeside campus of the **University of Alaska Southeast,** which offers associate, bachelor's, and master's degree programs in education, fisheries management, business administration, and several other fields of study. You would be hard put to find a more dramatic setting for a college campus. Two sights of interest on or near the campus: The **William A. Egan Library,** at the far end of the drive, contains an impressive collection of Northwest Coast Native art commissioned as part of the percent-for-art public building program. The individual pieces range from cedar-bark paper masks to carved house posts. As you leave the campus, stop at the log-and-shingled **Chapel by the Lake.** The simple, varnished spruce logs are a perfect foil for the grandeur framed by the front window. The Presbyterian chapel was completed in 1958.

From Auke Lake, Glacier Highway stretches northward for another 30 miles to terminate at Echo Cove at mile 40. If you have time, by all means make the entire drive. The road is good and offers exceptional views of water, mountains, forest, and wildflower-strewn fields. Side roads lead from the highway to waterfront residential neighborhoods such as **Fritz Cove, Lena Point,** and **Amalga Harbor. Auke Bay,** 12 miles from town, is a small commercial community and boat harbor with a convenience store. Showers are also available at the harbor office. There's a lot of eagle activity here as well, which makes this a great spot to rent a kayak for a few hours. In summer you can count on good burgers and shakes at the **Hot Bite** stand in the harbor parking lot.

The **Auke Village Recreation Area,** a short distance beyond the boat harbor, was for centuries the site of a winter village of the Auke Tlingit. Mining activity in Juneau drew the Indians into town where the jobs were, and the village was mostly deserted by 1900. Now the site is again populated—with picnickers, campers, anglers, and boaters who revel in the gentle beach and glorious view. Covered shelters guarantee a pleasurable outing even on liquid-sunshine days, and there is a quiet campground nearby. An unusual totem pole stands opposite the site on the highway. The **Yax-te pole** was raised in 1941 to commemorate the old village site. The Yax-te—what we call Ursa Major or the Big Dipper—was a crest of a clan of Indians near Klawock on Prince of Wales Island. After a battle the crest was given to one of the Auke chiefs, who adopted it for his clan. The top figure on the pole is Raven. Below him several tiny faces peer out from the wood. They represent different birds that assisted Raven in his adventures, except for the bottom face, which represents an Auke princess. The last figure on the pole, resembling a bear, is Yax-te.

At mile 23 you arrive at another scenic chapel, the Roman Catholic **Shrine of Saint Therese.** A gravel causeway extends to a small island with a stone church tucked into a wooded path on the sea. The shrine was built in 1938 and, like Chapel by the Lake, is in great demand for weddings. **Eagle Beach** (mile 28) has picnic facilities and wonderful beach walking and views.

South out of Juneau **Thane Road** begins at South Franklin Street and continues for 5 miles beyond the Cruiseship Terminal. Uphill on the left you will pass the shell of the Alaska-Juneau mill and, on your right, the tailings from the A-J Mine. Several years ago Juneau residents played a form of golf on this "million-dollar golf course," now a barge landing site and industrial park. Thane is now residential, but in former years quite a community of warehouses, shops, offices, boardinghouses, and even a school grew up around the great Alaska-Gastineau mill at Sheep Creek. There is a small **fish hatchery** at Sheep Creek. The nearby **Thane Ore House** (mile 4) serves grilled salmon, deep-fried halibut, and barbecued ribs at its "Miner's Cookhouse" on the beach, with entertainment from the Gold Nugget Revue.

Across the Douglas Bridge you turn left for a 2-mile drive to the small community of **Douglas.** (You will pass an old Tlingit cemetery on the left.) Primarily residential, Douglas has its own library (attached to the fire hall), post office, cafe, and professional theater. The award-winning **Perseverance Theatre** presents a full season of theater (September through May) at its Third Street home. At the end of town, the road angles left to the boat harbor and **Sandy Beach** in Savikko Park. Bring the family here for a picnic (covered shelters with fireplaces), softball game, tennis match, or walk on the beach. A trail to the Treadwell mining ruins starts from Sandy Beach—you can obtain a walking tour map of historic Treadwell at the Juneau-Douglas City Museum.

In the other direction Douglas Highway extends a dozen miles to the north end of Douglas Island and **Eaglecrest** (907–586–5284) municipal downhill ski area, which has dominated the winter recreational scene since its opening in 1976. Facilities include a beginner's tow and two chairlifts, Nordic ski trails, an equipment rental shop, and a day lodge and snack bar. Skiing usually starts by mid-December and closes in early April, but snowfall varies considerably from year to year. Some winters provide excellent skiing and others almost none.

There are 260 miles of **hiking trails** in the Juneau vicinity. The extensive network of city, state, and federal trails encompasses a variety of terrain, from beach walks to ridge walks. Many of the trails are legacies of former mining efforts. Hikers might want to acquire these trail guides: *Juneau Trails* (U.S. Forest Service) and *Short Walks around Juneau* (Mary Lou King), available from bookstores.

One of the most popular walking and hiking areas, **Perseverance Basin,** is accessed via Basin Road right in downtown Juneau. Basin Road begins at the intersection of Sixth and East Streets in Juneau, curves up and around a tree-covered knoll, then follows Gold Creek into Last Chance Basin. Houses rim the first section of the road, before the pavement ends, and then a wooden bridge hangs high above the tumbling waters of Gold Creek. On the opposite side of the creek, an old avalanche scar grows brilliant green with the advance of summer. Sometimes you can spot black bears there, testing the new vegetation. You can drive to this spot, but it is a much better walk, and an easy one after the first few uphill yards.

The gravel road continues for nearly a mile and a half through Gold Creek Valley. Mountains rise on both sides, Mount Juneau on the left, Mount Roberts on the right, white on top, dark green below. Gold prospectors cut this road through the mountains in the winter and spring of 1881. The valley opens up into Last Chance Basin, and some old mine buildings come into view. Ahead is Snowslide Gulch. Joe Juneau and Richard Harris labored to the top and looked down into the promised land of Silver Bow Basin. I never walk this road without thinking of the events of 1880 and 1881 and of the gritted-teeth determination of the men who passed this way.

You can see some of the gold-mining era's tools, machinery, and miners' personal items at the Gastineau Historical Society's **Mining Museum** near the end of Basin Road. The museum is housed in one of several old A-J structures accessible from a parking area via footbridge and stairs on the side of Mount Roberts.

At the end of Basin Road, the Perseverance Trail begins a gentle climb to beautiful Ebner Falls and Perseverance Basin (easy hike); other trails branch off to Mount Juneau (tough climb; experienced hikers only) and Granite Creek Basin. See local trail guides for details.

You only have to follow Perseverance Trail for thirty minutes to gain a spectacular view of this waterfall as it cascades down this lush valley toward Gold Creek. MICHELLE GURNEY

If you're driving out the road in late afternoon or early evening and feel an attack of the hungries coming on, turn right off the Egan Expressway onto Old Glacier Highway, turn right again at Hospital Drive, and then take a left onto Salmon Creek Lane. At the end of the lane, you'll find the **Gold Creek Salmon Bake at Salmon Creek.** (The reason for the strange name is the operation moved from Gold to Salmon Creek.) The specialty is king salmon liberally coated with a brown-sugar glaze and grilled over an alder fire. You sit at wooden tables and benches under heated canopies. Menu items include not only salmon but barbecued ribs and (often) halibut, plus baked beans, fresh salads, and sourdough bread. Dinner also comes with beer, wine, or soft beverages.

A short walk up the creek leads to the **Juneau Raptor Center** (visitors welcome; recuperating eagles, owls, and hawks in residence), and beyond that a small dam and assorted mining relics.

There are many wonderful excursions available out of Juneau. For example: **Alaska Discovery** (5310 Glacier Highway; 907–780–6226) offers one-day sea-kayaking trips exploring the coastal islands of Lynn Canal north of Juneau. (Also contact them about kayak and backcountry trips to Admiralty Island and Glacier Bay National Park.) Alaska Travel Adventure's **Mendenhall River Float Trip** starts with a stunning pass of Mendenhall Glacier and provides good family fun—no white water (907–789–0052). **Alaska Rainforest Tours** (907–463–3466) offers guided nature walks and day hikes with an experienced hiker and naturalist.

You can schedule a floatplane **flightseeing tour of the Juneau Ice Field** to see the amazing expanse of ice and snow that feeds more than thirty glaciers. Wings of Alaska (877–789–0790) takes off right from the seaplane float at Merchants Wharf downtown as well as from the airport. Or take a **helicopter glacier tour.** Several companies now offer the opportunity to land and walk on a glacier. TEMSCO Helicopters (877–789–9501), which developed the original tours, flies to the Mendenhall Glacier, as does Northstar Trekking (907–790–4530). You see some very dramatic formations of the Juneau Ice Field, including a number of other glaciers, and look down into deep, blue pools and crevasses. Then you land on the Mendenhall Glacier and explore the surface features with a guide.

TEMSCO Helicopters' Glacier Tour sets you on top of Mendenhall Glacier to walk on the ice with a glacier guide. MARK KELLEY

An excursion to **Taku Glacier Lodge** (907-789-5932) combines floatplane flightseeing over part of the ice field with a salmon bake at a picturesque log wilderness lodge on the Taku River, a stone's throw from two spectacular glaciers.

Cruise excursions from Juneau include day and overnight trips to

Anchored on a grassy bluff above the Taku River, Taku Glacier Lodge commands one of the most impressive views in wilderness Alaska.

beautiful **Tracy Arm,** a deep fjord about 50 miles south of Juneau, where two glaciers descend to the sea (good place to see killer whales, seals, porpoises, and bears). Inquire about different day-cruise options to Tracy Arm at the visitor center. Alaska Sightseeing/Cruise West (800–426–7702) offers circle cruises to Tracy Arm and Glacier Bay, as does Alaska's Glacier Bay Tours and Cruises (800–451–5952). Auke Nu Tours (800–820–2628) also runs a daily ferry from Juneau to Gustavus, the gateway to Glacier Bay, and a whale-watching tour in Icy Straits.

Juneau is also the departure point for visiting the **Stan Price Bear Sanctuary** at Pack Creek on Admiralty Island. This wilderness sanctuary, managed jointly by the U.S. Forest Service and Alaska Department of Fish and Game, provides an amazing opportunity to observe and photograph brown bears as they fish for spawning pink and chum salmon at the stream mouth. July and August are the prime viewing months. During this period a number of bears can often be seen on the tide flats or from an observation tower on the stream. As many as thirty bears are believed to use the site over the course of a summer. Pack Creek is located in a wilderness area; facilities for humans are limited, and access is restricted in order to preserve the bears and the integrity of the area. Forest Service or Fish and Game personnel are on site to answer questions and brief you on rules of conduct regarding food and access to the area. Camping is not permitted at the bear sanctuary but is allowed at a small island nearby.

You must obtain a permit before visiting Pack Creek. The number of permits per day is limited and allocated among professional guide services and individuals. You will have to charter with one of several local flying services (or charter boats) to get to Pack Creek, or you can go with a guided group. (The Forest Service will provide a list of approved guides and air charter companies.) Despite the regulations, expense, and possible discomfort from a damp day, Pack Creek is the sort of experience you will remember for a long, long time. Permit costs during the peak season of July 5 through August 25 are $50 per day. Permits cost $20 during the shoulder seasons, from June 1 to July 4 and August 26 through September 10. Half-price discounts are available for juniors and seniors. For additional information or to request a permit, contact the U.S. Forest Service, 101 Egan Drive, Juneau, AK 99801; telephone (907) 586-8751.

Juneau has a large number of cafes and restaurants, including some familiar fast-food franchises, both in town and in the Mendenhall Valley. Mexican and pizza restaurants seem to be the perennial favorites. **Armadillo Tex-Mex Cafe** (431 South Franklin Street) packs in a local clientele, as does the **Fiddlehead Restaurant and Bakery** (429 West Willoughby Avenue), close to the Alaska State Museum. I also like **Olivia's de Mexico** (222 Seward Street), a modest basement cafe with simple, well-prepared dishes, and **Valentine's Coffee House** (111 Seward Street). On weekdays in summer, downtown streets sprout food carts to serve the noontime office crowd. The hamburger and taco-salad stands on Seward Street are reliable favorites. For fancier dining try the Fiddlehead's second-floor **Fireweed Room, The Twisted Fish,** or one of the many hotel restaurants.

Summer entertainment options include free concerts every Friday evening in Marine Park.

Special Events

Annual celebrations in the Juneau vicinity include the **Alaska Folk Festival** in April (a free, weeklong series of concerts and workshops); the **Juneau Jazz & Classics Festival** (May); the **Classic Car Show** and **Gold Rush Days** (June); parades and fireworks on the Fourth of July; and the three-day **Golden North Salmon Derby,** usually held in August. The **Juneau Public Market** kicks off the holiday shopping season over Thanksgiving weekend, and downtown merchants host a three-day **Gallery Walk** in early December. In February the University of Alaska stages **Winterfest,** with a variety of family outdoor activities.

HAINES
Population 1,811

It is hard to imagine a setting more stereotypically Alaskan than that of Haines. The jagged Cathedral Peaks of the Chilkat Mountains are massed behind the town, raw-edged reminders that an ungentle spirit is abroad in this far-northern land. Salt water is also close to hand in frigid, salmon-filled Chilkoot Inlet on the upper reaches of Lynn Canal.

Haines was the only town north of Hyder with highway connections to the outside until 1978, when the Skagway-Carcross leg of the Klondike Highway opened the way to Whitehorse and the Alaska road system. A steady stream of traffic and freight still passes through the community en route between the Alaska state ferry terminal and the Haines Highway.

Too many highway travelers look upon Haines simply as a ferry transit point. I recommend staying at least a couple of days. There is plenty of good lodging and four state campgrounds from which to choose, each more beautiful and isolated than the last. Plenty of RV parking, too. There are interesting sights, a flourishing art community, good hikes, and great fishing. All these things can be found to a greater or lesser degree in any community along the Inside Passage, but Haines has a come-hither quality that reaches out to the visitor and says, "Welcome."

If you spend one day in Haines, you will enjoy the sightseeing opportunities presented by Fort William H. Seward, Alaska Indian

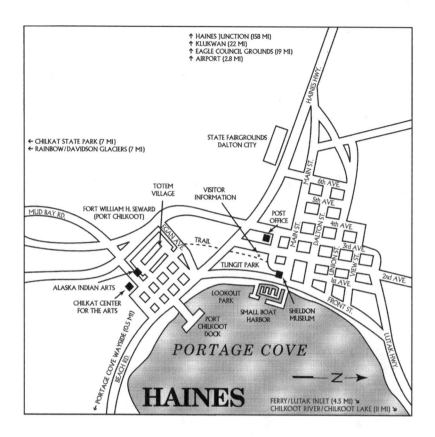

Arts, and great museums such as the Tsirku Canning Co., Hammer, and the Sheldon Museum and Cultural Center. At night there is the salmon bake at the Totem Village Tribal House. If you spend two days, you can take in some of the spectacular wilderness scenery along the way to Lutak Inlet or Chilkat State Park, just 7 miles down Mud Bay Road; hike Mount Ripinsky's north peak; or book a rafting or kayaking trip. If your stay extends to three days, you will start greeting people you pass on the street by name. If you stay four days, look out, because you may find yourself permanently hooked.

Background

Lynn Canal, one of the longest and deepest fjords on the North American continent, terminates at the northern end in two narrow fingers of water: Chilkat Inlet on the left and Chilkoot Inlet on the right (these two names, Chilkat and Chilkoot, will have you horribly confused before your stay in Haines is over). Haines lies between the inlets, on the 11-mile Chilkat Peninsula. Haines is approximately 75 miles northwest of Juneau and is separated from Skagway by about 14 miles of water.

At the time of the first European contact, all this territory was inhabited by the powerful and wealthy Chilkat Tlingit who lived in several villages in the area, of which the principal village was and continues to be Klukwan on the Chilkat River. The Chilkat controlled the passes leading through the Coast Mountains to the Alaska and Canadian Interior, trading the coveted eulachon oil to the Athapaskans in exchange for valuable hides from moose or caribou. The Chilkat were respected throughout the Tlingit nation for their wealth and strength and were particularly renowned for their skill at weaving Chilkat blankets.

The present settlement of Haines got its start in 1879 with the arrival of S. Hall Young, a Presbyterian missionary, with his naturalist friend John Muir. Muir was studying the surrounding wilderness, but Young was looking for a site to establish a mission. The two had journeyed from Wrangell in an open canoe in late October, which is a feat few would attempt today. The Tlingit chiefs offered Hall a site on Portage Cove, on a well-used portage trail between the Chilkat River and Chilkoot Inlet. The Tlingit name for the place was *Dei-shu,* or "End of the Trail." The mission school opened the following year. The settlement was named Haines for Mrs. F. E. Haines, secretary of the Presbyterian home mission board that had raised funds for the mission.

Hard on the heels of Haines Mission came the canneries. Several operated in Chilkat and Chilkoot Inlets starting in 1882, but only one, Haines Packing Company at Letnikof Cove, was a long-term success. Haines Packing Company continued operations as a cannery until 1972.

Haines next found itself caught up in the gold rush. In 1897 Jack Dalton, a shrewd businessman and sawed-off-shotgun-toting Wild West type who had come to Alaska in 1890, began driving livestock and pack horses over a trail to the Interior to stock the mining camps that had sprung up in Yukon Territory. The price was $2.00 a head for cattle and $2.50 a head for horses. The Dalton Trail, in reality a toll road, led from Pyramid Harbor on Chilkat Inlet to the vicinity of

Whitehorse, some 300 miles distant. The present-day Haines Highway follows the route of the trail quite closely.

The Dalton Trail was heavily used as a pack route into the Klondike, a longer but easier alternative to the Chilkoot and White Pass Trails, until the White Pass and Yukon railroad out of Skagway was completed in 1900. In 1898 a stop on the trail about 35 miles from Haines turned into a bonanza itself: Porcupine became the center of a rich mining district that produced gold until the mid-1930s, and Haines was the supply depot.

In 1902 the army stepped in with the construction of Fort William H. Seward at Port Chilkoot, 0.5 mile south of Haines Mission. Fort Seward housed two companies of soldiers. By 1904 Haines counted three hotels, two restaurants, several stores, and more than 400 residents. The army post was renamed Chilkoot Barracks in 1922 in commemoration of the famous trail to the Klondike and to avoid confusion with the town of Seward. Between 1922 and 1939 it was the only army post in Alaska. The post served as an induction and rest camp during World War II but was decommissioned in 1947 in favor of other military installations that had been built in Alaska. The property was purchased by a group of World War II veterans who established the community of Port Chilkoot, later merged with the city of Haines. The handsome white frame buildings of the old army post, ringing the grass parade grounds, are a serene sight. Most have been restored for use as private residences or commercial enterprises. The post was designated a National Historic Site in 1972, reverting to the original name Fort William H. Seward.

Two great transportation links were forged out of Haines in the 1940s. The 159-mile Haines Highway was built by the military during World War II to provide access from the Interior to tidewater. Approximating the route of the old Dalton Trail, the all-weather road extends from Haines to Haines Junction to link with the Alaska Highway, giving access to Anchorage, Fairbanks, and the Yukon Territory in Canada. The present Alaska Marine Highway System also had its birth in Haines as the brainchild of Steve Homer, one of the purchasers of the Port Chilkoot post. Homer envisioned a ferry system that would transport both passengers and freight between

Southeast ports and connect them with the Alaska Highway through Haines. He purchased a landing craft, named it the *Chilkoot,* and in 1948 initiated the first ferry service between Haines, Skagway, and Juneau. After three successful years Homer sold the *Chilkoot* to the territory of Alaska. The system proved so popular that a special ship, the 100-foot-long *Chilkat,* was commissioned, becoming the first vessel of the Alaska Marine Highway fleet.

Presently Haines relies primarily upon tourism and transportation to keep the economy fueled. Commercial fishing has always contributed to the economy, and a small lumber mill 4 miles north of town has operated intermittently. With noticeably drier weather than most parts of Southeast, striking wilderness scenery, excellent fishing, a magnificent state park, year-round highway and water access, and the world's largest gathering of bald eagles in residence October through January each year, Haines seems poised to become a significant visitor and recreational destination in the Southeast.

Getting There

You can reach Haines year-round by road via the 159-mile Haines Highway that links with the Alaska Highway at Haines Junction. U.S. and Canadian customs and immigration offices are located at mile 42 on the Haines Highway. Be sure to find out in advance how late they stay open (it has previously been until midnight only). Also check into Canadian regulations concerning such matters as car insurance, cash requirements, pets, and firearms before setting out for the border from Haines.

There is scheduled air service into Haines from both Juneau and Skagway, but no jet service. Alaska state ferries stop at Haines en route between Juneau and Skagway, both northbound and southbound. In summer the *Malaspina* makes a daily round-trip voyage from Juneau to Haines and Skagway, leaving Juneau early in the morning and returning around 10:00 P.M. Other state ferries also dock at Haines and Skagway throughout summer. The ferry terminal is located at Lutak Inlet, 4.5 miles north of Haines (shuttle transportation to town is available).

There are also privately operated ferries that connect Skagway

You will see some of the most spectacular scenery in the Inside Passage while touring the Lynn Canal en route to or from Haines. The octagonal-shaped Eldred Rock is one of two light-houses to see along the way. MICHELLE GURNEY

and Haines towns. Chilkat Cruises (888–766–2103) makes the trip in thirty-five minutes, up to twenty-eight times a day, on two 150-passenger catamarans. There is also a fast ferry that travels between Haines and Juneau daily (visit www.lynncanal.com to find ferry schedules for the Fjord Express). Neither ferry takes automobiles. A few large cruise ships and several smaller ones currently call at Haines. Write the Haines Visitors' Bureau to find out which ones. (See "Information Sources" at the end of this book.)

The northward sail up Lynn Canal rewards ferry and cruise-ship passengers with some of the most beautiful and diverse scenery of the Inside Passage, from the broad shoulders of the Chilkat Mountains to commercial fishing vessels, cruise ships, and tugs with barges. You pass two picturesque lighthouses: Sentinel Light and octagonal Eldred Rock. As you near the approach into Haines, you can see Davidson Glacier flowing toward Chilkat Inlet and, a little farther on, Rainbow Glacier, a "hanging glacier" that cascades over a cliff.

To See and Do

The **Haines Visitors' Information Center** (800–458–3579) is conveniently located at Second and Willard Streets downtown. There is lots of parking available, even for the largest motor homes, and the coffeepot is always on. Pick up walking-tour maps for Haines and Fort Seward.

Your first destination should be historic **Fort William H. Seward** at Port Chilkoot, only a few minutes' walk from Haines center. The neat parade green ringed with white pillared houses of the former army post is an anomaly in Southeast Alaska. The buildings, now in private hands, are identified with small plaques. The large homes at the top of the parade grounds originally constituted officers' row, housing captains, lieutenants, and their families. The white-painted buildings with beautiful oval gable windows have been turned into private residences, rental condominiums, shops, and bed-and-breakfast lodgings.

The bachelor officers' quarters, captains' quarters, and commanding officers' quarters were on the right side of the green as you face uphill. Now these buildings are part of the graceful **Hälsingland Hotel and restaurant.** Directly across the parade grounds from the hotel, the former post hospital now houses the workshops of Alaska Indian Arts Inc. The shingled, barnlike building behind the old hospital dates from the 1890s but not on this site. It was built originally as a cannery warehouse at Pyramid Harbor. The army dismantled the building and moved it to the present location in 1919 as the E & R (Education and Recreation) Hall. The building was renovated in 1967 as the **Chilkat Center for the Arts,** a convention hall and theater. The center also houses the Haines public radio station.

The nonprofit **Alaska Indian Arts** organization is dedicated to the preservation and furtherance of traditional Northwest Coast Indian arts. Artists work on the premises every weekday, carving totem poles, masks, silver jewelry, and other art pieces. Their artisans have produced totem poles for clients all over the world, and many in Alaska. In 1970 they carved Alaska's—and, at the time, the world's—tallest totem pole (132.5 feet) for Japan's Osaka World's Fair. The pole now stands in the village of Kake on Kupreanof Island. Visitors are welcome to tour the workshops and visit with the artists.

There is a showroom where you can purchase their work.

Alaska Indian Arts was founded by the late Carl Heinmiller, a retired army major and one of the group of veterans who purchased the Port Chilkoot post. Heinmiller also formed the **Chilkat Dancers,** who give scheduled evening performances in the Chilkat Center for the Arts. Searching for a way to involve the local youth in constructive projects, Heinmiller drew upon the knowledge of the local Tlingit population in Haines and Klukwan to help re-create traditional Tlingit dances with authentic costumes and masks. All children were encouraged to participate—Tlingit, Caucasian, old, young, boy, or girl. Gradually the idea took shape, and now, some forty years later, the Chilkat Dancers of Haines are known throughout the world for their stirring performances. The group performs four evenings a week in summer. You can't help but enjoy the fantastic carved wooden masks, elaborate Chilkat blankets, ermine headdresses, beaded dance shirts, and button blankets. Take your camera (with flash), as photographs are permitted.

Totem Village, located on the parade grounds of Fort William H. Seward, is also the work of Alaska Indian Arts. A salmon bake, with fresh salmon grilled over an alder fire, takes place here at the Raven Tribal House several evenings a week in summer. The totem poles in and around the house were some of the first ever carved by Alaska Indian Arts, and it is interesting to compare these early efforts with some of the later ones.

The two corner posts at the front were carved in the late 1960s. The top figure is Bear, with a small Frog on his chest. The center figure is Sea-Bear (with fins instead of legs), holding Halibut in his mouth. On the bottom is Bear again, holding a *tinneh*, a shield-shaped copper plate that was used as a form of currency by Southeast Natives in earlier days. In the carving the *tinneh* symbolizes wealth.

The freestanding pole at the front and to the left of the house was one of the first carved. From top to bottom the figures are Raven, as the founder of the world, Bear holding a tinneh, and Beaver holding the traditional stick (the staff of authority of a chief of the Beaver clan) but, untraditionally, in a vertical position. The lone face is the Sun, and the bottom figure is Whale, with the tail curled in front.

The back corner posts show a potlatch chief at the top, holding a staff and wearing his ringed potlatch hat. Raven is below him, easily identified by the wings and long, straight beak. The head at the bottom is Frog, known by the wide mouth with protruding tongue.

The tall center totem in back of the house is one of several copies of the small Friendship pole that can be seen in the city's Sheldon Museum. The original pole, only 28 inches high, was presented to Steve Sheldon of Haines in the 1920s by Chilkat Tlingit from Klukwan. Sheldon, a U.S. deputy marshal, had been instrumental in restoring goodwill between conflicting clans, and the totem symbolizes peace by representing both Eagle and Raven moieties on the same pole. From top to bottom the primary figures are Eagle (wearing hat), Raven (diving), Hawk, Bear, Frog, Wolf, and (very small) Eagle. Alaska Indian Arts carvers have produced two other copies of the original pole. One is displayed in Juneau in the foyer of the Alaska Court Building. A more recent pole, completed in 1977, stands before the Main Street school in Haines.

There are carved interior house posts, too. Inside the door to the right, you will recognize the figure of Beaver from his crosswise stick and crosshatched tail, with a small face in the tail joint. Hawk is below him, and Frog is on the bottom. Inside the door to the left is Raven on top, with a protruding beak. On the rear wall on the right is a special pole honoring Carl Heinmiller and his Tlingit name, *Ka Woosh' Gaaw,* which he translated as meaning the "sound of the Raven's wings." The diving Raven figure is dramatic on this post. The pole on the left was raised in honor of Heinmiller's daughter, Judy Heinmiller Clark. It is called "Looking in the Water" and, according to Heinmiller, was named for her "big, blue eyes." The pole recalls the story of Raven who looks in the water, sees his own image, and fears that he represents all of the evil in the world. The top figure is Raven, with a long bill, almost like a mosquito's. In the middle is an inverted figure with arms, representing imagination. On the bottom the inverted figure of Raven represents his image reflected in the water.

A 37-foot totem pole, **Raven: Guardian Spirit of the Clans,** stands outside the Chilkat Center for the Arts. Each of the figures of this unusual pole was carved by a different artist. From top to bottom the figures include Raven (carved by Greg Horner); Strong Man,

Corner post at Totem Village in Fort William H. Seward depicts Bear, Frog, and Halibut motifs.

holding Whale by the tail (by Dave Svenson); Bird figure, emerging from Whale's mouth (John Hagen); Beaver (Edwin Kasko); Man holding tinneh (Clifford Thomas); and Frog (Charles Jimmie). The pole was completed in 1980.

Fort Seward galleries include the **Sea Wolf** sculpture studio of lifelong Haines resident Tresham Gregg, situated on the parade green. Also check out **The Wild Iris,** featuring handcrafted gold and silver jewelry, prints, cards, hand-screened shirts and carry bags, and other items by owner-artists Fred and Madeleine Shields, and **Dejon Delights,** for smoked salmon.

From Port Chilkoot it is a short walk along Beach Road, following the shoreline to the north, to arrive at Haines proper. **Lookout Park** overlooks the Haines waterfront and small boat harbor, with benches, picnic areas, circular viewing platforms, a totem pole, and a Rube Goldberg steam-mining drill used in the Chilkat Valley around 1900. A topographical sign identifies mountain peaks, glaciers, and other natural features in the vicinity. The **City Boat Harbor** is home port for the Haines fishing fleet. You might see the gill-net fishermen spreading their nets on the dock to dry, or making repairs.

Across Beach Road from the harbor, the **Sheldon Jackson Museum and Cultural Center** houses an extensive local-history collection. The museum is named for Steve Sheldon, who adventured his way

A well-worn Haines gillnetter submits to a preseason overhaul at Letnikof Cove.

through Alaska at an early age and wound up in Haines, where he and his wife operated a series of businesses. He later became a U.S. deputy marshal and a U.S. commissioner. The Sheldons were enthusiastic collectors of Indian artifacts and other items of historical or artistic significance, and their collection forms the nucleus of the Sheldon Museum. One of the two Sheldon daughters, Elisabeth Hakkinen, of Haines, organized the collection into museum exhibits. You might encounter her bringing local history to life with her accounts of early-day Haines or offering a cup of Russian tea from the urn upstairs.

The museum's collection of more than 3,000 artifacts takes up two floors. Upstairs you will find a model Chilkat clan house; exhibits on Tlingit-style fishing, basketry, beadwork, and dance; and Chinese camphor-wood trunks. These colorful trunks, covered with pigskin and painted bright red, green, or blue with floral designs, were brought to Alaska by early traders. A special case houses the original lens from the Eldred Rock lighthouse (24 miles south of Haines in Lynn Canal), one of twelve manned lighthouses that formerly watched over the Inside Passage. The lens was in place from 1906 to 1973, when the station was automated.

Downstairs features industry, pioneer, and natural-history exhibits. Missionaries, canneries, gold prospecting, pioneer life, and the military are the focus for several displays. A corner of the room is devoted to Jack Dalton, the shrewd, early businessman who operated a toll road to the Interior and later built a hotel and a saloon in Haines. You see Dalton's pack saddles, yokes, and other equipment used on the Dalton Trail and the sawed-off shotgun he kept loaded with rock salt behind the bar of his saloon.

The museum puts you in perfect position to start the **Haines Walking Tour.** The 1.6-mile route from the museum to Lookout Park is easy walking, mostly on level ground. The tour is based on a historical building survey and provides an insider's look at past and present Haines. Count on spending forty-five minutes to one and one-half hours on your walk. You might reward your effort with a slice of buttermilk pie at the **Lighthouse Restaurant** overlooking the City Boat Harbor or an apricot bearclaw from the **Chilkat Bakery and Restaurant,** off Main Street on Fifth Avenue. **Whale Rider,**

Portage Cove lies beneath the splendid Chilkat Mountains. MICHELLE GURNEY

Uniquely Alaskan, The Far North, Form and Function, and **Windspirit,** near the Visitors Information Center, all feature Haines artists. The **Trading Post** specializes in furs and fur products from Alaska and the Yukon, including red fox and wolverine from the local Chilkat Valley, and handmade items.

A footpath leads from Main Street in Haines to Port Chilkoot. The trail crosses **Tlingit Park** beside an old tree-shaded cemetery and emerges near the Hotel Hälsingland at Fort William H. Seward. Continuing down Beach Road 0.5 mile in the other direction from Fort Seward, you come to the state-operated **Portage Cove State Recreation Site** (no motorized vehicles allowed), with tent sites, picnic tables, rest rooms, and a view of the passing ship traffic on Lynn Canal. A gentle trail follows the shore beyond the campground for about 2.5 miles to Battery Point.

For a greater understanding of the American bald eagle (a species greatly treasured and protected here and in the Chilkat Bald Eagle Preserve north of town), visit the nonprofit **American Bald Eagle Foundation** at Second Avenue and Haines Highway. A large diorama, which contains more than one hundred specimens of birds, wild animals, and fish, displays the diversity of life in the preserve and its surrounding area. A video presentation documents the annual arrival of thousands of the magnificent birds to the area. Out-the-road touring from Haines can take you in three different directions. Follow Lutak Highway to the north along Chilkoot Inlet to reach the state ferry terminal. You will pass the Haines Tank Farm, southern terminus of an old oil pipeline to military installations in Fairbanks. The highway leads to the wide **Chilkoot River,** which tumbles madly over stumps and boulders in its rush to the sea. You can easily imagine brown bears standing in the shallow water and scooping out the salmon that struggle upstream to spawn in Chilkoot Lake (mile 11 at the end of Lutak Road). There is a fish weir on the river to count the salmon as they travel upstream. The daily tally is noted on a blackboard alongside the road.

Go left at a fork in the road to reach the state campground and **Chilkoot Lake,** with good fishing for salmon and Dolly Varden. The facilities include campsites, picnic shelters, and a boat launch. Visitors have been known to drive all the way across the country and up the Alaska Highway to return to this spot. The right fork in the road leads across the river to a residential road on Lutak Inlet.

Driving south out of Haines on Mud Bay Road toward Chilkat

The face of Alsek Glacier looms behind rafters during a guided float trip on the Tatshenshini and Alsek Rivers. BART HENDERSON, CHILKAT GUIDES

State Park, you will be following the shore of Chilkat Inlet. You will be rewarded with views of the Chilkat Mountains, the Chilkat River, glaciers, wildflowers, and picturesque old cannery buildings at Letnikof Cove. If you're feeling ambitious, stop along the way and hike one of two routes up to the summit of Mount Riley (the second route cuts off from the Battery Point Trail). Here hikers will be rewarded with panoramic views (from 1,760 feet up) of the surrounding Chilkat and Chilkoot ranges.

A right turn off Mud Bay Road at mile 7 (follow the signs) takes you to **Chilkat State Park,** with forested campsites, rest rooms, and a hand-hewn ranger cabin that was built in Nenana (near Fairbanks in the Interior) of white spruce, disassembled, and trucked to the site. From the front deck of the cabin, you can practically reach out and touch the Davidson and Rainbow Glaciers. Follow the road another 500 yards and stop at the boat launch. This is the perfect lunch spot, with picnic tables and fire pits near the shore. There is also a 6.5-mile trail that will lead you through the park to Seduction Point at the tip of the Chilkat Peninsula. Back on Mud Bay Road, continue straight to reach Mud Bay on Chilkoot Inlet. Beach peas bloom here in summer, with lupine and wild roses.

The third road out of Haines, the Haines Highway (connecting with the Alaska Highway), parallels the Chilkat River, which is wide and shallow with many islands and lined with cottonwood trees. Before you get that far, stop in at **Mountain Market** (Haines Highway at Third Avenue). Haines locals gather over morning lattes at this espresso bar, bakery-deli, and natural-foods emporium. At Haines Highway and Sixth, less than a mile from the city center, you come to the entrance of the **Southeast State Fairgrounds** (see the special-events section at the end of this book) and **Dalton City** (907–766–2476), a gold rush theme park created from the movie set for *White Fang.* The Disney movie of the Jack London classic, filmed locally in 1990, left behind a couple dozen false-fronted buildings. State fair officials moved seventeen of them to the forty-acre fairgrounds, then set them up to look like an 1890s gold rush boomtown.

On the river flats near mile 19 are the famous **Eagle Council Grounds,** where an estimated 3,500 bald eagles gather in the cottonwoods along the river from October through January every year to take advantage of a late run of spawning chum salmon. In 1982 the state of Alaska set this area aside as the 49,000-acre Chilkat Bald Eagle Preserve to protect the birds and their habitat. You can observe and photograph the eagles from turnouts on the highway. **Alaska Nature Tours** (P.O. Box 491, Haines, AK 99827; telephone 907–766–2876) leads fall eagle-viewing tours from Haines; there are interpretive walks, birding treks, and guided hikes in summer.

At mile 22 you will see a turnoff for the Tlingit village of **Klukwan.** Klukwan, on the bank of the Chilkat River, has always been the principal village of the Chilkat Tlingit. This is a residential community, with two streets of homes and a log tribal house. Native heritage and cultural tours of Klukwan are offered: This is an opportunity for visitors to view totem poles and house screens normally off-limits to visitors. For information contact **Keet Gooshi Tours** (P.O. Box 997, Haines, AK 99827; telephone 907–766–2168). Klukwan is an acknowledged repository of fine Tlingit art.

Lee Heinmiller explains Chilkat blanket design during a performance of the Chilkat Dancers.

Outdoors enthusiasts will find several hiking trails to their liking in Haines. A brochure called *Haines Is for Hikers,* available at the visitor information center or book stands around Haines, contains maps of principal routes. The most strenuous leads to the top of 3,610-foot Mount Ripinsky, but this 3.6-mile hike to the summit can easily be completed in one full day. If you are more interested in rock climbing or ice climbing, you may want to get in touch with the **Alaska Mountain Guides and Climbing School** (P.O. Box 1081, Haines, AK 99827; telephone 907-766-3366 or 800-766-3396). The school offers an assortment of climbing courses as well as kayaking, rafting, ski mountaineering, canoeing, and glacier hiking trips.

Among the opportunities for visitors who prefer their adventure by water, **Chilkat Guides** (P.O. Box 170, Haines, AK 99827; telephone 907-766-2491) offers float trips (no white water) down the Chilkat or Klehini Rivers. The trips pass through the Chilkat Bald Eagle Preserve; you might also glimpse bears and moose. Chilkat Guides also operates multiday float trips on the spectacular Alsek and Tatshenshini Rivers. **Chilkoot Lake Tours** (P.O. Box 250, Haines, AK 99827; telephone 907-766-3779) has 28-foot pontoon boats that provide immense sightseeing comforts as well. In winter **Chilkoot Sled Dog Adventures** (P.O. Box 826, Haines, AK 99827; telephone 907-767-5667) offers family dogsled rides and overnight trips in Chilkat Bald Eagle Preserve. In summer the company schedules dogsled demos in the Fort Seward area. Call for times.

If your idea of adventure includes sampling local wines and ales, you may want to visit **Great Land Wines** (25 Small Tracts Road, P.O. Box 1083, Haines, AK 99827; telephone 907-766-2698) or the **Haines Brewing Company** (108 White Fang Way, Dalton City, SE Fairgrounds, P.O. Box 911, Haines, AK 99827; telephone 907-766-3823).

Evening entertainment in Haines includes the Chilkat Dancers, performing traditional Northwest Coast Indian dances on the Fort Seward parade grounds in conjunction with cruise-ship arrivals. Check the visitor center for times.

Special Events

The list of special events in Haines is topped by the **Southeast Alaska State Fair,** held the second or third week in August. Popular features of the five-day regional fair include craft exhibits, home-baked and home-canned foods, a horse show, and a parade. Reservations for the ferry are a must for the week of the fair, even for walk-on passengers.

The **Alaska State Community Theater Festival** (Actfest) occurs in April of odd-numbered years in the Chilkat Center for the Arts and brings plays from performing groups throughout the state. In May Haines really comes alive. There's an annual **Craftbeer and Homebrew Festival,** the **Chilkoot to Chilkat Biathlon** and the **King Salmon Derby,** which is held on Memorial Day weekend. In summer you can sign up for the annual **Kluane to Chilkat 160-mile bike relay,** or enjoy the **Summer Solstice Celebration,** the **Independence Day Celebration,** or a field day of games on **Fort Seward Day.** Take in the **State Fair and Bald Eagle Music Festival** in August, or compete in the **Sam Donajkowski Memorial Triathlon.** The **Alaska Bald Eagle Festival** is held in November, and the city hosts the annual **Alcan 200 Road Rally** in late January.

SKAGWAY
Population 862

Every day is showtime in this tiny outpost of the gold rush (812 miles from Bellingham via the Marine Highway)—in summer. The curtain comes down when the last cruise ship leaves in the fall, and the population dwindles to nearly nothing. Other towns might offer more grandiose scenery, fancier hotels, or better fishing, but Skagway knows how to entertain. Don't let the show fool you, though. For all the period costuming and honky-tonk veneer, Skagway is not a gold rush theme park—it's the genuine article. You can stay at hotels on Broadway that opened during the gold rush, and drink in saloons that served whiskey to stampeders. The ties to history are very direct. Quite a few families living in Skagway today set down their roots during that eventful era of '98.

Skagway is good fun for a day or two, especially if the weather is nice (which it probably will be since the precipitation averages only 26 inches a year—a desert compared with other parts of Southeast). You will enjoy the wooden sidewalks, meticulously restored storefronts,

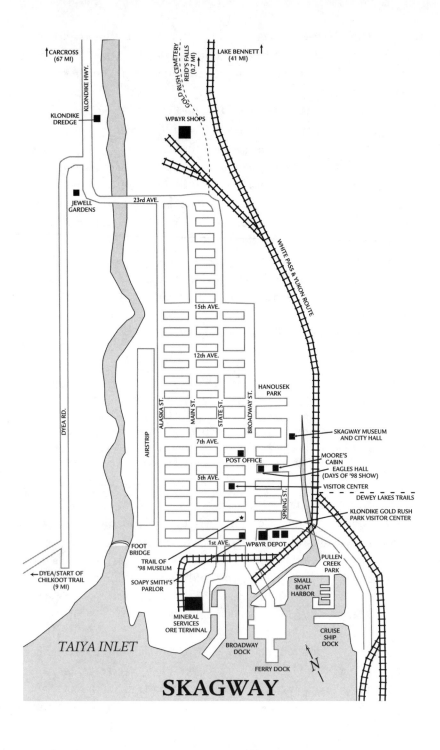

SKAGWAY

old-time hotels, and other trimmings of the Days of '98, topped off with an evening melodrama and a drink at the famous Red Onion Saloon.

Background

The historic gold rush town of Skagway is tucked up into the head of Taiya Inlet at the northern extreme of Lynn Canal, 90 air miles northwest of Juneau. The town occupies the level floor of a long, narrow valley at the mouth of the Skagway River. The Coast Mountains rise on every side, a seemingly impenetrable barrier to the goldfields of the Canadian Klondike. No one knows for certain the origin of the town's name. A popular explanation is that the name derives from a Tlingit word, *Skagua,* meaning "windy place" or "place where the north wind blows," as indeed it does in winter. Early residents spelled the name Skaguay, but the name was changed to the present form when the post office was established.

The first recorded settler in Skagway was a prescient riverboat captain named William Moore. Moore had been in Wrangell during the first gold strike to affect Alaska in 1861. He got his share of the bonanza by transporting prospectors by steamer up the Stikine River to the diggings in Canada. He was on the Stikine again in 1873 to move prospectors into the new Cassiar goldfields. By 1887 Moore was helping a survey party determine the boundary line between Alaska and Canada. With his son, he staked a homestead on the flats at the mouth of the Skagway River and began planning a wharf to accommodate the traffic he was sure would come knocking at the back door to the Yukon.

And come they did, ten years later, at a time when the nation was suffering a severe economic depression. When word reached a moody and out-of-work populace in July 1897 that a "ton of gold" had been brought out of the Klondike, West Coast docks groaned under the weight of fortune hunters waiting for steamers to take them north. Six days after the *Portland* docked in Seattle with the first samples of Klondike gold, the *Queen* was bound for Moore's wharf at the head of Lynn Canal with a cargo of impatient prospectors. The stampeders promptly overran Moore's property and set about the business of getting into the Klondike. A tent city sprang into place on the Moore homestead. By October the new boomtown of Skagway had streets, frame houses, dance halls, and three wharves under construction. The population passed 10,000 as wave upon wave of fortune seekers made their way north.

From Skagway the way to the Klondike led over the Coast Mountains through 2,900-foot White Pass to Lake Bennett in Canada, a trip of approximately 40 miles. Lake Bennett was the beginning of a system of interconnecting lakes and rivers that would float the prospectors the rest of the 500 miles to Dawson on the Yukon River. A more popular alternative was the Chilkoot Trail, which followed a parallel course through the mountains from Dyea, an old Indian village and trading post 9 miles from Skagway (by today's road) at the extreme northern tip of Taiya Inlet. This trail had long been used by the Chilkat Tlingit as a trading route to the Interior, and hundreds of prospectors had used it to traverse the mountains years before the big strike came. Both trails led to Lake Bennett, but the Chilkoot was shorter at only 32 miles.

With shorter came steeper, however; the final half-mile to the 3,550-foot summit of Chilkoot Pass was a tortuous forty-five-degree climb. In the winter steps were chopped into the snow, and the image of the long, black line of prospectors trudging single file up the "Golden Stairs" of Chilkoot Pass has come to symbolize the sacrifices made in the name of gold. Crossing the pass one time would have been plenty for anyone, but the stampeders were forced to assault the summit repeatedly, some as many as thirty times, to transport their gear (enough for a year's prospecting) and the 1,550 pounds of food and clothing that the Canadian government required them to have before crossing the border. At the end of the trail, the stampeders camped beside Lake Bennett, where they manufactured crude boats out of the surrounding stands of timber and waited for the spring breakup. When the lake ice broke up on 29 May 1898, more than 7,000 boats charged downriver to Dawson.

Skagway grew in reputation as a hard-bitten, lawless frontier town. Everyone was there for one reason only: to make money—big money—if not in the goldfields, then by providing services (some of them of the more reprehensible and unmentionable variety) to those who were on their way to the goldfields, or even by relieving the gold from those on their way back. The most notorious outlaw of the era was Jefferson Randolph "Soapy" Smith, a sleazy, two-bit con artist whose nickname derived from one of his better-known cons, which was to "give away" ordinary bars of soap purportedly wrapped in large-denomination bills for the price of a mere $5.00. Soapy enjoyed great success with this and other variations of the standard shell game but did not hesitate to use more direct methods to unburden prospectors of their grubstakes or their pokes of gold when appropriate.

Surrounded by the Chilkoot Mountains, Skagway maintains its gold rush image with carefully restored false-fronted buildings. MICHELLE GURNEY

The citizens grew increasingly outraged at Smith's brazen lawlessness, and in July 1898 Soapy's luck ran out. Two of his henchmen had robbed a prospector, J. D. Stewart, of $2,600 in gold dust, and Stewart screamed long and loudly for justice. The town citizens gathered down at the docks to discuss the situation. Frank Reid, the town surveyor, stood guard outside. When Soapy learned about the meeting, he took his rifle and set off for the dock but was halted. He struck at Reid with his rifle. Reid pushed it aside and fired his revolver, but his gun jammed. His first shot misfired. His second and third shots killed Smith instantly, but Reid took a bullet in the groin and died twelve days later. Both men are buried in Skagway's Gold Rush Cemetery.

During the first year of the rush, an estimated 20,000 to 30,000 '98ers crossed the two trails into Canada. It was not long before several enterprising individuals had built crude tramways to help transport goods to the summit. The most sophisticated on the Chilkoot Trail was an aerial tramway completed by the Chilkoot Railroad and Transportation Company in May 1898. The company charged 7½ cents a pound to haul supplies over the pass. In times of such fervor as the gold rush of 1898, though, big dreams are the order of the day, and the man who now stepped onto the stage had the biggest vision of all: to build a railroad over White Pass.

Michael J. Heney, an Irish railroad contractor, was sure that the railway could be built, and, after an all-night meeting in Skagway, a group of English financiers agreed. Construction began May 27, 1898, with picks, shovels, and blasting powder. The rails reached to the summit of White Pass by February 18, 1899, to Lake Bennett by July 6, 1899, and to Whitehorse by July 29, 1900: a total distance of 110 miles. Many stories attend the building of the White Pass and Yukon Route (which was quickly nicknamed the "Wait Patiently and You'll Ride") and the superhuman feats of Big Mike Heney, the "Irish Prince." One of them concerns Heney's reaction when his crew reached the summit of White Pass only to be halted by a Canadian border guard. Heney sent up an ambassador with a bottle of scotch in each pocket and a box of cigars under each arm. When the guard woke up a day or so later, so the story goes, Heney's crew was laying track a mile down the other side.

With completion of the railroad, the town of Dyea, which had vied with Skagway for the title of largest town in Alaska, folded. Most of the buildings were torn down for lumber. The White Pass and Yukon Route helped things along by buying up and dismantling the Chilkoot Railroad and Transportation Company tram to eliminate any competition from that direction. At present the most tangible reminder of the thousands of people who once passed through the town is the Slide Cemetery, where victims of an avalanche on the Chilkoot Trail in April 1898 lie buried.

Although the rush to the Klondike was nearly over by the time the railroad was completed—prospectors having been diverted to the Nome strike in 1899—the White Pass and Yukon operated steadily as a connecting link for passengers and freight between the coast and the head of navigable waters in the Yukon, bringing a sense of stability to the town of Skagway. From its boomtown origins, Skagway steadied to become one of Alaska's first two incorporated cities in 1900 (Juneau was the other). The thousands of occupants turned to hundreds of residents, and the population has remained at that level except for a period during World War II when the town swelled again as a supply depot for construction of the Alaska Highway.

Until 1982 the White Pass and Yukon railroad was the focal point of Skagway's economy, operating continuously, winter and summer, as an integrated ship-train-truck transportation system to bring goods into and out of the Yukon. In later years a major portion of the freight business consisted of hauling mineral concentrates (silver, lead, zinc, copper, and asbestos—not gold) out of Interior mines and shipping them south by water. In 1982 railroad officials announced that the White Pass and Yukon would suspend operations indefinitely: Closure of the Anvil Mines near Ross River in the Yukon and the subsequent loss of freight business made the railroad uneconomical. With a majority of permanent residents employed by the railroad, closure of the White Pass and Yukon Route struck at the heart of the community, and the already meager population dwindled. The summer-visitor industry continued to grow, however—currently more than 400,000 visitors arrive by cruise ship and highway each season. In 1989 the railroad reopened on a summer-excursion basis. At present the White Pass and Yukon operates a daily three-hour round-trip to the White Pass summit, and the sounds of the steam whistle once again echo through the valley.

And what of Captain Moore, who was unceremoniously pushed aside while his homestead was marked off into city streets? He did not make out too badly after all. After pursuing his claims through the courts, Moore was ultimately awarded one-quarter of the assessed value of all the original town lots in Skagway, and he sold his wharf to the railroad.

Getting There

Skagway is the northernmost stop on the Inside Passage for both cruise ships and Alaska state ferries. Both dock right in town. You can reach Skagway by car from Carcross via the Klondike Highway (connecting with the Alaska Highway at Whitehorse). If traveling this route, you must report to U.S. Customs and Immigration before entering Skagway. If you are outward-bound, you report to Canadian Customs in Fraser. Check ahead for office hours and Canadian regulations concerning firearms, pets, vehicle registration, and cash requirements (and be thankful you do not have to carry a ton of food with you the way the '98ers did!).

Gray Line of Alaska (800-544-2206) operates scheduled motor-coach service between Skagway, Whitehorse, and other cities in Alaska and the Yukon; smaller shuttle services are available as well. In summer you can also travel to Skagway aboard the historic White Pass and Yukon Route (800-343-7373) railroad from Fraser (with connecting bus service from Whitehorse to Fraser). Skagway Air Service (907-983-2218) operates a scheduled air taxi service (not jet) into Skagway and between Juneau and Haines. The airstrip is located alongside the Skagway River at the edge of town.

Another summer option: Haines and Skagway are 350 miles apart by road, but just 35 minutes apart by water. Chilkat Cruises (888-766-2013) operates two 150-passenger catamarans, known as the Fast Ferry, up to twenty-eight times daily between these two ports.

To See and Do

Approaching Skagway by water you'll cruise the length of Taiya Inlet. A perfect fjord, the passage is dark and brooding but very beautiful, the walls gradually closing together while the mountains drop to the sea. Your first sight of Skagway will be the brown ore terminal owned by the state of Alaska. Soon you will be able to pick out the gold onion dome on the Golden North Hotel, the oldest operating hotel in Alaska, dating from 1898. When the ship docks, look up at the rock walls above the wharf area. Painted there is the **registry for ships** that have called at Skagway since the town's beginning (the practice still continues). Skagway's cliffs have long served as natural billboards. The **painted advertisements** east of Fourth Avenue were the creations of gold rush shopkeepers. The clock was contributed by Kirmse's curio shop, which, established in 1897, now advertises as "Alaska's oldest gift shop." (Look for the colorful totem pole in front of the store on Broadway. The store clerks still use the original cash register to ring up sales.) The hands of the clock point to 8:20, the hour Lincoln was shot, which was the conventional setting for clocks not running.

Broadway, the main street, beckons with a cornucopia of curio shops, galleries, restaurants, and saloons, many housed in buildings original to the gold rush. This commercial core of Skagway is part of **Klondike Gold Rush National Historical Park.** There are four separate units to the park: a visitor center in Seattle's Pioneer Square (117 South Main Street), with historical exhibits and films (the '98ers departed from there on their 1,100-mile journey to Skagway); the 8-block historical district in Skagway; the town site of Dyea and the Chilkoot Trail; and the White Pass Trail.

In the Skagway sector, state, city, federal, and private funds are at work restoring many of the historic structures in town—fourteen of the fifteen historic buildings purchased have been restored. This is a three-step process, beginning with research and documentation, followed by "stabilization" of buildings in their present locations and conditions, and finally complete restoration to the original appearance. Some of these efforts may be taking place around you as you walk through the streets of Skagway. (One of the most recent, the **Mascot Saloon,** has been restored as a museum illustrating the role of saloons in gold rush history.) The park visitor center is located in the restored White Pass and Yukon depot at Broadway and Second

Avenue. The depot was hastily thrown together in 1898, of packing crates and other ready-to-hand materials. Inside you will find exhibits, films, brochures, and maps. National Park Service naturalists conduct forty-five-minute guided walking tours of historic Skagway several times a day. Tours leave from the visitor center. Or you can guide yourself through the historic district with a *Skagway Walking Tour* brochure and map, obtained from the visitor center. The basic self-guided tour takes sixty to ninety minutes.

The Skagway Visitors' Center is housed in a most remarkable structure: the **Arctic Brotherhood Hall** on Broadway near Second Avenue. This building, completed in 1899, was the headquarters and first hall of the Fraternal Order of the Arctic Brotherhood, a benevolent organization that, like many others, sprang into being during the gold rush era to provide a social outlet for men who were far from home. At the height of the gold rush, the organization counted thirty chapters, or "camps," in Alaska and Canada. The facade of the building is constructed of more than 20,000 pieces of driftwood arranged in a basket-weave pattern, with the date 1899 over the door and the brotherhood's emblem—the letters *AB*—in a gold pan full of gold nuggets, at the top.

The **Trail of '98 Museum,** 1 block east of Broadway on Seventh Avenue in the McCabe College/City Hall building, is packed with wonderful relics of the gold rush, from wagon wheels and a pilot's hand-drawn chart of the Yukon River from the stern-wheeler *Klondike* to games of chance, gold scales, rocker boxes, and an early-1900s menu board offering "plain steak" for 25 cents, rib steak for 35 cents, and sirloin for 40 cents. Every corner offers up treasures: a rusty stove and kettle that crossed the Chilkoot Trail, a small organ lovingly carried to Skagway in 1898. A furnished setting in one portion of the museum depicts "Victorian Life in Skagway." The museum devotes quite a bit of space to those famous Skagway characters, Jefferson Randolph Smith and Frank Reid, and you can purchase copies of the July 15, 1898, edition of the *Skagway News* reporting the events leading up to their deaths. The paper makes interesting reading, not just for the details of the story but for the steamer ads: "Quick Time. First-Class Accommodations. The Fast and Commodious Steamer 'Farallon,' Makes Regular Trips Between

The Arctic Brotherhood Hall, built in 1899, was the headquarters for the Fraternal Order of the Arctic Brotherhood during the gold rush era. Today it houses Skagway's visitor center. MICHELLE GURNEY

Skaguay, Dyea, Haines' Mission, Juneau, Wrangel and all Puget Sound Ports."

The museum has records of persons crossing the Canadian border in either direction during the critical stampede years, including information that appeared in the original logbooks kept by the Royal Canadian Mounted Police, plus passenger lists from White Pass Steamships and other records. When time permits, the staff will check the records for information about your ancestors who might have helped make gold rush history.

Skagway has a history of moving things around. Originally the tracks of the White Pass and Yukon railroad headed straight up Broadway toward the mountains, whereas the main commercial streets ran east and west. In 1908 several of the commercial proprietors decided to cluster their businesses along Broadway, where they are presently located. The **Lynch and Kennedy Dry Goods store,** on Broadway near Fourth Avenue, had to be cut into three pieces before it could be moved from its former location on Sixth Avenue. The building was an army barracks prior to the construction of Fort William H. Seward in Port Chilkoot in 1904. When the barracks was installed at the new address, a false front was added to make the building blend in with surrounding facades.

Almost every building in Skagway seems to have played a part in the gold rush, from **Soapy Smith's Parlor** (Second Avenue and Broadway; not open to the public) to the antique-filled **Golden North Hotel** (one of Alaska's oldest). The **Red Onion Saloon** dates from 1898 as a saloon and house of prostitution. The saloon, which serves from the original 19-foot mahogany bar, packs in locals as well as tourists. Staff members dress in authentic 1890s attire, and a small collection of bawdy-house miscellany is on display. When the Red Onion was moved to the present location, the building was installed backwards; evidently it fit better front-to-back. Farther up Broadway the **Skagway Inn Bed & Breakfast** (Broadway and Seventh) dates from 1897, first as a brothel, then as a boardinghouse and inn. (With twelve cozy rooms, all different and full of character, it's a great place to stay if you don't mind a bath down the hall.)

The oldest building of all is **Moore's Cabin** (Fifth Avenue, off Broadway), which was built by Captain Moore and his son Ben as part of the Moore homestead in 1888. The tiny house has been stabilized with new exterior logs, but the interior newspaper-lined walls remain unchanged. You can peer through the small window in the front door but will be able to make out little in the gloom. The gray frame house beside the cabin is the **Moore House,** later built by Ben Moore to house his family.

Another historical structure houses the Skagway city offices on Seventh Avenue. The building was constructed in 1899 as McCabe Methodist College, Alaska's first institute of higher learning, but it stayed open for only two terms. The building then housed U.S. District Court Number One.

Serious walkers with a couple of hours at their disposal can easily make their way to the **Gold Rush Cemetery,** about 2 level miles from downtown Skagway. The route lies straight up State Street from the waterfront. At Twenty-third Avenue, State Street curves around to the left to cross the Skagway River for the road to Dyea and the Klondike Highway. Your way lies straight ahead, following the sign to the Gold Rush Cemetery.

Most of the graves in the Gold Rush Cemetery date from 1898 to 1904. The two most famous are those of Frank Reid and Jefferson Randolph "Soapy" Smith. Soapy's grave is enclosed within four plain wooden posts, with iron pipes strung between and the simple inscription "Jefferson R. Smith, died July 8, 1898, age 38 years." This is not the original tombstone, which disappeared long ago. Reid has been given a massive monument and the words, "He gave his life for the honor of Skagway." The National Park Service publishes a brief *Gold Rush Cemetery Guide* containing biographies of some of the individuals buried there (available at the park visitor center). For additional information look in bookshops for *Gold Rush Cemetery* by local historian Glenda Choate (Lynn Canal Publishing). From the cemetery it is worth taking the five-minute climb to **Reid's Falls.** These 300-foot falls cascade deep in the forest.

Although Skagway, more than other Southeast destinations, lends itself to walking, there are interesting options for seeing the sights. For example, the **Skagway Street Car Company** (907–983–2908) conducts Skagway historical tours (including the Gold Rush Cemetery) in a fleet of vintage 1936–37 black-and-buttercup-yellow White Motor Company national park sightseeing vehicles. Costumed

Tour the town in style with the Skagway Street Car Company. MICHELLE GURNEY

chauffeurs breathe life into the cast of Skagway pioneers with polished vignettes from gold rush history. The two-hour tour concludes with a slide show/performance, *The Skagway Story,* at the Skagway Mercantile building on Second Avenue, off Broadway.

The host of shops along Broadway offer every imaginable trinket and souvenir, from the tacky to the sublime. The venerable **Kirmse's** and **Corrington's Alaskan Ivory** are emporiums of gold, jade, ivory, and soapstone. The wonderfully bizarre **Corrington Museum of Alaskan History,** in the back of the store, sketches periods and themes of Alaskan history—aviation, World War II, the Iditarod Race—through artifacts, photographs, and carved ivory models. Thirty-two scrimshawed walrus tusks, commissioned by proprietor Dennis Corrington to commemorate events in Alaska's past, form the core of the collection.

Dedman's Photo Shop and Art Gallery specializes in books pertaining to Skagway and the Chilkoot Trail. Some of the paintings in the upstairs art gallery are by Dedman's owner, third-generation Skagway resident Barbara Kalen, who specializes in scenes of the White Pass and Yukon railroad. **Inside Passage Arts, David Present**

One of the most famous graves in the Gold Rush Cemetery reads: "He gave his life for the honor of Skagway." The epitaph belongs to Frank Reid, town surveyor turned hero after he shot and killed the infamous Soapy Smith. MICHELLE GURNEY

Gallery, and **The Cabbage Rose** all deserve a browse.

All that shopping builds up an appetite, and a rich selection of cafes, restaurants, and snack shops stand ready to oblige. The **Sweet Tooth Cafe,** a Skagway institution, opens at 6:00 A.M. with fresh donuts and cinnamon rolls. A more recent addition, **Mabel G. Smith's** (Fifth Avenue, off Broadway), serves espresso and desserts. **Haven,** which sits just off the beaten path on Ninth Avenue and State Street, is an excellent option as well. This cafe offers espresso and light fare and the highly recommended cafe de menthe—iced or otherwise. This is also a great spot to relax on a rainy evening; there are lots of board games and old issues of *National Geographic* to help you pass the time.

Entertainment options include the long-running (more than seventy-five years) *Days of '98* show, a lively melodrama based on the town's early history that features Soapy Smith and the other Skagway characters. Some strictly-for-fun gambling (for kids, too—bring the whole family) precedes the evening show, which plays in the Eagles Hall at Broadway and Sixth. (There's a daytime version as well.)

Check with the Gray Line desk in the Westmark Hotel or the Red Onion Saloon about the schedule of shows for **Madame Jan's Gold-panning Camp,** located about 3 miles from Skagway at a spot called "Liarsville." The lighthearted gold-camp experience begins with a warm welcome from the luscious Miss Lil. Gathered around the campfire you'll hear some yarns, drink hot cider, meet a musher and team of dogs, and learn how to pan for gold. The show lasts about one hour.

You can also spend a few hours enjoying your own gold-mining experience with **Klondike Gold Dredge Tours.** The dredge features the very piece of technology that was responsible for mining over 70 percent of all gold taken from Alaska and the Yukon. In fact, you are guaranteed to hit gold yourself thanks to a little instruction from their experienced panners. You can walk to the dredge from town (1.7 miles); however, they have several pickup locations in Skagway, and you just need to call them at (907) 983–3175 to arrange a ride.

As you make your way toward "pay dirt," you will spot some lovely gardens on your left. Run by local green thumb Charlotte Jewell, **Jewell Gardens** is a nice place to spend an hour or so. Walk along the boardwalk "stem" to reach the flower gardens, where you will also see a miniature Skagway town site with a model train racing through it, as well as an assortment of giant vegetables. The gardens are open from May to September. Tea parties are by reservation only and are held in a solarium overlooking the gardens. Call (907) 983-2111 for a booking.

From Skagway you can embark on many interesting excursions. **Southeast Tours** (Fifth and Broadway, P.O. Box 637, Skagway, AK 99840; www.southeasttours.com) and **Chilkoot Charters and Tours** (340 Seventh Avenue, P.O. Box 1336, Skagway, AK 99840; 907-983-3400; www.skagwaysbesttour.com) offer daily tours of the White Pass summit area, horse adventures where you will have the opportunity to explore a gold claim and prospector's cabin, dogsled adventures, and mountain-biking treks. From May through September the **White Pass and Yukon Route railroad** operates twice-daily, three-hour excursion trains to the White Pass summit, as well as through-service to Fraser, British Columbia, with connecting motorcoach service to Whitehorse (independent passengers should book forty-five days in advance to avoid disappointment). You travel in the original dark green coaches, each named for a Yukon lake. The train climbs from sea level to 2,885 feet in 21 miles, one of the steepest railroad grades in the world. (Sit on the left leaving Skagway for the best view.) For schedules and information write The White Pass and Yukon Route, P.O. Box 435, Skagway, AK 99840; telephone (800) 343-7373 or (907) 983-2217. The railroad also provides a daily shuttle for Chilkoot Trail hikers (see below).

TEMSCO Helicopters (907-983-2900) will take you **helicopter flightseeing** to area glaciers. You fly over Dyea and part of the Chilkoot Trail, investigate a remote glacier-hung valley, then land on the surface of a glacier. You disembark onto the "river of ice," where a guide escorts you to view crevasses, moulins, and other features of the glacier terrain—pretty amazing. Several operators run van tours to the White Pass summit. Call the visitor center (907-983-2854) for names and numbers. **Alaska Direct** (907-983-2854) provides year-round transportation service between Skagway and Whitehorse.

Hikers will want to pick up a Skagway trail map from a visitor center. The **Dewey Lakes trail system** starts across the railroad

Vintage sightseeing vehicles contribute to the historical flavor of Skagway, at the head of Taiya Inlet. The landmark Golden North Hotel dates from the 1898 gold rush. SARAH EPPENBACH

tracks between Third and Fourth Avenues. Signs point the way to several different lakes and falls on trails varying from 0.5 to 5 miles in length. A suspension footbridge over the Skagway River at First Avenue gives access to an easy 1-mile trail to picnic areas at Yakutania Point and Smugglers Cove.

The trail of trails, of course, is the historic **Chilkoot Trail** that leaves from Dyea, 9 miles from Skagway via a dirt road (take a cab or scheduled bus). Largely abandoned after the opening of the White Pass railroad, the Chilkoot was reopened for hikers in the 1960s. The present-day trail, much improved over the original with footbridges and occasional shelters, measures 33 miles from Dyea to Lake Bennett, with an elevation gain of 3,739 feet.

At Bennett **Chilkoot Water Charters** (403–821–3209) provides daily boat shuttle service in summer (on a first-come, first-served basis unless you reserve ahead) between Bennett and the Yukon community of Carcross. From Carcross you can catch a bus back to Skagway. If, due to weather or mechanical delay, the boat option goes awry, you can hike a trail from nearby Lake Lindeman to the White Pass and Yukon rail tracks and then follow them to a junction with the Klondike Highway at Log Cabin. **Frontier Excursions** (907-983-2512) schedules morning and afternoon hiker pickups at Log Cabin. Call them before leaving Skagway for your trek to obtain current pickup times.

Although you will be passing through untamed country, the Chilkoot Trail is more of a walk through history than a wilderness adventure. You will encounter many other people along the trail—in recent years some 3,500 people have hiked the route every season. Camping is allowed in designated areas only; open fires are not allowed. Shelters must be shared and are for drying out only and not for overnight use.

All along the trail you will see objects left behind by the thousands of prospectors who traveled the route in 1897 and 1898 and the remains of the sizable communities that sprang up along the way. For example, Sheep Camp at mile 13 at one time had a population of 6,000 to 8,000 people waiting out winter storms so that they could cross over the pass. There were hotels, saloons, and restaurants to serve them. Lindeman City, over the border almost to Bennett, was a tent town of 10,000 transients in the spring of 1898, but little now remains. At trail's end at Lake Bennett, you pass the weathered log facade of Saint Andrews Church, which prospectors built during the winter of 1898-99 while waiting to journey down to the Yukon. The interior furnishings have been lost to time and souvenir hunters.

I hiked the trail in 1975 with five other women and three dogs. It was quite far along in the season, late September or early October, and the trail saw considerably less traffic then, so we met only one or two other parties along the entire route. The rain pummeled us unpityingly, and we holed up at Lake Lindeman for two or three days to dry ourselves out. When the sun finally emerged, we went out and filled our packs with the largest, roundest, sweetest blueberries I have ever seen. Hiking the Chilkoot was one of the most memorable—and best—outdoor experiences of my life. I vividly recall the moment the clouds lifted from The Scales and we got our first look at the pass. I assumed there had been an avalanche or earthquake because the way seemed completely blocked by a mountain of enormous boulders. I had not cottoned to the fact that the photographs showing stampeders ascending the steep but steady slope to the top of the pass were taken in *winter*. We were crossing Chilkoot Pass in summer, without the leveling cloak of snow.

If you contemplate hiking the Chilkoot Trail, plan well in advance. You need three to five days for a hike as opposed to a forced march. Access to the trail is limited, and trail hikers must pay a fee and have reservations before crossing the border into Canada. Reservations can be made by calling Parks Canada (800–661–0486). For additional information about hiking the trail, contact Klondike Gold Rush National Historical Park (see "Information Sources" at the end of this book).

Special Events

In March Skagway hosts the **Buckwheat Ski Classic,** with amateur and professional Nordic ski races at White Pass. Organizers claim this is a ski race for "the lazy, the infirmed, and a few who are fast." (Contact Wendy Anderson at the Skagway News Depot, P.O. Box 498, Skagway, AK 99840.) **Windfest,** at the end of March, waves goodbye to winter with a chili cook-off, dances, and similar festivities. April brings both the **Skagway Film Festival** and an **International Mini Folk Festival.**

Family and friends return to Skagway from across the nation for the Norman Rockwell–style scene on the Fourth of July. **The Independence Day and Ducky Derby** features a parade, children's races, a horseshoe toss, and a pie-eating contest, but no fireworks. Join in a toast to an infamous conman at **Soapy Smith's wake** on July 8.

Skagway's prolific gardens, publicized nationally as early as 1905, take center stage during the annual **Flower and Garden Show** in August. In mid-September hundreds of runners from Alaska, Canada's Yukon, and the Lower 48 gather in ten-person teams for Southeast's biggest race, the **Klondike Road Relay** from Skagway to Whitehorse. Stay on in Skagway afterward to enjoy **National Hippie Week.**

CHAPTER NINE

OFF THE
MAIN LINE

sing the *Aurora* and *LeConte*—the smaller vessels of the
Alaska Marine Highway fleet—it is easy to sample some of
the fishing towns, vacation retreats, Native villages, and
logging communities along the Inside Passage. Away from the bustle
of urban centers and tourist crowds, you will have the chance to
become acquainted with local residents because people have time to
talk with you out in the bush. If you like to fish, hike, canoe, kayak,
watch birds, or photograph the wild, you can use the small port as a
base to explore the adjacent country. A few of the destinations (Metlakatla, for instance) make excellent day excursions: over in the morning, a quick look around, and back the same day, with a great cruise
in the bargain. Or you can take the ferry to any of the ports and hop
a floatplane back. The possibilities are limitless once you make the
commitment to diverge from the established path and experience
rural Alaska.

All the following communities are accessible via Alaska state ferry
as well as scheduled and charter air taxi services. Depending on the
destination, ferry service may be available several times a week or
once every one or two weeks, so check the schedule in advance.
Travel in these villages and small towns is not for the faint-of-heart
or luxury-minded but for the adventuresome and self-sufficient.
Facilities and services may be limited. Several communities prohibit
the sale and serving of alcohol. Check the lodging directory at the
back of the book for available accommodations.

HYDER
Population 100

Way up at the head of the Portland Canal, the 90-mile-long fjord that forms the southern boundary between Southeast Alaska and Canada, lie a tiny community named Hyder and its Canadian neighbor, Stewart. Publicized as the "friendliest ghost town in Alaska," Hyder developed as a supply depot for intermittent mining activities on both sides of the border. Presently the economy depends on tourism. With excellent highway access (from Cassiar Highway 37 in British Columbia) as well as weekly ferry access (from Ketchikan, summer only), Hyder occupies a unique niche in the southern part of the Panhandle.

The neighborly association with Stewart only adds to the uniqueness. Town residents share a Canadian area code (250 instead of 907 like the rest of Alaska) and price their goods in Canadian dollars (but shops and businesses trade in both U.S. and Canadian currencies). Parents may send their children to Canadian schools; billet them out to Ketchikan, the nearest Alaskan community; or school them at home. Some Hyder residents set their clocks to Pacific time; others to Alaska time.

Hyder is the only community in this book that I have not visited, and I hope to correct that. Local residents report a choice of good restaurants and motels, a triplet of bars, five gift shops, a sporting-goods store, a library, a museum/information center, and other traveler services. Weary road warriors, they claim, can fuel up on a home-cooked meal and the "lowest gas prices for 1,000 miles around." Visitors rave about the mountain and glacier scenery surrounding Hyder. You can drive to the **Salmon Glacier** (20 miles away). From July through September you are likely to see grizzly and black bears, along with bald eagles and spawning salmon, at **Fish Creek Bridge Viewing Area** (4 miles from Hyder). There are charter fishing boats, mountain bikes, and flightseeing available from Stewart.

Hyder and Stewart coordinate an annual **International Days** celebrating Canada Day and Independence Day. The festival begins June 30 and culminates July 4 with a fireworks display. The days between are packed with games, races, food booths, tournaments, dances, and many other events.

The Alaska state ferry *Aurora* currently makes the ten-hour passage between Ketchikan and Hyder/Stewart every Tuesday in summer (the ship actually docks in Stewart). The ferry lays over for a few hours and returns to Ketchikan. There is also scheduled air taxi service from Ketchikan.

METLAKATLA
Population 1,421

The Tsimshian community of Metlakatla is located on the west coast of the Annette Island Indian Reserve. The island, approximately 20 miles long and 12 miles across, is at the southern tip of the Southeast island chain, only 20 miles north of the U.S. and Canadian border. Ketchikan is the nearest large port. The state ferry *Aurora* makes the round-trip between Ketchikan and Metlakatla five days a week. The journey takes approximately one and one-half hours each way. On Saturdays visitors can take a morning ferry to Metlakatla, spend the day there, and catch an evening ferry back to Ketchikan.

Metlakatla was founded by Father William Duncan, a missionary who led his Tsimshian followers from their former home in British Columbia to establish a model community on this Southeast Alaska island in 1887. The United States government created the Annette Island Indian Reserve in 1891. The community elected not to participate in the Alaska Native Claims Settlement Act of 1971 in favor of retaining its status as a reservation.

Like many other communities in Southeast, Metlakatla is supported by timber and fish. The Annette Hemlock Mill produces cants (squared-off logs with the bark removed) that are later sawn into general construction lumber. Annette Island Packing Company, the community fish-processing plant, operates a cold-storage plant. The cannery has been in continuous operation since 1890. Many of the salmon come from Metlakatla's four fish traps, the only such traps allowed in the state. On the journey from Ketchikan, you may pass one of them: a large, floating assembly of heavy-gauge chicken

Metlakatla's four floating fish traps are the only ones allowed in the state.

wire and logs. The salmon are guided into the trap through a series of funneling enclosures. Traps used to be the primary means of harvesting salmon, but the method proved too efficient and the salmon stocks were depleted. The traps were outlawed when Alaska became a state in 1959.

Metlakatla has been opening itself up to tourism in recent years. The Metlakatla Community is running a bus tour of the area, which includes **Father Duncan's cottage and museum,** the **Annette Island Packing plant,** and the white, twin-steepled **William Duncan Memorial Church** (not the original, which burned down in 1948). The missionary lived in the cottage until his death in 1918, and he is buried beside the church. The visit also includes presentations about the tribal longhouse and Tsimshian art and culture, including dance performances.

Ferry travelers might want to take a pleasant walk along Walden Point Road, which leads past some stunted trees and muskeg and on to the Annette Hemlock Mill and then the cannery. Continue down the road to the center of town. There is a good camera view of the entire cannery complex from the floatplane dock. Hike Yellow Hill for a panoramic view of lakes, mountains, or the ocean.

There is a grassy bank overlooking the harbor where you can enjoy a picnic while watching the bald eagles. Taquan Air Alaska (1007

Water Street, Ketchikan, AK 99901; telephone 800-770-8800) offers flightseeing. Promech Airlines (1515 Tongass Avenue, Ketchikan, AK 99901; telephone 907-225-3845) also offers daily flights between the two communities; however, Pacific Air (877-360-3500) may be the most active. In recent years some of the smaller cruise lines have begun calling on Metlakatla.

Metlakatla has a hotel, bed-and-breakfast inns, an art studio, a furniture and gift shop, a pizzeria, a small cafe, and several snack bars. Tours by vans are also available. Metlakatla's paved roads are bicycle-friendly, and bikes are available for rent. Information is available from the community's tourism department (Department of Tourism, P.O. Box 8, Metlakatla, AK 99926; telephone 907-886-8687; www.tours.metlakatla.net).

PRINCE OF WALES ISLAND

Prince of Wales is the largest island in Southeast, measuring 135 miles long by 45 miles wide. The island lies 45 miles west of Ketchikan, an approximate two-and-one-half-hour ride on the *Aurora*. The ferry, which makes the trip several times a week, docks at **Hollis** (population 170), a former gold-mining town and logging camp that is now limited to the ferry terminal, a small float, and a few other services. Prince of Wales has been logged extensively and is undergoing further timber harvest by several Alaska Native corporations, but the island still offers opportunities for travelers. The logging has left the island with more than 1,000 miles of roads—the most extensive road network in Southeast Alaska—which has put some excellent fishing, camping, and kayaking within reach of the family car. But logging is not a gentle or low-profile industry, and it has also left scars.

Sportfishing is excellent on Prince of Wales. Besides the salmon and halibut fishing available off 990 miles of saltwater coast, there are many interior lakes and streams harboring rainbow, steelhead, and cutthroat trout. One of the region's major fly-in fishing lodges, **Waterfall Resort,** is located on the outer coast of the island (see "Wilderness/Fly-in Fishing Lodges" in the lodging directory).

In recent years a massive system of limestone caves has been discovered on the north end of the island in the vicinity of **El Capitan Peak.** Forest Service geologists and an army of international volunteers are in the process of cataloging the caves, but this much is certain: This is a world-class discovery. Bone deposits dating back more than 44,500 years have been found, not to mention an aquatic insect species still in residence that has lived in the dark recesses so many millennia it no longer has eyes or skin color. Evidence of human visitors goes back 3,300 years.

At present two caves in the northern portion of the island are accessible to modern-day tourists. **El Capitan Cave,** with more than 11,000 feet of mapped passage, is the longest known cave in Alaska and the deepest in the world. From late May through mid-September, the Forest Service conducts guided tours through 1,000 feet of the most spacious horizontal passage. Four two-hour tours are conducted Thursdays through Sundays. You need reservations because tours are limited to parties of six. No children under seven and no children with backpacks. Caution: Dress warmly for the chilly forty-degree temperature you'll encounter, and wear boots or comfortable walking shoes. The walking surface in the cave may be rocky, muddy, or uneven. There are places you'll have to crouch a bit to get through an entrance. The Forest Service provides only hard hats; you need to bring two flashlights and extra batteries (it's very dark in there!).

El Capitan is located 11 miles north of Whale Pass. From the ferry terminal at Hollis, it's a 94-mile, three-and-a-half-hour road trip. Access to the cave from the parking lot is provided by a 360-step wooden staircase, climbing about 300 feet. A viewing deck at the cave entrance provides excellent views of El Capitan Passage and an additional view of nearby Kosciusko Island.

Cavern Lake Cave, located at Cavern Lake (about 2.5 miles north of Whale Pass) was formed by outflow from the lake. Salmon, swimming up 108 Creek (yes, that's its name) migrate through cave waters into the lake. *Do not,* says the Forest Service, *attempt to do likewise;* drowning or hypothermia could result. Instead view the cave from the observation deck or at the entrance. Don't disturb the entrance area because an American dipper nests within the cave. Call the Forest Service, Thorne Bay Ranger District Office

Memorial and mortuary poles were brought to Klawock from several abandoned villages on Prince of Wales Island.

(907–828–3304) for reservations and directions for both caves.

From Hollis the road leads westward to connect with a network of old and new logging roads. A turnoff to the south leads to the village of **Hydaburg** (population 425), the principal community of Haida Indians in Southeast. The village was established in 1911–12, when several Haida villages in the vicinity joined together to form a school. At Hydaburg you will find a wonderful collection of old totem poles but few visitor facilities.

Craig (population 2,200), 31 miles from Hollis, is situated on a tiny island connected by a short causeway to Prince of Wales. This is a lively community. Loggers and fisherfolk come together to blow off steam at the Craig Inn on Saturday nights. The community was formerly the site of several fish salteries, followed by canneries, and a sizable seine fleet still ties up at the dock. The largest community on Prince of Wales, Craig offers a full range of services: bank, grocery stores, hotels, restaurants, bars, library, swimming pool, recreation center, and shops. **Alaska Gifts** carries a large selection of Alaska books—more than 500 titles. A new totem pole was raised in Craig in recent years. The Healing Heart totem pole was carved by Stan Marsden, and it is located on the Craig-Klawock Highway in a park off East Hamilton Drive. The pole was raised in memory of Marsden's son, Jim.

The nearby community of **Klawock** (population 800), a Tlingit Indian village 24 miles from Hollis, was the site of the first salmon cannery in Alaska in 1878, which operated for fifty-one years. The town has an important collection of totem poles—memorial and mortuary poles that were gathered from abandoned sites farther north on the island, from the village of Tuxekan in particular. The poles are arranged in a park overlooking the town. One of the most striking poles has a 12-foot Killer Whale mounted crosswise atop the figure of Brown Bear. Another unusual pole recalls Raven's efforts to destroy a giant clam that was threatening the people. The clam is shown halfway up the pole. Klawock facilities include the comfortable **Fireweed Lodge** and several bed-and-breakfast inns. For visitors with wheels, **Log Cabin Resort** is a good place to park the motor home and stay for awhile. Tours of the **Prince of Wales Fish Hatchery** on the Klawock River are available daily, noon to 4:30 P.M., telephone (907) 755–2231.

The road to **Thorne Bay** (population 450) winds northwest from Klawock for 35 miles (59 miles from Hollis) through the interior forest. You will see many signs of logging and wildflowers rimming the road, especially Alaska cotton, fireweed, and bunchberry. Thorne Bay used to be the largest logging camp in Alaska, with a school, church, post office, and shops. Louisiana-Pacific has since packed up most of the logging operation, but the community voted in 1982 to incorporate as a city. There is a grocery and sporting-goods store but few other services. Overnight accommodations consist of bed-and-breakfast lodgings and **McFarland's Floatel,** a floating resort and beachside cabin complex (888–828–3335). A short drive out of Thorne Bay takes you to Sandy Beach overlooking Clarence Strait; you can sometimes spot cruise ships steaming past in the distance. You can also check out the fishing and wildlife at the Thorne River.

Facilities are few up on the north end of Prince of Wales. **Coffman Cove** and **Whale Pass** are logging-camp communities. Lodging and RV facilities are available. At the extreme northern tip of the island, the fishing villages of **Port Protection** and **Point Baker**—by choice unconnected to and thus unreachable by the

Float houses bob in the sunset at Thorne Bay, a former Louisiana-Pacific logging camp.

island road system—look toward the sea, straining to preserve their privacy and independence.

Except for the stretch between Hollis and Craig/Klawock, the roads on Prince of Wales Island are not paved, and some, especially on the north end, are extremely rough. Be sure you have at least one spare tire and ascertain in advance the availability of fuel along your route. As you tour the island, bear in mind that these are logging roads; you have to share the right-of-way with trucks that will not slow down for long. Be prepared to give way.

Taking a car or camper on the ferry from Ketchikan is undoubtedly the most straightforward approach to exploring Prince of Wales, but there are alternatives. You can fly into Klawock and rent a car from Shaub-Ellison Tire & Fuel (907-826-3450) or Wilderness Rent-a-Car (907-826-5200 or 800-949-2205). There is both wheeled and floatplane service into Klawock from Ketchikan and floatplane service into Craig, Thorne Bay, and other communities. Or fly one way and ferry the other—shuttle service between the Hollis ferry dock and Craig/Klawock is available (Hollis Transporter: 907–826–3151). Contact the Prince of Wales Island Chamber of Commerce (P.O. Box 497, Craig, AK 99921; telephone 907–826–3870; www.princeofwalescoc.org) for additional information about island communities and services. Also, write for the *Prince of Wales Island Road Guide* from the Alaska Natural History Association, c/o SEAVC, 50 Main Street, Ketchikan, AK 99901; telephone (907) 228–6214. Enclose $4.00 plus $1.50 shipping.

Special Events

In May there's a **Fine Art Show and Jazz Fest.** At the end of July most of the island gets together for the annual **Prince of Wales Fair and Logging Show.** The event includes an old-fashioned crafts fair and logging competition, including a chain-saw toss. Call the Prince of Wales Chamber of Commerce for details (907–826–3870).

KAKE
Population 710

The Tlingit community of Kake lies on the northwest corner of Kupreanof Island. Alaska state ferries stop twice a week on a route that includes Petersburg, Sitka, Juneau, and smaller communities; and scheduled air service is available from Juneau, Sitka, and Petersburg. Kake Tribal Corporation, the largest employer in the community, operates logging and cold-storage enterprises.

The community has actively entered the modern visitor trade with the addition of two lodges. The **Keex' Kwaan Lodge** (P.O. Box 316, Kake, AK 99830; telephone 907–785–3434; www.kake alaska.com) is a twelve-room facility, two rooms of which are accessible by wheelchair. The hunting-and-fishing lodge was specifically designed to blend with the historic canneries located nearby. All rooms are wired for computer, fax, and modem use. Visitors can also stay at the modern **Waterfront Lodge** (P.O. Box 222, Kake, AK 99830; telephone 907–785–3472), which has sixteen rooms. Kake is also a handy place to stop for a few hours or overnight if you are touring Southeast by private boat and need to refuel and replenish supplies. There are several stores and restaurants, plus rooms available for overnight stays in addition to the lodges. Kake offers good fishing for all species of salmon, halibut, and trout, and some of the world's largest gatherings of humpback whales occur nearby. Inquire about fishing and whale-watching guides at both lodges. The local hatchery in the community is "tourist friendly," and there's excellent bear watching in the nearby creek (but only from a distance, please!).

Kake is the home of Alaska's tallest totem pole (136 feet), which was carved by Alaska Indian Arts in Haines for Expo '70 in Osaka, Japan. The pole is anchored with guy wires to the top of a bluff overlooking central Kake. The community has been enjoying something of a cultural renaissance in recent years with the formation of the Keex' Kwaan Dancers, an annual cultural camp, and the revival of many traditional arts and crafts.

Kake lies on a gentle curve of beach as did Tlingit villages of old. Aluminum skiffs are drawn up on shore.

The water boils past the dock on turbulent Kootznahoo Inlet in Angoon.

ANGOON
Population 572

Angoon is the sole permanent community on 1,709-square-mile Admiralty Island southwest of Juneau. The village straddles a finger of land on the west coast of the island, fronting on a crescent of beach on Chatham Strait while turbulent Kootznahoo Inlet rushes past the back door. Angoon remains a stronghold of Tlingit culture within the unspoiled wilderness of Admiralty Island National Monument/Kootznoowoo Wilderness, where the villagers coexist with the island bear and bald eagles, as they have for centuries.

Industry came to Angoon in the nineteenth century with the Northwest Trading Company of Portland, Oregon, which built a shore-based whaling station on Killisnoo Island, 3 miles to the south of Angoon. The whale carcasses were processed into oil, bone meal, and fertilizer. Later a herring-reduction plant operated on the same site. A second whaling station was established on the southeast tip of Admiralty in 1907. Although both ventures were short-lived, the whaling industry brought disaster to the village of Angoon in an incident that is remembered with bitterness today. In 1882 a Tlingit shaman was killed accidentally when a harpoon gun exploded aboard a Northwest Trading Company vessel. The Tlingit community demanded that the trading company compensate for the life of the shaman with a payment of 200 blankets. When the company refused, the situation escalated and then ended with navy vessels coming from Sitka to shell and burn the village houses and canoes. Angoon was rebuilt gradually over the next decade.

The people of Angoon did obtain $90,000 in reparations from the government in 1973. In 1982, one hundred years after the shelling, a memorial potlatch was held to commemorate the unfortunate event and to dedicate three new totem poles, the first steps in what villagers hope will be a major restoration of the community housefronts to a semblance of their 1882 appearance.

Angoon's present-day economy is based primarily upon fishing, especially hand-trolling. Many of the rhythms of the old lifestyle are still apparent in this isolated community. Subsistence fishing takes precedence in August and September, when villagers move up Kootznahoo Inlet into Mitchell Bay to set their beach seines and take the salmon the state allows them to catch for personal use. With the regular service provided by the state ferry system—usually the *LeConte,* which arrives some three times a week on the run between Juneau and Sitka—Angoon is slowly and carefully entering the tourist trade. The attractions are primarily the outdoor recreational opportunities available in and around Angoon and the access the community provides to the vast Kootznoowoo Wilderness. The concentration of wildlife on Admiralty Island is phenomenal. Admiralty has the highest brown bear population in Southeast (the Tlingit name for Admiralty, *Kootznahoo,* is translated to mean "bear fort," or "fortress of the bears"). Estimates suggest one brown bear for every square mile. An average of two eagle nesting trees per mile along the 678 miles of shoreline gives Admiralty Island the highest known concentration of bald eagles on the continent. Humpback whales are commonly seen in Mitchell Bay at the upper reaches of Kootznahoo Inlet.

Boaters need to be cautious. The tidal rapids in the inlet can be

Three stone faces and a salmon mark a grave near the Angoon ferry terminal, where ferries stop several times a week.

extremely dangerous for small craft. Visitors should consult with locals regarding the times and location of the rapids that develop.

Angoon is the terminus for the Cross-Admiralty Canoe Route from Mole Harbor on Seymour Canal on the eastern shore of the island. The 32-mile route bisects the island via a series of midland lakes and short portages, with Forest Service cabins strategically placed along the way. Allow six to ten days for a leisurely trip. Consult Margaret Piggott's *Discover Southeast Alaska with Pack and Paddle* (The Mountaineers) for a thorough description of this route, and write for the Forest Service brochure and map, *Admiralty Island National Monument/Kootznoowoo Wilderness Canoe Route*. **Alaska Discovery** offers guided canoe and camping trips on the Cross-Admiralty route. Write Alaska Discovery, 5449 Shaune Road, Suite 4, Juneau, AK 99801; telephone (907) 780-6226.

Angoon's limited visitor accommodations include the water-front **Favorite Bay Inn Bed & Breakfast** (907-788-3123), near the boat harbor and floatplane docks, which offers personable lodging in a 1930s-era home that once served as a general store. The inn rents kayaks and canoes for local exploration. The **Kootznahoo Inlet Lodge** (907-788-3501) has rooms for daily rentals or longer and a restaurant. The lodge overlooks the old floatplane dock on Kootznahoo Inlet. Small boats are usually moored there, too.

At any hour there always seems to be somebody bringing in a load of salmon, halibut, octopus, or other bounty from the sea. If you walk out on the dock and look down into the clear water, you will see some beautiful examples of metridium, a large, white sea anemone that clings to the pilings. Groceries, fuel, and other services are available in the village. A fifteen-minute walk along a well-maintained forest path will take you to the cemetery (go up the hill past the Salvation Army building at the north end of town), or you can follow along the shingle beach. You will see Orthodox crosses side by side with cherubic angels and totemic carvings. The beach lends itself to tide-pool investigations and a leisurely picnic lunch.

South of the village on Kootznahoo Inlet, you will come to the small boat harbor where the commercial fishing boats tie up. The ferry docks at Killisnoo Harbor opposite Killisnoo Island, approximately 3 miles south of Angoon. There is an old graveyard with some impressive carvings above the beach to the right of the dock (as you face the water). One has three faces and a salmon carved in low relief. Killisnoo Island has several summer cabins and **Whalers Cove Sportfishing Lodge** (907-788-3123), a sportfishing lodge with restaurant and private cabins on the beach.

HOONAH
Population 860

Hoonah is one of three communities on Chichagof Island that can be reached by Alaska state ferry. Hoonah, the largest Tlingit settlement in Southeast, lies on the northeast corner of the island in Icy Strait, just 20 miles from Glacier Bay. Hoonah legends indicate that their people migrated from Glacier Bay to the present site long ago. Like so many traditional Indian villages that were located near the resources of the sea, Hoonah became a cannery center in the early part of the twentieth century. Hoonah Cold Storage continues to be an economic force in the community, but logging is now the primary industry. Huna Totem Corporation, formed under the Alaska Native Claims Settlement Act of 1971, is logging the surrounding lands and exporting timber to Japan.

Hoonah has something to offer visitors looking for an out-of-the-way experience. Lodging is available at the **Wind 'N Sea Inn** (907–945-3438) and **Sportsman's Bed and Breakfast** (907–945-3218). **Royal Charters and Tours** offers sightseeing and fishing adventures (907–945-3773). **Harbor Lights** and **Hoonah Trading Post** are places downtown where visitors can buy any essentials. You can also pick up a sandwich at the **Harbor Lights Deli** or order a burger at **Dixie D's** down at the harbor. If you need information, the Hoonah city offices can help. Farther south the **George Hall Jr. Memorial Boat Harbor** provides docking, shower, and laundry facilities.

The town is only three hours by ferry from Juneau. The ferry docks about a mile northwest of the town center. As you stroll up the dirt road toward town, you will pass identical wooden frame houses in weathered pastels. The structures were put up under a government housing program after a fire devastated the old village in 1944. Canoes, totem poles, and many valuable pieces of art were destroyed as well. Newer housing developments are on the south side of town. You will pass Thompson Dock, where **Hoonah Cold Storage** buys and processes salmon, halibut, and crab. The Cold Storage has operated on this site for at least twenty years. You are welcome to look around if they are not too busy. (Stop in at the office first and ask permission.) You can buy fresh fish from the Cold Storage, too.

Proceeding north past the ferry terminal, on the right side of the road, you will pass a graveyard with old Orthodox crosses and at least one large carved totem among the berry bushes and evergreens. In approximately 2 miles you will come to the old Hoonah Packing cannery, which processed salmon until 1944. The complex of buildings is used by Excursion Inlet Packing Co. to outfit its seine fleet. The fleet goes out to seine for salmon in early July. The big seiners, with names like *Gypsy Queen, Mary Joanne,* and *Karen Jean,* are a wonderful sight.

TENAKEE SPRINGS
Population 104

Tenakee Inlet, which cleaves Chichagof Island from the northeast shore, was once the site of both crab and salmon canneries. The hamlet of Tenakee Springs, at the north shore of the inlet, developed as a winter retreat for fishermen and prospectors who had discovered that hot sulfur springs bubble out of the earth there at temperatures of 106 to 108 degrees.

By 1900 small, hand-hewn cabins had sprouted along the beach. At present Tenakee Springs provides a relaxed alternative lifestyle for approximately one hundred Southeasterners who flee the confines of city life for this haven of genteel rusticity. Some full-time residents are retirement age, whereas others are raising families and working

Tenakee Springs offers a relaxed and alternative lifestyle. Life centers around the hot sulfur bath.

the land. Many homeowners live in Juneau and Sitka and use Tenakee for a weekend and vacation retreat.

From shipboard—Alaska state ferries make the eight-hour trip from Juneau a couple times a week—Tenakee appears as a long row of dollhouses on stilts along the water. The cabins are arranged along a dirt and gravel path that reaches nearly 8 miles in either direction from the center of town, but most fall within a 2-mile stretch. No vehicles are allowed in the community except an oil truck and a fire truck, although there is an increasing preponderance—some say an alarming preponderance—of three- and four-wheel ATVs (all-terrain vehicles).

The atmosphere in Tenakee is one of studied neglect. Overalls and comfortable surroundings set the tone, and no one is too keen on development. Tenakee has electricity and telephones but no city water or sewer system. Some cabins have indoor plumbing, but there are many outhouses stationed over the tide. A walk on the path in either direction yields many arresting images for the camera or canvas: rusted oil drums perched outside each cabin on special wooden platforms, old-fashioned wringer washing machines out on the porch, luxurious flower and vegetable gardens, piles of crab pots, hand-hewn and notched log cabins, and various contraptions for hauling things from the ferry or floatplane dock or buckets of water from the creek or cold spring.

Tenakee is not without commercial enterprise. **Snyder Mercantile,** at the entrance to the ferry dock, carries all necessary provisions, including marine fuels (hours vary). Sometimes you can buy fresh Tenakee-grown vegetables and day-old eggs. There is a library, post office, school, and city hall. You can even get a therapeutic massage. The **Blue Moon Cafe** gives you a burger and super fries, if Rosie feels like cooking. In the Shamrock Building you'll find **The Bakery,** offering fresh-baked goodies and sandwiches. Local arts and crafts are also sold there.

More important than any of these places is the **bathhouse,** which is the focal point of Tenakee. The painted concrete bathhouse, at the end of the ferry dock opposite Synder Mercantile, was built to enclose the principal spring in 1940. The water flows into the natural rock bath at the rate of seven gallons per minute. Bath hours are

A stroll along the Tenakee path leads past hand-notched cabins and luxurious gardens.

posted: men from 2:00 to 6:00 P.M. and 10:00 P.M. to 9:00 A.M.; women 6:00 to 10:00 P.M. and 9:00 A.M. to 2:00 P.M. These hours are strictly adhered to; mixed bathing is but a wishful dream on the part of the more free-thinking visitors. Life in Tenakee revolves around the bath. It is customary to bathe at least once every day and often twice. Women bring the children and bathe them, too; sometimes they bring the laundry as well. There is an outer dressing room (with a stove for winter use) with hooks for your clothes and benches where you can lie down and cool off when you emerge from the bath. A short flight of steps leads down to an inner door, opening onto the steamy interior of the bath.

The bath itself is a small, deep, rectangular pool. A concrete floor surrounds the bath and channels the overflow to the outside of the bathhouse. The rules are the same as in a Japanese bath; no soap in the water and wash yourself *before* getting in to soak. You start by sitting on the concrete floor. Pick up one of the plastic jugs you will see lying around (often old Wesson Oil bottles). Dip the jug in the bath and pour the hot water over your body. After you have scrubbed, shampooed, and rinsed via the jug, lower yourself gingerly into the bath for a good soak. (Be sure to remove your silver jewelry before bathing because the water will turn it black.) Before you leave Tenakee, a small donation to the bathhouse fund at Snyder Mercantile is appropriate to help with the upkeep.

Other recreational activities in Tenakee include walking up and down the path; fishing for crab, salmon, and halibut and consuming same; picking salmonberries, raspberries, and thimbleberries; cooking; watching bald eagles and humpback whales cavort off the front deck; and reading an armload of trashy novels brought for the purpose. Tenakee is a form of therapy.

A devastating fire in summer 1993 destroyed several cabins and the waterside Tenakee Inn. The owners of the inn have decided not to rebuild their visitor accommodations. Snyder Mercantile, however, rents Tenakee-style rental cabins with cooking facilities at very reasonable prices (especially the big one, which has a fireplace and sleeps six). Reservations are essential during summer and the fall hunting season. Lodging is also available at the **Tenakee Hot Springs Lodge** (907–736–2400).

PELICAN
Population 163

The ferry pulls into this small fishing and fish-processing town on Lisianski Inlet, on the northwest corner of Chichagof Island, about twice a month—once a month in winter—on a special run from Juneau. If the schedule is suitable, you can make a fun (and very long) day of it by catching the ferry out in the morning for the trip to Pelican, looking around during the two-hour stopover, and returning to Juneau. Or you can take the ferry out and fly back. The ferry trip takes approximately seven hours in each direction.

Pelican can hum during the fishing season with the comings and goings of the commercial fleet and the activity of Pelican Cold Storage, which processes salmon, halibut, crab, herring, black cod, and other species. A Pelican institution is **Rose's Bar and Grill,** where fisherfolk gather to let off steam. Namesake Rose Miller sold the bar, but the institution, the name, and the stories live on. Pelican's **library,** a small but effective niche of books, provides a warm island of sanity amid the chaotic swirl of cold-storage life.

Walking down the wide wooden boardwalk that serves as a street in Pelican, a visitor can pick up breakfast or lunch at the **Inlet Cafe.** If you're in need of something more substantial, **Pelican Wetgoods,** a liquor store, also runs a steam bath for visitors and locals.

Pelican is not an old community; it dates from the 1930s when a fish buyer, Kalle Raatikainen, established a fish-processing operation and named the settlement after his fish-packing boat. Seasonal accommodations include **Big Mick's Little Inn** (907-735-2252), **Boardwalk Bed and Boat** (907-735-2476), **Beyond the Boardwalk B&B** (907-735-2463), **Otter Cove Bed and Breakfast** (907-735-2259), and **Lisianski Lodge** (800-962-8441), 2 miles up the inlet.

GLACIER BAY NATIONAL PARK AND PRESERVE

Sixteen separate glaciers flow out of the Saint Elias Mountains into the two arms of Glacier Bay. Those persons privileged to look upon the ice-locked wilderness of the upper bay, described by the great naturalist John Muir as "icy wildness unspeakably pure and sublime," journey back to a time when the present Southeast rain forests were not yet established and the simplest form of vegetation strove for a tentative hold on the denuded land. In addition to viewing the fantastic glaciers and icebergs of Glacier Bay, visitors often see wildlife. Humpback and orca whales frequent the area. Brown bears may be spotted along the shore and mountain goats on the cliffs high above. Some 200 species of birds have been recorded within the park.

The park headquarters is at Bartlett Cove, at the entrance to the bay. The facilities there include a dock, the fifty-five-room Glacier Bay Lodge with restaurant and lounge, a campground, and a visitor

A visitor to Glacier Bay National Park takes a walk out on a short spit at Bartlett Cove, looking for whales spouting in the distance. DIRK MILLER

center (located upstairs in the lodge), with excellent exhibits illustrating the natural and human history of Glacier Bay. Park naturalists present evening programs at the lodge, guide hikes on a trail through the rain forest at Bartlett Cove, and provide commentary on commercial tour vessels cruising the bay. A nine-and-a-half-hour day cruise into the west arm of Glacier Bay departs daily from Bartlett Cove dock.

There are many different ways to experience the splendor of Glacier Bay during the May-through-September visitor season. Most (but not all) of the luxury cruise ships include a day of Glacier Bay cruising on their regular Inside Passage itinerary. A couple of companies offer overnight cruises into Glacier Bay on smaller vessels, which give you more time in the park. **Glacier Bay Tours and Cruises** (800–451–5952) offers one- to six-day cruises aboard the *Spirit of Adventure* and the *Wilderness Explorer*. The *Spirit of Adventure* travels within Glacier Bay, and the *Wilderness Explorer* also cruises to and from Juneau and Icy Straits. **Alaska Sightseeing/Cruise West** (907-586-6300/800-426-7702) offers multiday cruises that include Glacier Bay routes departing from Juneau, Ketchikan, and Seattle. Local charter operators also offer day and overnight excursions in the area. Alaska state ferries do not travel into the bay.

Then there's the option of taking your own boat into Glacier Bay. For the past several years, the Park Service has limited the number of motorized vessels, including cruise ships, entering the bay in order to minimize the disturbance to the humpback whales that feed there in summer. If you wish to take your own boat into the bay during the June 1 to August 31 permit period, you need to write or call ahead for a seven-day vessel permit. You can request a permit up to sixty days in advance. Write Glacier Bay National Park and Preserve, P.O.

Sixteen separate glaciers flow from the mountains into the twin arms of Glacier Bay. ALASKA DIVISION OF TOURISM

Box 140, Gustavus, AK 99826; or telephone the backcountry and boater permit number, (907) 697–2627. You also can radio Bartlett Cove (KWM 20 Bartlett Cove) on VHF Channel 12 (or 16 as a backup) when you are in the area to see if a permit is available.

You can even kayak through Glacier Bay with one of the kayak and camping packages (including day trips from Bartlett Cove) offered by **Alaska Discovery** (5449 Shaune Road, Suite 4, Juneau, AK 99801; telephone 907–780–6226). For kayak rentals in Glacier Bay, contact **Glacier Bay Sea Kayaks,** P.O. Box 26, Gustavus, AK 99826; telephone (907) 697–2257.

You can fly into the area by air taxi or scheduled jet service on Alaska Airlines (summer only). The airport is located in the rural community of Gustavus, 9 miles by road from Bartlett Cove. Local air services provide flightseeing over Glacier Bay from Gustavus or Bartlett Cove. There is no road access into Glacier Bay or Gustavus from other Southeast communities—you must arrive by boat or plane. A private ferry that runs between Juneau and Gustavus offers another way for visitors to get to the area. The Gustavus ferry, run by **Auk Nu Tours** (76 Egan Drive; Juneau, AK 99801; 907–463–5701/ 800–820–2628), takes about three hours one way. It leaves Juneau in the morning and arrives at the Gustavus dock in the early afternoon. The ferry returns to Juneau in the evening. A round-trip ticket was $138 plus tax in 2003. An optional three-hour whale-watching cruise to Icy Strait is also available.

For details concerning sightseeing, camping, fishing, boating, kayaking, and other aspects of the park, contact Glacier Bay National Park and Preserve, P.O. Box 140, Gustavus, AK 99826; telephone (907) 697–2230. Visitors interested in backcountry camping should be sure to inquire about the availability of fuel.

GUSTAVUS
Population 429

Gustavus is a small, rural, year-round community whose residents enjoy a slower-paced lifestyle that is the envy of their friends in more urban areas of Southeast. Several Juneau residents have built weekend or summer cabins in Gustavus and go there to unwind in the better

Two old boats sit high and dry in the Gustavus boat harbor. DIRK MILLER

weather that Gustavus usually enjoys. The flat terrain, bordered by the clear water of Icy Strait and surrounded by mountain vistas, makes gardening a treat; in fact, Gustavus provided meat and garden produce for nearby canneries in the early part of the last century. Strawberries, both wild and cultivated, are something of a Gustavus specialty.

Although Gustavus serves as the gateway and support community to Glacier Bay National Park, the community also deserves consideration as a destination in its own right. Gustavus offers an increasingly wide range of accommodations, topped by some renowned country inns, and a long list of local charter services for salmon and halibut fishing and whale-watching trips in Icy Strait. Other services include a grocery store, a cafe, a hardware and building-supply store, car rental, and galleries featuring the works of local artists. Several of the inns and lodges provide Gustavus-style bicycles (simple to operate, don't go too fast) for their guests.

An ideal visit to Gustavus might include the day cruise up the bay from Bartlett Cove, a half-day of fishing and/or whale watching, some excellent meals, and several hours of walking or pedaling along the level roads to work them off. Contact the **Gustavus Visitors Association** (P.O. Box 167, Gustavus, AK 99826; telephone 907–697–2285;

A Park Service naturalist unravels some of the mysteries of Glacier Bay aboard Alaska Sightseeing vessel Spirit of Glacier Bay. *A variety of cruise ships visit the area John Muir described as "icy wildness unspeakably pure and sublime."*

www.gustavus.com) for a map and brochure of local services and visitor opportunities. All the major lodging establishments can arrange charter excursions, including the day cruise up Glacier Bay; and **Puffin Travel** (907–697–2260), a local travel bureau, coordinates travel arrangements for Gustavus/Glacier Bay and the entire northern Panhandle. The available accommodations in Gustavus range from full-package inns to cabin rentals and bed-and-breakfast lodgings, plus the **Glacier Bay Lodge** at Bartlett Cove (see the lodging directory at the back of the book for a more complete listing). The latter includes a few dormitory rooms for visitors seeing Glacier Bay on a minimum budget. At the other end of the scale, the celebrated country inns pamper visitors with fluffy comforters and private baths plus a parade of culinary treats from the garden and sea.

One of Alaska's most celebrated kitchens is at the **Gustavus Inn,** which has been operated by various members of the Lesh family since the mid-1960s. When I first visited the inn in 1969, Jack and Sally Lesh were running the old homestead, raising a family, reporting the weather, driving the school bus, operating the single telephone in the community, and preparing the finest meals in Southeast Alaska for a grateful and loyal clientele, some of whom would fly over from Juneau on a summer evening solely for the pleasure of sitting at Sally's table. Nowadays the second generation—David and JoAnn Lesh—is running the inn. The rooms have been

The country inns of Gustavus are renowned for bountiful meals of homegrown produce and local seafood. The celebrated Gustavus Inn is a former homestead.

refurbished and others added. But the kitchen is still renowned throughout Alaska for the produce picked from the inn's own extensive gardens, the fresh-caught salmon/halibut/crab, the home-baked breads and wild-berry desserts, and the tried-and-true family recipes. Meals are still served family style, giving you an opportunity to get acquainted with your neighbors and hosts. And the old homestead still overflows with warmth.

A more recent addition to the Gustavus lodging scene is Glacier Bay's **Bear Track Inn,** a hand-built, fourteen-room, spruce-log lodge located several miles out of town on Rink Creek. The inn is spacious and comfortable, built to accommodate large groups of visitors along with individual travelers. It's a family operation run by the Olneys: Janie and John and son Michael. The Bear Track is breaking the mold of Gustavus's visitor industry by branching out into winter tourism, specifically helicopter skiing and snowboarding in the nearby Chilkat Mountains. The Onleys are teaming up with Out of Bounds Adventures, a Juneau heli-skiing firm that specializes in Chilkat skiing, for their winter operations.

The **Glacier Bay Country Inn** stands secluded on 160 peaceful acres of trees, fields, and gardens, a mile off the main road. The proprietors, Sandi and Ponch Marchbanks, have taken care with the

Glacier Bay's Bear Track Inn is one of the newer accommodations to sprout up in Gustavus, the gateway to the national park. COURTESY GLACIER BAY'S BEAR TRACK INN

pleasant rooms and are doing their part to enhance the community's culinary reputation. The dining room looks out to mountains, trees and wildflowers, and passing bald eagles. An equally tranquil scene surrounds the cozy, five-room **Annie Mae Lodge,** another in the roster of Gustavus inns. The front deck of the natural-wood lodge looks out to fields and wildflowers surrounding the banks of the Good River.

REMOTE INNS AND WILDERNESS LODGES

In addition to the communities available to the visitor via the Alaska Marine Highway System, there are several remote lodges that require a floatplane or private boat for access. They are not reachable by cruise ship, ferry, or road. Although an expensive proposition—as much as several hundred dollars per person per day—these secluded inns offer the traveler a uniquely Alaskan experience. Situated on

Waterfall Resort is located at a former cannery site. Cannery workers' cottages are now luxurious guest quarters.

freshwater lakes or saltwater shores, the wilderness resorts offer outstanding fishing, exploring, and photography together with good food and superlative Alaskan hospitality. Rates generally include round-trip floatplane transportation, all meals, lodging, guide service, boats, and equipment. Fishing resorts clean, freeze, and package your fish for the trip home. Most are closed over winter; write for details. Some to consider are listed in the lodging directory at the back of this book.

Yes Bay Lodge, a family fishing resort, caters equally to local residents, private boaters, and visitors from afar. It is situated on an inlet on the mainland, 50 miles northwest of Ketchikan, and offers guided saltwater and freshwater fishing. Meals are served family style, with an emphasis on Alaska seafood. The Hack family, who operate the lodge, have lived at Yes Bay year-round for more than twenty years. The lodge can arrange fly-in fishing to nearby lakes. The lodge provides all the fishing gear you need and can process your catch afterward.

The most elaborate resort in the Ketchikan area is **Waterfall Resort,** 62 miles west of Ketchikan on the outer coast of Prince of Wales Island (but not on the road system). Waterfall has been built out of what was one of the largest canneries in Southeast Alaska. Twenty-six cabins have been transformed from cannery workers' housing into luxurious guest quarters, each with full bath, wet bar, and refrigerator. There are also newly built condominiums. Family-style meals served in the former mess hall capitalize on the abundant local seafood (200-pound halibut have been caught off the dock).

Primarily a fishing resort, Waterfall offers first-class fishing for salmon, halibut, and steelhead. You can also hike to the waterfall (1.5 miles on a cedar boardwalk), watch big-screen TV, play billiards, and photograph old cannery buildings. A small store carries fishing gear, groceries, and a modest collection of Native artifacts.

On the opposite coast of Prince of Wales Island, Doug and Donna Ibbetson operate **Boardwalk Wilderness Lodge** in a sheltered cove near Thorne Bay. Guests stay in a hand-hewn log lodge with a hot tub and pursue river and saltwater fishing and crabbing.

Northwest of Prince of Wales Island, the mass of Chichagof and Baranof Islands forms a triangular barrier against the outside coast.

Near the slender southern tip of Baranof Island lies the fishing village of Port Alexander, a small community of independent-spirited souls, accessed by private boat or floatplane from Sitka or Petersburg. Longtime residents Paul and Gayle Young offer the small **Rainforest Retreat** in this coastal paradise of old-growth rain forest, muskeg meadows, and intertidal beaches. The accommodations consist of a modern, spacious cabin with picture windows overlooking the bay and mountains, plus additional facilities in the main house. The Youngs invite you to share their daily activities or explore on your own. The facility includes a kitchen where guests prepare food that they have brought along. By special arrangement, the Youngs will prepare three healthful meals a day, with emphasis on whole grains and seasonal garden produce. This is not a fishing lodge or a high-service facility, but a place to relax and enjoy an authentic and spectacularly scenic corner of Southeast Alaska.

Pybus Point Lodge is situated at an old cannery site on Pybus Bay, on the southeast tip of Admiralty Island. The low-key lodge looks out to no other signs of human intrusion: only mountains, water, islands, and trees. The facilities include a main log lodge with kitchen, dining room, and living room warmed by a huge, custom-designed wood stove, plus pine-finished, two-bedroom cabins with private baths and individual woodstoves.

Although primarily a guided-fishing-and-hunting lodge, guests include families with children. Besides the cannery relics, the area offers much to see and enjoy, from abandoned fox farms on nearby islands to sea lion rookeries and waterfalls. In summer humpback whales frequent the area, and brown bears fish the creeks at the end of the salt chuck. Bald eagles feed off the fish trimmings within easy camera range. The kitchen makes good use of the local bounty: fresh crab, shrimp, and fish, fish, fish. You fly in by floatplane from Petersburg.

Thayer Lake Lodge is tucked onto the shore of a freshwater lake in the midst of Admiralty Island National Monument Wilderness. Bob and Edith Nelson of Ketchikan began constructing the lodge in 1947 and have hosted summertime guests there every year but one since 1952. Facilities consist of a comfortable main lodge with two upstairs guest rooms plus two independent lakefront cabins. You

Floatplanes carry mail and freight as well as passengers into isolated hamlets like Elfin Cove; they depart with boxes of frozen fish caught by vacationers.

choose between the Nelson family's cooking at the lodge or self-service in the cabins. The second generation of Nelsons, Erik and Cecilia, now run the Thayer Lake operation.

Cutthroat in 9-mile Thayer Lake are not trophy-worthy but are plentiful with spinning gear or fly rod. Thayer Lake Lodge is less strictly a fishing resort, however, than a contemplative wilderness experience. The acres of forest surrounding the lodge have heard few human voices. Canoes and aluminum skiffs are at your disposal for exploring the lake: Paddle gently about, investigate muskeg meadows, amble along 6 miles of gentle, maintained forest trails, drop a line into the water, listen to the call of the loons. Then settle back and enjoy the company of your hosts. After forty summers on the lake, the Nelsons have achieved a singular peace with their primitive wilderness surroundings. Ask Bob to explain the workings of his handmade wooden waterwheel.

Lodge and cabins are comfortably rustic, with hand-built spruce bunks, rock fireplaces, and full bath facilities. Trips down Thayer Creek to Chatham Strait are available. Thayer Lake Lodge is reached by floatplane from Juneau or Angoon. There is also a trail from the vicinity of Angoon. Many guests fly in to the lodge and top off their wilderness adventure with a guided walk/float trip back to Angoon. The Nelsons also offer guided trips to the Stan Price Bear Sanctuary at Pack Creek.

Elfin Cove, a fishing hamlet with a resident population of around thirty, is located on the northwest corner of Chichagof Island, on Cross Sound. Like Pelican, also on Chichagof, the community is close to the Fairweather fishing grounds on the outside coast. There are two harbors. The outer harbor, with a view of Brady Glacier across Cross Sound, contains the floatplane dock, fuel dock, and the cash buyers who purchase fish from incoming fishing crews. The inner harbor, connected to the outer by a narrow channel called The Gut, is edged with a wooden boardwalk lined with tiny cabins and, increasingly, larger vacation homes. Fishing and pleasure boats can tie up at either of two protected floats. On summer nights the inner harbor fills with fishing boats, sailboats, and private cruisers from Southeast ports and elsewhere. Access is by private boat or float-plane only—Wings of Alaska makes one scheduled flight daily from Juneau in summer.

With singular salmon and halibut fishing only minutes away,

Boardwalk buildings overlook the inner harbor of tiny Elfin Cove on Chichagof Island.

Elfin Cove has developed into a major fly-in sportfishing center. Four substantial fishing lodges and a couple of smaller outfits operate out of the community. They are largely self-contained; guests fly in on day one and out on day five or day six and have little contact with the rest of the community in between. Their meals are provided at their respective lodges (whose dining rooms are not open to the general public).

The major fishing lodges are **Elfin Cove Lodge,** which overlooks the floatplane dock and Brady Glacier; **Tanaku Lodge,** situated across the outer harbor from the community; **Cross Sound Lodge;** and **Cove Lodge.** The latter offers accommodations on a bed-and-breakfast basis as well as the full fishing package. Tanaku Lodge has expanded to a capacity of twenty-four guests and also has a large hot tub. Elfin Cove contains a small grocery store, liquor store, Laundromat, sportfishing shop, variety store, and self-service library. Meals are available at Coho's Bar and Grill. There are no skiff rentals at Elfin Cove, but you can arrange for day-fishing or sightseeing charters.

Around the corner to the west from Elfin Cove, Lisianski Inlet knifes into the mass of Chichagof Island. The boardwalk fishing village of Pelican lies within the protected waters of the inlet. Two miles from town is **Lisianski Lodge,** run by Gail Corbin (formerly Pelican's magistrate). The facilities include a few rooms upstairs in the spruce-log cabin, a separate guest cabin with kitchen and private baths, and an interesting assortment of watercraft.

You have the option of chartering aboard the *Goodtime Charley,* a 26-foot C-Dory operated by Gail's son, Denny, or other boats. Do-it-yourselfers can rent kayaks. You eat Gail's home cooking family style in front of the window, where you can keep an eye out for passing sea otters and humpback whales.

There's nothing at all fancy about Lisianski Lodge. Staying there might be described as an "Alaskan homestead vacation"—you sort of fit in with what's going on (berry picking, fish smoking, picking wild goose-tongue down by the creek). Like hiking? Wildflowers? Photography? Gail loves an excuse to go bushwhacking through the muskegs and forests behind the lodge and across the inlet. Salmon or halibut fishing, beachcombing, or wildlife watching could also be on the agenda. If you're lucky, you might get the opportunity to go to White Sulphur Hot Springs on the outer coast.

A fifty-year-old beachfront cabin offers visitors a taste of homesteading at Lisianski Lodge near Pelican. SARAH EPPENBACH

SOUTHEAST ALASKA LODGING DIRECTORY

This lodging directory has been compiled from select listings provided by the visitor bureaus of Southeast Alaska as well as other sources and does not necessarily reflect the personal recommendations of the author. Prices shown for hotels and motels include the lowest and highest rates, if possible.

MAIN-LINE PORTS OF THE INSIDE PASSAGE

HAINES

Hotels/Motels

Beach Roadhouse: Eight units with private baths, kitchenettes. 1 mile Beach Rd., P.O. Box 1293, Haines, AK 99827; (907) 766-3060; e-mail: frontdesk@beachroadhouse.com; www.beachroadhouse.com; $50+.

Captain's Choice Motel: Great views, close to restaurants. Second Ave. N, P.O. Box 392, Haines, AK 99827; (907) 766-3111; e-mail: capchoice.usa.net; www.capchoice.com; $50+.

Eagle's Nest Motel: 1 mile Haines Hwy., P.O. Box 250, Haines, AK 99827; (907) 766-2891, (800) 354-6006; e-mail: eaglesnestmotel@ wytbear.com; www.eaglesnest.wytbear.com; $50+.

Fort Seward Lodge: 39 Mud Bay Rd., P.O. Box 307, Haines, AK 99827; (907) 766-2009, (800) 478-7772; e-mail: ftsewardlodge@ wytbear.com; www.ftsewardlodge.com; $50+.

Hotel Hälsingland and Officer's Inn B&B: 13 Ft. Seward Dr., P.O. Box 1649, Haines, AK 99827; (907) 766-2000, (800) 542-6363; e-mail: reservations@hotelhalsingland.com; www.hotelhalsingland.com; $50+.

Mountain View Motel: 57 Mud Bay Rd. and Second Ave., P.O. Box 62, Haines, AK 99827; (907) 766-2900, (800) 478-2902; e-mail: budget@mountainviewmotel.com; $50+.

Thunderbird Motel: 216 Dalton St., P.O. Box 589, Haines, AK 99827; (907) 766-2131, (800) 327-2556; e-mail: mbr@thunderbirdmotel.com; www.thunderbird-motel.com; $50+.

Bed-and-Breakfasts

Bear Den Apt.: 8½ Main St., P.O. Box 361, Haines, AK 99827; (907) 766-2117; e-mail: alaskabearden@hotmail.com; www.alaskabearden.com; $75+.

Cherry House: P.O. Box 666, Haines, AK 99827: (907) 766-3440; e-mail: degon@alaskasmokery.com; www.alaskasmokery.com/cherry; $75+.

Chilkat Eagle B&B: 67 Soapsuds Alley, P.O. Box 387, Haines, AK 99827; (907) 766-2763 (call collect); e-mail: eaglebb@wytbear.com; www.kcd.com/eaglebb; $50+.

Fort Seward Bed & Breakfast: #1 Ft. Seward Dr., P.O. Box 5, Haines, AK 99827; (907) 766-2856, (800) 615-NORM; e-mail: norm@fortsewardbnb.com; www.fortsewardbnb.com; $75+.

Fort Seward Condos: #4 Ft. Seward Dr., P.O. Box 75, Haines, AK 99827; (907) 766-2708; www.fortsewardcondos.com; $75+.

Little Crooked House B&B: 61 Helms Loop, P.O. Box 758, Haines, AK 99827; (907) 766-3933, (866) 298-6287; e-mail: crookedhouse@ alaskafloattrips.com; www.alaskafloattrips.com/ b&b_littlecrookedhouse.htm; $50+.

Officers' Inn Bed & Breakfast: Fort Seward, P.O. Box 1589, Haines, AK 99827; (907) 776-2000, (800) 542-6363, (800) 478-2525 in AK, VT, BC; $50+.

On the Beach B&B: P.O. Box 1553, Haines, AK 99827; (907) 766-3992; $50+.

River House on the Chilkat: 3 River Rd., P.O. Box 1173, Haines, AK 99827; (907) 766-3215, (888) 747-7422; e-mail: riverhouse@wytbear.com; $75+.

Sheltered Harbor B&B: 57 Beach Rd., P.O. Box 806, Haines, AK 99827; (907) 766-2741; $75-$100.

Summer Inn Bed & Breakfast: 117 Second Ave., P.O. Box 1198, Haines, AK 99827; (907) 766-2970; e-mail: summerinnb&b@wytbear.com; www.summerinn.wytbear.com; $50+.

Tanani Bay Luxury Suite: 46 Dolphin St., P.O. Box 1235, Haines, AK 99827; (907) 766-3936; e-mail: tananibay@wytbear.com; www.tananibay.com; $75+.

Hostels/Cabins

Bear Creek Cabins: 1.5 Small Tracts Rd., P.O. Box 1293, Haines, AK 99827; (907) 766-2259; e-mail: bearcreekcabin@yahoo.com; www.kcd.com/hostel; hostel bunks $18, cozy cabins $42.

Cabin Fever: 8 mile Mud Bay Rd., P.O. Box 541, Haines, AK 99827; (907) 766-2390; e-mail: jhill541@yahoo.com; $75+.

Chilkat Outback Cabins and Glacier View Lodge: P.O. Box 731, Haines, AK 99827; (907) 767–5522, (907) 766–2334; $75+.

Dalton Street Cottages: Sixth and Union St., P.O. Box 1528, Haines, AK 99827; (907) 766–3223; e-mail: dalton@kcd.com; www.kcd.com/dalton; $75+.

Klehini Cabins: Mile 33¼ Haines Hwy., HC 60 Box 3317, Haines, AK 99827; (907) 767–5642; e-mail: rockbuddy52@hotmail.com; $50–$75.

JUNEAU

Hotels/Motels

Alaskan Hotel & Bar: 167 S. Franklin St., Juneau, AK 99801; (907) 586–1000, (800) 327–9347; e-mail: akhotel@ptialaska.net; www.ptialaska.net/~akhotel; $60.

Alaska's Capital Inn: 113 W. Fifth St., Juneau, AK 99801; (888) 588–6507; e-mail: innkeeper@alaskacapitalinn.com; www.alaskacapitalinn.com; $115+.

Aspen Hotel: 1800 Shell Simmons Dr., Juneau, AK 99802; (907) 790–6435, (888) 559–9846; e-mail: info@aspenhotelak.com; www.westernsteelhotels.com; $149–$179.

Best Western Country Lane Inn: 9300 Glacier Hwy., Juneau, AK 99801; (907) 789–5005, (888) 781–5005; www.countrylaneinn.com; $79.

Breakwater Inn: 1711 Glacier Ave., Juneau, AK 99801; (907) 586–6303, (800) 544–2250; e-mail: breakwaterinn@gci.net; www.breakwaterinn.com; $69.

Driftwood Lodge: 435 W. Willoughby Ave., Juneau, AK 99801; (907) 586–2280, (800) 544–2239; e-mail: driftwood@gci.net; www.driftwoodalaska.com; $85.

Frontier Suites Airport Hotel: 9400 Glacier Hwy., Juneau, AK 99801; (907) 790–6600, (800) 544–2250. e-mail: frontiersuites@gci.net; www.frontiersuites.com; $89.

Goldbelt Hotel: 51 Egan Dr., Juneau, AK 99801; (907) 586–6900, (888) 478–6909; e-mail: tourcenter@goldbelt.com; www.goldbelttours.com; $89.

GreatLand Hotel: P.O. Box 35403, Juneau, AK 99803; (907) 586–6101; e-mail: greatland-alaska@gci.net; www.greatland-alaska.com; $89.

Inn at the Waterfront: 455 S. Franklin St., Juneau, AK 99801; (907) 586–2050; e-mail: an1898inn@aol.com; $60.

Juneau Super 8 Motel: 2295 Trout St., Juneau, AK 99801; (907) 789–4858, (800) 800–8000; e-mail: super8ju@ptialaska.net; www.super8.com; $70+.

The Prospector Hotel: 375 Whittier St., Juneau, AK 99801; (907) 586-3737, (800) 331-2711; e-mail: prospect@ptialaska.net; www.prospectorhotel.com; $80.

The Silverbow Inn, Bakery and Restaurant: 120 Second St., Juneau, AK 99801; (907) 586-4146, (800) 586-4146: e-mail: info@silverbowinn.com; www.silverbowinn.com; $85.

Travelodge–Juneau Airport: 9200 Glacier Hwy., Juneau, AK 99801; (907) 789-9700, (888) 660-2327; e-mail: tlodgeak@aol.com; www.travelodge.com; $85.

Westmark Baranof Hotel: 127 N. Franklin St., Juneau, AK 99801; (907) 586-2660, (800) 544-0970; e-mail: wbaranof@ptialaska.net; www.westmarkhotels.com; $129.

Lodges

Aldersheim Lodge: P.O. Box 20862, Auke Bay, AK 99821; (907) 790-5002, (907) 723-4447.

Alexis Suites and Ocean Spa: P.O. Box 32377, Juneau, AK 99803; (907) 789-7473; e-mail: grundy@gci.net; $189+.

Pearson's Pond Luxury Suites and Adventure Spa: 4541 Sawa Circle, Juneau, AK 99801-8723; (907) 789-3772, (888) 6-JUNEAU; e-mail: book@pearsonspond.com; www.pearsonspond.com.

A Whale's Eye Lodge & Charter: P.O. Box 210166, Auke Bay, AK 99821; (907) 723-2920; e-mail: walseye@starband.net; www.alaskaone.com/whaleseye; $110+.

A sign warns visitors to watch out for fishermen at Forget-Me-Knot Cottage, a lodge on Shelter Island near Juneau. DIRK MILLER

Bed-and-Breakfasts

AK Fireweed House B&B: 8530 N. Douglas Hwy., Juneau, AK 99801; (907) 586-3885, (800) 586-3885; e-mail: firewd@ak.net; www.fireweedhouse.com; $89+.

Alaska Tours and Lodging: P.O. Box 35403, Juneau, AK 99803; (907) 780-5150.

Alaska Travelers Accommodations: 4672 S. Tongass Hwy., Ketchikan, AK 99901; (907) 247-7117, (800) 928-3308; www.alaskatravelers.com. A reservation service for lodging and B&Bs throughout Southeast Alaska.

Alaska Twin Lakes B&B: 4018 Ridge Way, Juneau, AK 99801; (907) 780-5132; e-mail: twinlakes@gci.net; $55+.

Alaska Victorian B&B: 434 W. Willoughby, Suite B, Juneau, AK 99801; (907) 586-4200, (866) 586-4200; e-mail: reservations@ alaskavictorian.com; www.alaskavictorian.com; $95.

Alaska Wolf House B&B: P.O. Box 21321, Juneau, AK 99802; (907) 586-2422, (888) 586-9053; e-mail: akwlfhs@ptialaska.net; www.alaskawolfhouse.com; $95+.

Alaskan Bear B&B: 4436 Glacier Hwy., Juneau, AK 99801; (907) 780-6420; e-mail: elliottj@alaska.net; www.alaskanbear.com; $65+.

Auke Lake Bed & Breakfast: 9040 Glacier Hwy., Juneau, AK 99801; (907) 790-3253, (800) 790-3253; e-mail: info@admiraltytours.com; www.admiraltytours.com; $95+.

Aurora View Inn on the Mountain: 2917 Jackson Rd., Juneau, AK 99801; (888) 580-8439; e-mail: auroravu@ptialaska.net; www.ptialaska.net/~auroravu; $89+.

A Beachside Luxury Inn: 3120 Douglas Hwy., Juneau, AK 99801; (907) 463-5531, (888) 879-0858; e-mail: beachside@gci.net; www.beachsidevilla.com; $69+.

Bed & Breakfast Association of Alaska, INNside Passage Chapter: P.O. Box 22800, Juneau, AK 99802; (907) 247-2583; www.accommodations-alaska.com or www.inns-alaska.com.

Best Western Grandma's Feather Bed: 2358 Mendenhall Loop Rd., Juneau, AK 99801; (907) 789-5566; www.grandmasfeatherbed.com; $89+.

Blueberry Lodge on the Tidelands: 9436 N. Douglas Hwy., Juneau, AK 99801; (907) 463-5886; e-mail: jayjudy@alaska.net; www.blueberrylodge.com; $95+.

Cashen Quarters Bed & Breakfast: 303 Gold St., Juneau, AK 99801; (907) 586-9863; e-mail: www.cashen.quarters@acsalaska.net; www.cashenquarters.com; $75.

Channel B&B: P.O. Box 20437, Juneau, AK 99802; (907) 463-5683; e-mail: cmwear@hotmail.com; $95+.

Cinnamon Inn & Suite: P.O. Box 240411, Douglas, AK 99824; (907) 789-INNS; e-mail: hjs01234@aol.com; www.cinnamoninn.com; $85+.

Cliff House Bed and Breakfast: 124 W. Sixth St., Juneau, AK 99801; (907) 586-2179; e-mail: jhoman@ptialaska.net; $105.

A Cove House B&B: 220 Fritz Cove Rd., Juneau, AK 99801; (907) 789-2571; e-mail: info@acovehouse.com; www.acovehouse.com; $110+.

A Cozy Log Bed & Breakfast: 8668 Dudley St., Juneau, AK 99801; (907) 789-2582; e-mail: cozylog@alaska.net; www.cozylog.net; $65+.

Crondahls Bed & Breakfast: 626 Fifth St, Juneau, AK 99801; (907) 586-1464; e-mail: judy@juneaucrondahls.com; www.juneaucrondahls.com.

Eagle's Nest Bed & Breakfast: P.O. Box 20537, Juneau, AK 99802; (907) 586-6378.

Gill's Horizon Vacation Rental and B&B: 10730 Horizon Dr., Juneau, AK 99801; (907) 586-2829; e-mail: gills@alaska.com; www.gillshorizon.com; $85+.

Glacier Trail Bed & Breakfast: 1081 Arctic Circle, Juneau, AK 99801; (907) 789-5646; e-mail: stay@juneaulodging.com; www.juneaulodging.com; $110.

The Highlands B&B: 421 Judy Lane, Juneau, AK 99801; (877) 463-5404; e-mail: info@juneauhighlands.com; www.juneauhighlands.com; $140+.

Hummingbird Hollow B&B: P.O. Box 32798, Juneau, AK 99803; (907) 789-7400; e-mail: hummingbirdhollow@ak.net; www.hummingbirdhollow.net; $99+.

Indian Cove B&B: P.O. Box 210092, Auke Bay, AK 99821; (907) 789-2726; e-mail: signell@email.msn.com; www.indiancove.com; $65+.

Mountain View B&B: 9719 Trapper's Lane, Juneau, AK 99801; (877) 552-2647; e-mail: info@mountainviewbb.com; www.mountainviewbb.com; $89+.

Mt. Juneau Inn Bed & Breakfast: 1801 Old Glacier Hwy., Juneau, AK 99801; (907) 463-5855; e-mail: mtjuneauinn@alaska.com; www.mtjuneauinn.com; $79.

Mullins House Bed & Breakfast: 526 Seward St., Juneau, AK 99801; (907) 586-3384; $80.

A Russian Classic—The Jorgenson House: P.O. Box 33102, Juneau, AK 99803-3102; (907) 789-9532; e-mail: jorgenson@gci.net; $125.

Sally's Bed & Breakfast: 465 Whittier St., P.O. Box 22093, Juneau, AK 99801; (907) 780-4708; e-mail: sbb@alaska.net; www.alaska.net/~sbb; $80.

Salmonberry Inn: 5025 Thane Rd., Juneau, AK 99801; (907) 586-3451; e-mail: paula@salmonberryinn.net; www.salmonberryinn.net; $80.

Sepel Hallow Bed & Breakfast: 10901 Mendenhall Loop Rd., Juneau, AK 99801; (907) 789-5220; e-mail: sepelhall@alaska.com; home.gci.net/~sepelhall; $90.

Serenity Inn Luxury B&B: P.O. Box 210902, Auke Bay, AK 99821; (907) 789-2330, (800) 877-5369; e-mail: serenity@ptialaska.net; www.ptialaska.net/~serenity; $99.

The Williwaws: 19100 Williwaw Way, Juneau, AK 99801; (907) 789-2803, (888) 837-9617; e-mail: dmalick@earthlink.net; www.williwaws.com; $125-$175.

Hostels

Juneau International Hostel: 614 Harris St., Juneau, AK 99801; (907) 586-9559.

KETCHIKAN

Hotels/Motels

Best Western Landing: 3434 Tongass Ave., Ketchikan, AK 99901; (907) 225-5166, (800) 428-8304; e-mail: bwlanding@kpunet.net; www.landinghotel.com.

The Cedars Lodge: 1471 Tongass Ave., Ketchikan, AK 99901; (907) 225-1900, (800) 813-4363; e-mail: info@cedarslodge.com; www.cedarslodge.com.

Gilmore Hotel: 326 Front St., Ketchikan, AK 99901; (907) 225-9423, (800) 275-9423; e-mail: gilmor23@kpunet.net; www.gilmorehotel.com.

Ingersoll Hotel: 303 Mission St., Ketchikan, AK 99901; (907) 225-2124, (800) 478-2124.

The Narrows Inn: 4871 Tongass Ave., P.O. Box 8296, Ketchikan, AK 99901; (907) 247-2600, (888) 686-2600; e-mail: narrows@ aptalaska.net; www.narrowsinn.com.

New York Hotel & Cafe: 207 Stedman St., Ketchikan, AK 99901; (907) 225-0246, (866) 255-0246; e-mail: reservations@ thenewyorkhotel.com; www.thenewyorkhotel.com.

Super 8 Motel: 2151 Sea Level Dr., Ketchikan, AK 99901; (907) 225-9088, (800) 800-8000; www.super8.com.

WestCoast Cape Fox Lodge: 800 Venetia Way, Ketchikan, AK 99901; (907) 225-8001, (866) 225-8001; www.westcoasthotels.com.

Lodges/Resorts

Salmon Falls Resort: 16707 N. Tongass Hwy., P.O. Box 5700, Ketchikan, AK 99901; (907) 225-2752, (800) 247-9059; e-mail: fishing@salmonfallsresort.net; www.salmonfallsresort.net.

Bed-and-Breakfasts

Alaska's Hidden Cove Adventure Rentals: P.O. Box 1420, Ward Cove, AK 99928; (907) 225-7934, (866) 822-2683; e-mail: contact@akhiddencove.com; www.akhiddencove.com.

Anchor Inn by the Sea: 4672 S. Tongass Hwy., Ketchikan, AK 99901; (907) 247-7117, (800) 928-3308; e-mail: akseashore@att.net; www.alaskatravelers.com/anchor.htm.

Anne's Secret Garden Suite: P.O. Box 7012, Ketchikan, AK 99901; (907) 225-4577, (888) 302-0845; e-mail: stay@secretgardenbeds.com; www.secretgardenbeds.com.

Blueberry Hill B&B: P.O. Box 9508, Ketchikan, AK 99901; (877) 449-2583; e-mail: stay@blueberryhillbb.com; www.blueberryhillbb.com.

Captain's Quarters B&B: 325 Lund St., Ketchikan, AK 99901-9202; (907) 225-4912, (800) 987-5337; e-mail: captbnb@ptialaska.net; www.ptialaska.net/~captbnb.

Classic Stop Bed and Breakfast: 216 Madison St., P.O. Box 5863, Ketchikan, AK 99901; (907) 225-3607; e-mail: ekhenderson@worldnet.att.net; home.att.net./~ekhenderson.

Corner B&B: P.O. Box 5023, Ketchikan, AK 99901; (907) 225-2655; e-mail: cjwilsie@ptialaska.net; www.cornerbnb.com.

Crazy Wolf B&B: 607 Mission St., Ketchikan, AK 99901; (907) 225-9653, (888) 331-9653; e-mail: crazywolf@kpunet.net.

Edgewater B&B: 1626 Water St., P.O. Box 9302, Ketchikan, AK 99901; (907) 247-3343; e-mail: host@edgewaterbb.com; www.edgewaterbb.com.

Erickson's Bed & Breakfast: 2122 Third Ave., Ketchikan, AK 99901; (907) 225-9219, (877) 255-3948; e-mail: davenjoy@ptialaska.net.

Guest Suites at Pier 29: 1649 Water St., Ketchikan, AK 99901; (907) 225-7500, (800) 478-7510; e-mail: guestsuites@kpunet.net; www.guestsuitesatpier29.com.

Ketchikan Bed and Breakfast/Ketchikan Bed and Breakfast Association: P.O. Box 5015, Ketchikan, AK 99901; (907) 225-8550.

Ketchikan Reservation Service/Bed & Breakfast Lodging: 412 D-1 Loop Rd., Ketchikan, AK 99901; (907) 247-5337, (800) 987-5337.

Lundberg's South Shore Inn: 7446 S. Tongass Hwy., Ketchikan, AK 99901;
(907) 225-0909, (888) 732-0220; e-mail: lundberg.l@att.net;
home.att.net/~lundberg.l.

Madame's Manor Victorian Bed & Breakfast: 324 Cedar St.,
Ketchikan, AK 99901; (907) 247-2774, (888) 893-5338; e-mail:
stay@madamesmanor.com; www.madamesmanor.com.

Nantucket House: 600 Front St., Ketchikan, AK 99901;
(907) 247-3731; e-mail: welcome@nantuckethousebb.com;
www.nantuckethousebb.com.

Nichols Passage B&B: 3032 S. Tongass Hwy., Ketchikan, AK 99901; (907)
225-4698; e-mail: carsonnichols@kpunet.net.

Tuck 'Em Inn Bed & Breakfast: P.O. Box 574, Hillcrest Rd., Metlakatla, AK
99926; (907) 886-7853; e-mail: winterr@aptalaska.net;
www.alaskanow.com/tuckem-inn.

Ward Cove B&B: 7937 William Rd. (8 mile N. Tongass),
Ketchikan, AK 99901; (907) 247-8608; e-mail: h.rambosek@att.net;
www.wardcovebnb.com.

WayPoint Inn at Herring Bay: 7866 S. Tongass Hwy., Ketchikan, AK
99901; (907) 225-8605; e-mail: info@waypointinn.com;
www.waypointinn.com.

Hostels

Backpackers Hostel Eagleview: 2303 Fifth Ave., Ketchikan, AK 99901;
(907) 225-5461; e-mail: seaeagle@ktn.net.

Ketchikan Youth Hostel: P.O. Box 8515, Ketchikan, AK 99901;
(907) 225-3319; e-mail: ktnyh@eagle.ptialaska.net.

PETERSBURG

Hotels/Motels

Beachcomber Inn: 384 Mitkof Hwy., P.O. Box 570, Petersburg, AK 99833;
(907) 772-3888.

Scandia House: 110 N. Nordic Dr., P.O. Box 689, Petersburg, AK 99833;
(907) 772-4281, (800) 722-5006; e-mail: scandia@alaska.net;
$90-$175

Tides Inn: 307 N. First St., P.O. Box 1048, Petersburg, AK 99833;
(907) 772-4288, (800) 665-8433; e-mail: tidesinn@alaska.net.

Lodges

Green Rocks Lodge (Kupreanof Island): P.O. Box 104, Petersburg, AK
99833; (907) 772-3336.

Bed-and-Breakfasts

A Lille Hus Bed & Breakfast Box: 102 Dolphin St., P.O. Box 814, Petersburg, AK 99833; (907) 772-4810.

Alaska Pad: Box 748, Petersburg, AK 99833; (907) 772-3659; e-mail: norheim@mitkof.net.

Bear Necessities Guesthouse: P.O. Box 923, Petersburg, AK 99833; (907) 772-2279; e-mail: bearbnb@alaska.net; www.alaska.net/~bearbnb.

Bed and Breakfast at the Water's Edge: P.O. Box 1201, Petersburg, AK 99833; (907) 772-3736, (800) TO-THE-SEA; e-mail: bbsea@alaska.net; www.alaska.net/~bbsea; $85-$95.

Brum Hus Bed & Breakfast: P.O. Box 427, Petersburg, AK 99833; (907) 772-3459; e-mail: brumhus@alaska.net.

Cottrell's Sugar Shack: P.O. Box 947, Petersburg, AK 99833; (907) 772-4615.

Das Hagedorn Haus: 400 Second St., P.O. Box 1333, Petersburg, AK 99833; (907) 772-3775; e-mail: trask@alaska.net; www.alaska.net/~trask; $80+.

Feathered Nest B&B: P.O. Box 683, Petersburg, AK 99833; (907) 772-3090; e-mail: altab@mitkof.net; www.featherednestbandb.com; $75+.

Heather and Rose Guest Hus: P.O. Box 478, Petersburg, AK 99833; (907) 772-4675; e-mail: hrosehus@alaska.net; www.alaska.net/~hrosehus; $80+.

Morning Mist: P.O. Box 566, Petersburg, AK 99833; (907) 772-3557; e-mail: mornmist@alaska.net; www.alaska.net/~mornmist.

Nordic House Bed & Breakfast: 806 S. Nordic Dr., P.O. Box 573, Petersburg, AK 99833; (907) 772-3620; e-mail: nordicbb@alaska.net; www.nordichouse.net.

Rainsong B&B: P.O. Box 968, Petersburg, AK 99833; (907) 772-3178; e-mail: riemer@mitkof.net.

Seafarer's Shakk: P.O. Box 94, Petersburg, AK 99833; (907) 772-3974; e-mail: sonja@alaska.net; www.alaska.net/~sonja; $70+.

Waterfront B&B: P.O. Box 1364, Petersburg, AK 99833; (907) 772-9300; e-mail: h20frbnb@alaska.net; www.alaska.net/~h20frbnb.

Hostels

Petersburg Bunk and Breakfast Hostel: P.O. Box 892, Petersburg, AK 99833; (907) 772-3632; e-mail: info@bunkandbreakfast.com; www.bunkandbreakfast.com.

SITKA

Hotels/Motels

Cascade Inn & Boat Charters: 2035 Halibut Point Rd., Sitka, AK 99835;
(907) 747-6804, (800) 532-0908; e-mail: cascade@ptialaska.net;
www.travelsitka.com/cascade; $85-$100.

Sitka Hotel: 118 Lincoln St., Sitka, AK 99835; (907) 747-3288;
e-mail: stay@sitkahotel.com; www.sitkahotel.com;$50-$110.

Super 8 Motel: 404 Sawmill Creek Blvd., Sitka, AK 99835;
(907) 747-8804, (800) 800-8000; www.super8.com; $78-$117.

Westmark Shee Atika: 330 Seward St., Sitka, AK 99835; (907) 747-6241,
(800) 544-0970; e-mail: westmark@ptialaska.net;
www.westmarkhotels.com; $98-$131.

Lodges

Baranof Expeditions-Cape Ommaney Lodge: P.O. Box 3107, Sitka, AK
99835; (907) 747-3934; e-mail: boyce@ptialaska.net;
www.baranofexpeditions.com.

Baranof Wilderness Lodge: Summer: P.O. Box 2187, Sitka, AK 99835;
(907) 738-3597. Winter: P.O. Box 42, Norden, CA 95724;
(800) 613-6551; e-mail: mtrotter@flyfishalaska.com;
www.flyfishalaska.com.

Berry Island Adventures-Raven's Nest House: P.O. Box 597,
Sitka, AK 99835; (907) 747-5165; e-mail: info@berryisland.net;
www.berryisland.net.

Dove Island Lodge Sitka Sportfishing Charters, LLC: P.O. Box 1512, Sitka,
AK 99835; (907) 747-5165; e-mail: sitkasportfish@aol.com;
www.aksitkasportfishing.com.

Fishermen's Inn: P.O. Box 8092, Port Alexander, AK 99836; (907)
568-2399; e-mail: kmullifish@aol.com; www.fishermensinn.com.

Homestead Outfitters, LLC: P.O. Box 691, Sitka, AK 99835; (907)
738-1050, (800) 995-0461.

Middle Island Recreation Cabin: P.O. Box 1982, Sitka, AK 99835; (907)
747-5169; e-mail: jehly@ptialaska.net; www.ptialaska.net/~jehly.

Quest Alaska Lodges: 1910 Eighth Ave. N.E., Aberdeen, SD 57402;
(605) 229-8685; e-mail: jason@questalaskalodges.com;
www.questalaskalodges.com.

Rockwell Lighthouse: P.O. Box 277, Sitka, AK 99835; (907) 747-3056.

Wild Strawberry Inn: 724 Siginaka Way, Sitka, AK 99835;
(907) 747-8883, (800) 770-2628.

Bed-and-Breakfasts

Alaska Ocean View B&B: 1101 Edgecumbe Dr., Sitka, AK 99835; (907) 747-8310, (888) 811-6870; e-mail: info@sitka-alaska-lodging.com; www.sitka-alaska-lodging.com; $69-$159.

Alaska Swan Lake Bed & Breakfast: 206 ½ Lakeview Dr., Sitka, AK 99835; (907) 747-5746; e-mail: p.fager@worldnet.att.net; www.sitka.org/swanlake; $85.

Angler's Landing Bed & Breakfast: 206 Lance Dr., Sitka, AK 99835; (907) 747-6055; e-mail: angler@ptialaska.net; www.ptialaska.net/~angler.

Annahootz Bed and Breakfast: P.O. Box 2870, Sitka, AK 99835; (907) 747-6498, (800) 746-6498; e-mail: cdhanson@att.net; www.sitka.org/annahootz; $95.

Ann's Gavan Hill Bed & Breakfast: 415 Arrowhead St., Sitka, AK 99835; (907) 747-8023; e-mail: annlowe@ptialaska.net; www.annsgavanhill.com; $70-$80.

Baranof Island Bed & Breakfast: 401 Charters St., Sitka, AK 99835; (907) 747-8306; e-mail: mail@baranofislandbedandbreakfast.com; www.baranofislandbedandbreakfast.com; $65-$85.

Bear Den Bed & Breakfast: 1906 Dodge Cir.; (907) 747-3350; e-mail: danlin@gci.net; $65-$95.

Biorka B&B: 611 Biorka St., Sitka, AK 99835; (907) 747-3111; e-mail: biorkabnb@alaska.com; www.bnbcity.com/inns/20025.

A Crescent Harbor Hideaway: 709 Lincoln St., Sitka, AK 99835; (907) 747-4900; e-mail: bareis@ptialaska.net; www.sitkabedandbreakfast.com.

Eddystone Inn: 2898 Sawmill Creek Rd., Sitka, AK 99835; (907) 747-3313; e-mail: janeteddy@hotmail.com; www.eddystoneinn.com; $85-$150.

Finn Alley Inn Bed & Breakfast: 711 Lincoln St., Sitka, AK 99835; (907) 747-3655; e-mail: seakdist@ptialaska.net; www.ptialaska.net/~seakdist/finn.htm; $85-$105.

Hannah's Bed and Breakfast: 504 Monastery St., Sitka, AK 99835; (907) 747-8309; $60-$85.

Helga's Bed and Breakfast: P.O. Box 1885, Sitka, AK 99835; (907) 747-5497; e-mail: helgasbb@eagle.ptialaska.net; www.ptialaska.net/~jgarrison/index.htm.

Karras Bed and Breakfast: 230 Kogwanton St., Sitka, AK 99835; (907) 747-3978; e-mail: keet-hit@worldnet.att.net.

Raven Frog Bed & Breakfast: 1502 Edgecumbe Dr., Sitka, AK 99835; (907) 747-8700; e-mail: bandb@ravenfrog.com; www.ravenfrog.com; $60-$100.

Seaview Bed and Breakfast: 203 Harbor Dr., Sitka, AK 99835; (907) 747-3908; $55-$65.

Sitka's Nest: 408 Lake St, Sitka, AK 99835; (907) 747-5000, (907) 747-7140; e-mail: mail@sitkanest.com; $60-$100.

Sitka's Scenic B&B: 100 Johnson St, Sitka, AK 99835; (907) 747-8790, (907) 738-3405; e-mail: sitkascenicbbb@webtv.net; www.ptialaska.net/~kendavis; $75-$85.

Sitka Woodside Lodging: 411 Wortman Lp., Sitka, AK 99835; (907) 747-8287; e-mail: sdenherder@gci.net; www.home.gci.net/~sdenherder; $85-$100.

Where Eagles Roost: 2713 Halibut Point Rd., Sitka, AK 99835; (907) 747-4545; e-mail: whereeaglesroost@gci.net; $80.

Other

Sheldon Jackson College Summer Housing: 801 Lincoln St, Sitka, AK 99835; (907) 747-5220; dormitory rooms.

SKAGWAY

Hotels/Motels

At the White House: Eighth and Main, P.O. Box 41, Skagway, AK 99840; (907) 983-9000; e-mail: whitehse@aptalaska.net; www.atthewhitehouse.com; $108+.

Gold Rush Lodge: Sixth and Alaska, P.O. Box 514, Skagway, AK 99840; (907) 983-2831, (888) 983-3509; e-mail: info@goldrushlodge.com; www.goldrushlodge.com; $75-$105.

Golden North Hotel: Third and Broadway, P.O. Box 431, Skagway, AK 99840; (907) 983-2294, (907) 983-2451; e-mail: gnhsbc@ aptalaska.net.

Historic Skagway Inn: Seventh and Broadway, P.O. Box 500, Skagway, AK 99840; (888) 752-4929; e-mail: stay@skagwayinn.com; www.skagwayinn.com; $89-$124.

Sgt. Preston's Lodge: Sixth and State, P.O. Box 538, Skagway, AK 99840; (907) 983-2521; e-mail: sgt-prestons@usa.net; $60-$130.

Westmark Inn: Third and Spring, P.O. Box 515, Skagway, AK 99840; (907) 983-6000, (888) 544-0970; www.westmarkhotels.com; $89-$139.

Wind Valley Lodge: Twenty-second and State, P.O. Box 345, Skagway, AK 99840; (907) 983-2236; $79-$89.

Bed-and-Breakfasts

Alaskan Sojourn: 488 Eighth Ave., P.O. Box 564, Skagway, AK 99840;
(907) 983-2030; e-mail: ijourneynorth@hotmail.com;
www.aptalaska.net/~akfoto; $20-$40.

Mile Zero Bed & Breakfast: Ninth and Main, P.O. Box 165, Skagway, AK
99840; (907) 983-3045; e-mail: mile0@aptalaska.net;
www.mile-zero.com; $105.

Hostels/Cabins

Cindy's Place: Dyea Rd., P.O. Box 479, Skagway, AK 99840;
(907) 983-2674, (800) 831-8095; e-mail: croland@alaska.net;
www.alaska.net/~croland; $30-$99.

Chilkoot Trail Outpost: Mile 8.5 Dyea Rd., P.O. Box 286, Skagway, AK
99840; (907) 983-3799; e-mail: khosford@aptalaska.net;
www.chilkoottrailoutpost.com; $100-$125.

Skagway Bungalows: Mile 1 Dyea Rd., P.O. Box 287, Skagway, AK 99840;
(907) 983-2986; e-mail: saldi@aptalaska.net;
www.aptalaska.net/~saldi; $99.

Skagway Home Hostel: Third and Main, P.O. Box 231, Skagway, AK
99840; (907) 983-2131; e-mail: schave@aptalaska.net;
www.hostels.net; $15-$40.

WRANGELL

Hotels/Motels

Harding's Old Sourdough Lodge: 1104 Peninsula Ave., P.O. Box 1062,
Wrangell, AK 99929; (907) 874-3613, (800) 874-3613; e-mail:
bruce@akgetaway.com; www.akgetaway.com; $75-$195.

The Roadhouse Lodge: Mile 4, Zimovia Hwy., P.O. Box 1199, Wrangell,
AK 99929; (907) 874-2335; e-mail: ddolson@aptalaska.net.

The Stikine Inn: 107 Front St., P.O. Box 990, Wrangell, AK 99929;
(907) 874-3388, (888) 874-3388; e-mail: inn@stikine.com;
www.stikine.com; $90+.

Thunderbird Hotel: 223 Front St., P.O. Box 110, Wrangell, AK 99929;
(907) 874-3322.

Bed-and-Breakfasts

Anchor B&B: P.O. Box 1463, 325 Church St., Wrangell, AK 99929;
(907) 874-2078; e-mail: anchorbb@aptalaska.net;
www.aptalaska.net/~anchorbb.

Fennimore's by the Ferry: P.O. Box 957, Wrangell, AK 99929; (907)
874-3012; e-mail: wrgbbb@aptalaska.net; www.fennimoresbbb.com.

Grand View B&B: P.O. Box 927, Wrangell, AK 99929; (907) 874-3225; e-mail: judy@grandviewbnb.com; www.grandviewbnb.com.

Merritt's Bed & Breakfast: P.O. Box 912, Wrangell, AK 99929; (907) 874-3054.

Rooney's Roost Bed and Breakfast: 206 McKinnon St., P.O. Box 552, Wrangell, AK 99929; (907) 874-2026; e-mail: rroost@aptalaska.net; www.rooneysroost.com.

Zimovia B&B: P.O. Box 1424, Wrangell, AK 99929; (907) 874-2626; e-mail: zimoviabnb@rgbwebs.com; www.rgbwebs.com/zimoviabnb.

Hostels

Wrangell Hostel: Wrangell First Presbyterian Church, P.O. Box 439, Wrangell, AK 99929; (907) 874-3534.

OFF THE MAIN LINE

ANGOON

Favorite Bay Inn: P.O. Box 101, Angoon, AK 99820; (907) 788-3123, (800) 423-3123; e-mail: favoritebayinn@juno.com; www.favoritebayinn.com; $89+.

Kootznahoo Inlet Lodge: P.O. Box 134, Angoon, AK 99820; (907) 788-3501.

ELFIN COVE

(Also see Wilderness/Fly-in Fishing Lodges)

Icy Straits Adventures (cabin rental): P.O. Box 13, Elfin Cove, AK 99825; (907) 239-2255. Winter: P.O. Box 240941, Douglas, AK 99824; (907) 364-2181.

Shearwater Lodging and Charters: P.O. Box 57, Elfin Cove, AK 99825; (907) 239-2223.

GLACIER BAY/GUSTAVUS

Country Inns

These establishments operate on the American Plan: Daily rates include lodging and three full meals.

Annie Mae Lodge: P.O. Box 55, Gustavus, AK 99826; (907) 697-2346, (800) 478-2346 (in Alaska); e-mail: anniemae@cheerful.com; www.anniemae.com; $130–$400.

Glacier Bay Country Inn: P.O. Box 5, Gustavus, AK 99826;
(907) 697-2288, (800) 628-0912; $99-$3,521.

Gustavus Inn: P.O. Box 60, Gustavus, AK 99826; (907) 697-2254,
(800) 649-5220. Winter: 7920 Outlook, Prairie Village, KS 66208;
(913) 649-5220; e-mail: dave@gustavsinn.com; www.gustavusinn.com;
$140+.

Lodges

Alaska Seair Adventures: P.O. Box 299, Gustavus, AK 99826;
(907) 697-2215.

Fairweather Lodge and Adventures: P.O. Box 148, Gustavus, AK 99826;
(907) 697-2334.

Glacier Bay Lodge: 76 Egan Dr., Juneau, AK 99801; (907) 586-8687,
(800) 451-5952. Winter: 520 Pike St., Suite 1400, Seattle, WA 98101;
(206) 623-2417.

Glacier Bay's Bear Track Inn: P.O. Box 255, Gustavus, AK 99826;
(907) 697-3017, (888) 697-2284; $300-$616.

Bed-and-Breakfasts

Aimee's Guest House: Box 40 Shooting Star Way, Gustavus, AK 99826;
(907) 697-2330.

Blue Heron B&B: P.O. Box 77, Gustavus, AK 99826; (907) 697-2337;
e-mail: blueheronbnb.net; www.blueheronbnb.net; $100+.

Good Riverbed & Breakfast: P.O. Box 37, Gustavus, AK 99826;
(907) 697-2241.

Meadow's Glacier Bay Guest House: P.O. Box 93, Gustavus, AK 99826;
(907) 697-2348, (877) 766-2348; $99+.

A Puffin's Bed and Breakfast: P.O. Box 3, Gustavus, AK 99826;
(907) 697-2260, (800) 478-2258 (in Alaska).

Salmon River Rentals: P.O. Box 13, Gustavus, AK 99826;
(907) 697-2245.

Spruce Tip Lodge: P.O. Box 299, Gustavus, AK 99826; (907) 697-2215;
e-mail: sprucetiplodge@hotmail.com; $110+.

TRI Bed & Breakfast: P.O. Box 214, Gustavus, AK 99826;
(907) 697-2425; e-mail: trigbay@pluto.he.net;
www.glacierbaylodging.com; $85.

Whalesong Lodge: P.O. Box 389, Gustavus, AK 99826; (907) 697-2288,
(800) 628-0912.

HOONAH

F.I.S.H.E.S: P.O. Box 245, Hoonah, AK 99829; (907) 945-3327; e-mail: fishes@hoonah.net; $300.

Hubbard's Bed and Breakfast: P.O. Box 205, Hoonah, AK 99829; (907) 945-3414.

Sportsman's Bed & Breakfast: Hoonah, AK 99829; (907) 945-3218.

Tina's Room Rentals: P.O. Box 234, Hoonah, AK 99829; (907) 945-3442.

HYDER

Grand View Inn: 27 Hyder Ave., Hyder, AK 99923; (250) 636-9174.

Kathy's Korner B&B: 503 Main St., P.O. Box 42, Hyder, AK 99923-0042; (250) 636-2393; $40-$75.

Sealaska Inn: Premier and Nevada Sts., Hyder, AK 99923; (888) 393-1199.

KAKE

Keex' Kwaan Lodge: P.O. Box 207, Kake, AK 99830; (907) 785-3434.

Nuggett Inn: P.O. Box 516, Kake, AK 99830; (907) 785-6469.

Waterfront Lodge: P.O. Box 222, Kake, AK 99830; (907) 785-3472.

METLAKATLA

Metlakatla Hotel and Suites: P.O. Box 670, Metlakatla, AK 99926; (907) 886-3456, (800) 353-3455.

PELICAN

(Also see Wilderness/Fly-in Fishing Lodges)

Beyond the Boardwalk B&B: (360) 297-3550 August 27 to May 20, (907) 735-2463 May 21 to August 26; e-mail: twhited@tscnet.com; www.fishpelicanalaska.com.

Big Mick's Little Inn: P.O. Box 614, Pelican, AK 99832; (907) 735-2252; e-mail: pelbar@ptialaska.net.

Boardwalk Bed and Boat: P.O. Box 707, Pelican, AK 99832; (907) 735-2476 in season, (360) 546-0725 November to March; e-mail: sdindigo@attbi.com; www.boardwalkbandb.com.

Lisianski Inlet Wilderness Lodge & Charters: P.O. Box 765, Pelican, AK 99832; (907) 735-2266, (800) 962-8441; e-mail: kuhook@aol.com; www.alaskaecoadventures.com.

Paddle House: 1873 Shell Simmons Dr., Juneau, AK 99801-9398; (907) 463-3466, (800) 463-4453; e-mail: artour@alaska.com.

Otter Cove B&B: P.O. Box 618, Pelican, AK 99832; (907) 735-2259, (888) 687-2683; www.northernlightsdesign.com/ottercove; $75+.

PRINCE OF WALES ISLAND
(Also see Wilderness/Fly-in Fishing Lodges)

Fireweed Lodge: P.O. Box 116, Klawock, AK 99925; (907) 755-2930.

Haida-Way Lodge: P.O. Box 90, Craig, AK 99921; (907) 826-3268, (800) 347-4625.

Klawock Bay Inn: P.O. Box 137, Klawock, AK 99825; (907) 755-2929.

Log Cabin Resort and R.V. Park: P.O. Box 54, Klawock, AK 99925; (907) 755-2205, (800) 544-2205.

McFarland's Floatel: P.O. Box 19149, Thorne Bay, AK 99919; (888) 828-3335.

Prince of Wales Lodge: P.O. Box 72, Klawock, AK 99925; (907) 755-2227.

Ruth Ann's Hotel: P.O. Box 145, Craig, AK 99921; (907) 826-3378.

TENAKEE SPRINGS

Snyder Mercantile: P.O. Box 505, Tenakee Springs, AK 99841; (907) 736-2205.

Tenakee Hot Springs Lodge: P.O. Box 3, Tenakee Springs, AK 99841; (907) 736-2400/2245, fishing packages available.

WILDERNESS/FLY-IN FISHING LODGES

Most wilderness and fly-in sportfishing lodges offer multiday packages that include lodging, all meals, equipment, and guided fishing or other activities. When comparing rates, check whether or not the package includes round-trip floatplane transportation, and how many full days of guided fishing or other activities are included. The sample rates listed below are based on double occupancy in 2001. Most lodges offer a selection of packages—write for details and current prices.

ADMIRALTY ISLAND

Admiralty Island Wilderness Homestead: 4 Crab Cove, Funter Bay, AK 99850; (907) 789-4786; e-mail: nwart@ptialaska.net;

www.ptialaska.net/~nwart/; $350 per person per day, all-inclusive.

Pybus Point Lodge: P.O. Box 33497, Juneau, AK 99803; (907) 790-4866; $1,995 per person, four days/four nights during July and August.

Thayer Lake Lodge: P.O. Box 8897, Ketchikan, AK 99901; (907) 788-3203, (907) 247-8897. Winter: $170 per person per night (full meals), $135 per cabin per night (housekeeping rate; cook your own meals).

ANGOON

Favorite Bay Sportfishing Lodge: P.O. Box 149, Angoon, AK 99820; (866) 788-3355; e-mail: favorite@ptialaska.net.

Whalers Cove Lodge: P.O. Box 101, Angoon, AK 99820; (800) 423-3123; e-mail: whalerscovelodge@juno.com; www.whalerscovelodge.com.

CHICHAGOF ISLAND: ELFIN COVE

The Cove Lodge: P.O. Box 17, Elfin Cove, AK 99825; (907) 239-2210 (summer), (800) 382-3847 (all year). Winter: 961 W. Nebraska Ave., St. Paul, MN 55117; (651) 489-5002; $2,395 per person, four nights/three days.

Cross Sound Lodge: P.O. Box 85, Elfin Cove, AK 99825; (907) 239-2210, (800) 323-5346. Winter: P.O. Box 1167, Haines, AK 99827; $2,495 per person, five nights/six days.

Eagle Charters: P.O. Box 77, Elfin Cove, AK 99825; (907) 239-2242, (888) 828-1970. Winter: 4200 NE 60th St., Vancouver, WA 98661; e-mail: kulavik@aol.com; www.eaglecharters.com; $125.

Elfin Cove Lodge: P.O. Box 72, Elfin Cove, AK 99825; (800) 482-6258, (800) 422-2824. Winter: P.O. Box 4007, Renton, WA 98057; (206) 813-0600. e-mail: tanaku@msn.com ; $2,895 per person, five nights/four days.

Gull Cove Lodge: P.O. Box 22, Elfin Cove, AK 99825; (907) 697-2720; e-mail: mowich@alaska.net; www.gullcove.com.

Tanaku Lodge: P.O. Box 72, Elfin Cove, AK 99825; (907) 239-2205; www.tanaku.com; $2,495 per person, three nights/four days.

CHICHAGOF ISLAND: PELICAN

Lisianski Lodge: P.O. Box 776, Pelican, AK 99832; (907) 735-2266; $150 per person per day (includes lodging and three meals; guided fishing and other activities extra).

JUNEAU VICINITY: SHELTER ISLAND

Forget-Me-Knot Cottage and Charters: P.O. Box 33081, Juneau, AK 99803; (907) 789-9334; $175 per person per day, two-person minimum.

KETCHIKAN VICINITY

Yes Bay Lodge: P.O. Box 8660, Ketchikan, AK 99901; (907) 225-7906, (800) 999-0784; www.yesbay.com; $2,620 per person, four nights/three days.

PRINCE OF WALES ISLAND

Boardwalk Wilderness Lodge: P.O. Box 19121, Thorne Bay, AK 99919; (907) 828-3918, (800) 764-3918; $2,420 per person, three nights/three days.

Sportsman's Cove Lodge: P.O. Box 2486, Olympia, WA 98507-2486; (360) 956-3333, (800) 962-7889; $2,400 per person, four nights/five days.

Waterfall Resort: P.O. Box 6440, Ketchikan, AK 99901; (907) 225-9461, (800) 544-5125; $2,960 per person, three nights/four days.

SITKA VICINITY

Rainforest Retreat: P.O. Box 8005, Port Alexander, AK 99836; (907) 568-2229; $40 per person per day (guests bring and prepare their own food).

ANNUAL CELEBRATIONS, FESTIVALS, AND SPECIAL EVENTS

January

Alcan 200 Road Rally, Haines. A snow machine race from the U.S./Canada border.

Polar Bear Swim, Wrangell.

February

Festival of the North and Wearable-Art Show, Ketchikan. Month-long arts, music, and drama festival.

Tent City Winter Festival, Wrangell (first weekend in February). Food and craft fair and contests celebrating gold rush days.

Devil's Thumb Days, Petersburg. Winter carnival.

Winterfest, Juneau. Outdoor events and family activities.

March

Coffman Cove Salmon Derby (March through July).

Double Ironman Triathlon, Ketchikan.

Prince of Wales Island Trade Show, Craig (two days). Local merchants demonstrating wares and services; food booths and prizes.

Buckwheat Ski Classic, Skagway (late March). Amateur and professional Nordic ski races.

Windfest, Skagway (end of March). Dances, chili cook-off, other festivities.

April

Alaska Hummingbird Festival, Ketchikan.

Craig/Klawock Salmon Derby (April through June).

Thorne Bay Salmon Derby (April through July).

Alaska Folk Festival, Juneau. Weeklong series of free concerts and workshops with Alaska folk musicians.

Alaska State Community Theater Festival, Haines (odd-numbered years). Juried theater productions from Alaskan communities.

Gathering of the People, Sitka. Cultural exchange that attracts Alaska Native dance groups from across the state.

Garnet Festival, Wrangell.

Skagway Film Festival and International Mini Folk Festival, Skagway.

May

Mayfest. Monthlong schedule of special events and activities taking place throughout Southeast Alaska.

Chilkoot to Chilkat Biathlon, Haines.

Classic Car Show, Juneau.

King Salmon Derby, Ketchikan and Haines (weekends in late May, early June).

Wrangell Salmon Derby, Wrangell.

Muskeg Meadows Annual Gold Tournament, Wrangell.

Little Norway Festival, Petersburg (third weekend of May). Folk dances, contests, Norwegian food celebrating Norwegian Independence Day.

Salmon Derby, Petersburg (Memorial Day weekend).

Sitka Salmon Derby (continues in June).

Juneau Jazz & Classics Festival. Ten-day schedule of performances and workshops by visiting national artists.

Great Alaska Craftbeer and Homebrew Festival, Haines. Craft-beer and home-brew judging, tasting.

June

Sea Art Walk, Ketchikan.

Sitka Summer Music Festival, Sitka (three weeks). Chamber-music performances by visiting national artists.

Sitka Writer's Symposium, Sitka. Guest writers and lecturers.

Kluane to Chilkat International Bicycle Relay (mid-June). Relay teams pedal 160 miles from the Yukon to Haines.

Gold Rush Days, Juneau. Gold panning, logging events.

International Days, Hyder (June 30–July 4). Joint Independence Day celebration with Stewart, British Columbia.

Summer Solstice Celebration, Haines.

July

Independence Day celebrations, communities throughout Southeast Alaska.

Timber Carnival, Ketchikan (July 4). Competitive logging events.

Prince of Wales Island Fair and Logging Show, Thorne Bay (late July).

Loggers' Rodeo, Wrangell (July 4). Competitive logging events.

Fort Seward Day. A "Field Day" of games in Haines.

August

The Bear and Beer Festival, Wrangell (third week in August). Honor the bears of Anan and toast the local brews.

Blueberry Festival, Ketchikan. Summer street fair.

Southeast Alaska State Fair, Haines (second or third week of August). Five-day regional fair with exhibits and events.

Golden North Salmon Derby, Juneau (three days).

Master Anglers Tournament, Haines.

Bald Eagle Music Festival, Haines.

Flower and Garden Show and Competition, Skagway (third weekend in August).

Sam Donajkowski Memorial Triathlon, Haines.

September

Great Alaska Sportfishing Championship, Ketchikan.

Klondike Trail of '98 Road Relay, Skagway. Ten-person relay teams running from Skagway to Whitehorse.

National Hippie Week, Skagway.

October

Seafood Fest, Petersburg.

Octoberfest, Petersburg. Arts and crafts fair.

Alaska Day Festival, Sitka (around October 18). Five-day celebration of Alaska Purchase, featuring costume ball, parade, reenactment of transfer ceremonies.

November

Holiday Fest, Sitka (November through January). Various holiday festivities including Russian Christmas and Starring.

Juneau Public Market (Thanksgiving Day weekend). Mega arts, crafts, and merchandising fair.

Bald Eagle Festival, Haines. Three-day event celebrating the peak of the winter gathering of eagles.

Sitka Whalefest. Educational lectures from biologists, experts, and speakers, along with a trade fair and concert.

Winter arts fair and Festival of Lights, Ketchikan.

December

Annual Art Walk and Wearable Art Show, Ketchikan.

Festival of Lights and Christmas tree ceremony, Wrangell and Petersburg.

Gallery Walk, Juneau. Evening gallery showcase and Christmas festivities.

INFORMATION SOURCES

General

Alaska Department of Fish and Game: P.O. Box 25526, Juneau, AK 99802-5526; (907) 465-4100; www.state.ak.us/adfg/geninfo/ contact/contact.htm.

Alaska Division of Tourism: P.O. Box 110801, Juneau, AK 99811-0801; (907) 465-2010; Fax: (907) 465-2287; www.dot.state.ak.us/amhs.

Alaska Marine Highway System: 6858 Glacier Hwy., Juneau, AK 99801-7909; (907) 465-3941, (800) 642-0066; TDD/VOICE: (800) 764-3779; www.dot.state.ak.us/amhshome.html.

Alaska Pass: P.O. Box 351, Vashon, WA 98070-0351; (206) 463-6550, (800) 248-7598; Fax: (800) 488-0303; www.alaskapass.com.

Alaska Wilderness Recreation and Tourism Association: 2207 Spenard Rd., Suite 201, Anchorage, AK 99503; (907) 258-3851; www.awrta.org.

Bed & Breakfast Association of Alaska: P.O. Box 22800, Juneau, AK 99801; (907) 247-2583; Fax: (907) 247-2584; e-mail: artours@ alaska.net; www.accommodations-alaska.com.

Southeast Alaska Tourism Council: P.O. Box 20710, Juneau, AK 99802-0710; (907) 586-4777, (800) 423-0568; Fax: (907) 463-4961; e-mail: gotoalaska@aol.net; www.alaskainfo.org.

U.S. Forest Service Southeast Alaska Visitor Center: 50 Main St., Ketchikan, AK 99901; (907) 228-6214; Fax: (907) 228-6234; TDD: (907) 228-6237.

U.S. Forest Service (Tongass National Forest information): 648 Mission St., Federal Building, Ketchikan, AK 99901-6591; (907) 225-3101; Fax: (907) 586-7928; www.fs.fed.us/r10/tongass.

White Pass & Yukon Route: P.O. Box 435, Skagway, AK 99840; (907) 983-2217, (800) 343-7373; from Northwest Canada: (800) 478-7373; e-mail: info@whitepass.net; www.whitepassrailroad.com.

Ferry Terminals

Bellingham Terminal: (360) 676-8445.

Haines Terminal: (907) 766-2111; recorded schedule information: (907) 766-2113.

Juneau Terminal: (907) 789-7453; recorded schedule information: (907) 465-3940.

Ketchikan Terminal: (907) 225-6182; recorded schedule information: (907) 225-6181.

Petersburg Terminal: (907) 772-3855; recorded schedule information: (907) 772-3855.

Prince Rupert, British Columbia Terminal: (604) 624-9627.

Sitka Terminal: (907) 747-8737; recorded schedule information: (907) 747-3300.

Skagway Terminal: (907) 983-2941.

Wrangell Terminal: (907) 874-3711.

Local Visitor Bureaus

Gustavus Visitors Association: P.O. Box 167, Gustavus, AK 99826; (907) 697-2285; www.gustavus.com.

Haines Visitors' Bureau: P.O. Box 530, Haines, AK 99827; (907) 766-2234, (800) 458-3579; e-mail: hcvb@haines.ak.us; www.haines.ak.us.

Hyder Community Association: P.O. Box 149, Hyder, AK 99923; (250) 636-9148; Fax: (250) 636-2714.

Juneau Convention and Visitors' Bureau: One Sealaska Plaza, Suite 305, Juneau, AK 99801; (907) 586-1737, (888) 581-2201; Fax: (907) 586-6304; e-mail: info@traveljuneau.com; www.traveljuneau.com.

Ketchikan Visitors' Bureau: 131 Front St., Ketchikan, AK 99901; (907) 225-6166, (800) 770-3300; e-mail: kvb@ktn.net; www.visit-ketchikan.com.

Petersburg Visitor Center: P.O. Box 649, Petersburg, AK 99833; (907) 772-4636; Fax: (907) 772-3646; e-mail: pcoc@alaska.net; www.petersburg.org.

Prince of Wales Chamber of Commerce: P.O. Box 497, Craig, AK 99921; (907) 826-3870; e-mail: powcc@aptalaska.net; www.princeofwalescoc.org.

Prince Rupert Convention and Visitors' Bureau: P.O. Box 669, Prince Rupert, BC, Canada V8J 3Sl; (604) 624-5637, (800) 667-1994; Fax: (604) 627-8009.

Sitka Convention and Visitors' Bureau: P.O. Box 1226, Sitka, AK 99835; (907) 747-5940; Fax: (907) 747-3739; e-mail: scvb@sitka.org; www.sitka.org.

Skagway Convention and Visitors' Bureau: P.O. Box 1025, Skagway, AK 99840; (907) 983-2854; Fax: (907) 983-3854; e-mail: infoskag@aptalaska.net; www.skagway.org.

Wrangell Chamber of Commerce/Visitors' Bureau: P.O. Box 1350, Wrangell, AK 99929; (907) 874-2381; www.wrangell.com.

National Parks and Monuments

Admiralty Island National Monument/Kootznawoo Wilderness: 8461 Old Dairy Rd., Juneau, AK 99801; (907) 586-8790; Fax: (907) 586-8795.

Glacier Bay National Park and Preserve: P.O. Box 140, Gustavus, AK 99826-0140; (907) 697-2230.

Klondike Gold Rush National Historical Park: P.O. Box 517, Skagway, AK 99840; (907) 983-2921, (907) 983-9224.

Misty Fiords National Monument: 3031 Tongass Ave., Ketchikan, AK 99901; (907) 225-2148.

Sitka National Historical Park: 106 Metlakatla St., Sitka, AK 99835; (907) 747-0110; www.nps.gov/sitk.

INDEX

ABOUT THE AUTHORS

Sarah Eppenbach

Sarah Eppenbach is a travel and food writer and the originator of this classic guide to Alaska's Southeast. Having moved to Lopez Island, Washington, she and her husband maintain a second home in Juneau. She writes for such magazines as *Travel & Leisure, Travel Holiday,* and *Alaska Airlines.*

Michelle Gurney

Editor Michelle Gurney has a great love of the outdoors and a passion for travel writing. A Canadian, she is the author of a number of travel features for newspapers across Canada and is co-author of *Hiking Yoho, Kootenay, Glacier, and Mt. Revelstoke National Parks* (A FalconGuide/The Globe Pequot Press).